*"Penelope Wilcock has done it again! She gets [...]
way that fills the imagination, challenges the h[...]
just to think about faith but to do something t[...]*
*home groups talking for hours and dreaming together about what they can do
to make a difference in the world. The studies will help you see the big picture
of God's purposes in the world and they will draw you out of self-centred,
stuck, me-focused faith. There is something here for everyone. If you want
to follow a character then you'll find a banquet of material from Adam to
Zacchaeus. If you need fresh insight into the Gospel then the studies around
Matthew will deepen you, those around Luke will move you, those around
Mark will put a fresh spring in your step and those around John will cause
you to worship. Want to change the world? The justice studies are replete with
life and bursting with energy. Don't just one copy of this book, buy a dozen for
your home group and dive into a journey that will change your life."*

– Malcolm Duncan, Gold Hill Baptist Church

*"Clear, provocative, focussed and accessible, these pithy stand-alone studies are
a treasure-trove for home groups and other discussion-based gatherings. Each
study takes a single character or theme, freeing your group to respond in a very
focussed way to the issues raised. The questions offer great flexibility – they
can be quickly dealt with in a short-form setting, or can be the basis of longer
discussions and explorations. The range is inspiring – a tour of the Bible in
100 bites. Recommended!"*

– Gerard Kelly, The Bless Network

Penelope Wilcock has pastored ten Methodist congregations, worked as a school chaplain and a hospice chaplain, been involved in ministry with prisoners, and initiated a Fresh Expression of Church. She blogs at Kindred of the Quiet Way (*www.kindredofthequietway. blogspot.co.uk*)and is a regular columnist in *Woman Alive* magazine. She believes in the hidden working of the gospel in the context of the daily lives of ordinary people as the revolution that will change the world.

She lives a quiet life on England's Sussex coast.

By the same author

Fiction

The Hawk and the Dove series (Crossway):
>*The Hawk and the Dove* (trilogy)
>*The Hardest Thing to Do*
>*The Hour Before Dawn*
>*Remember Me*
The Clear Light of Day (David C. Cook)
Thereby Hangs A Tale (Kingsway)

Pastoral resources

Spiritual Care of Dying and Bereaved People (SPCK; revised and expanded edition, BRF)
Learning To Let Go (Lion)

Christian lifestyle

The Road of Blessing (Monarch)
In Celebration of Simplicity (Monarch)

100

STAND-ALONE

BIBLE STUDIES

To grow healthy home groups

Penelope Wilcock

MONARCH
BOOKS

Oxford, UK & Grand Rapids, Michigan, USA

Published by Monarch Books (an imprint of Lion Hudson plc)
Lion Hudson plc, Wilkinson House, Jordan Hill Road,
Oxford OX2 8DR, England
Email: monarch@lionhudson.com www.lionhudson.com/monarch
and by Elevation (an imprint of the Memralife Group)
Memralife Group, 14 Horsted Square, Uckfield, East Sussex TN22 1QG
Tel: +44 (0)1825 746530; Fax: +44 (0)1825 748899;
www.elevationmusic.com

ISBN 978 0 85721 419 5
e-ISBN 978 0 85721 420 1

First edition 2013

Acknowledgments

Unless otherwise stated, Scripture quotations are taken from the Holy Bible, New International Version Anglicized. Copyright © 1979, 1984, 2011 Biblica, formerly International Bible Society. Used by permission of Hodder & Stoughton Ltd, an Hachette UK company. All rights reserved. "NIV" is a registered trademark of Biblica. UK trademark number 1448790
Other versions used:
Extracts from The Authorized (King James) Version. Rights in the Authorized Version are vested in the Crown. Reproduced by permission of the Crown's patentee, Cambridge University Press.
Scripture taken from the New King James Version. Copyright © 1982 by Thomas Nelson, Inc. Used by permission. All right reserved.
Scripture quotations from the Good News Bible published by the Bible Societies and HarperCollins Publishers, © American Bible Society 1994, used with permission.
New English Bible © Oxford University Press and Cambridge University Press 1961, 1970.
Revised English Bible © Oxford University Press and Cambridge University Press 1989.

A catalogue record for this book is available from the British Library

Printed and bound in the UK, February 2013, LH27

Contents

About this book   **9**

"Tell me about it!"
— Bible characters in moments we can identify with (25 studies)   **23**

Adam	24
Eve	26
Abraham	28
Ruth	30
Cain	32
Elijah	34
Esther	36
The widow of Zarephath	38
David	40
Jeremiah	42
Peter	44
Dorcas	46
Paul	48
Martha	50
Judas	52
Barnabas	54
Mary the mother of Jesus	56
John the Baptist	58
Andrew	60
The boy with five loaves and two fishes	62
Pontius Pilate	64
Zacchaeus	66
Deborah	68
Joseph	70
Jacob	72

Themes from the four Gospels — key features from the four Gospels (20 studies)   **75**

Matthew

The faithful Israel and the new Moses   76
The teacher of righteousness   78
The holy mountain   80
The fulfilment of the Law   82
The Zoroastrians   84

Mark

The Son of God   86
The reinterpretation of leadership   88
Transfiguration – sight and insight   90
The unvarnished Jesus   92
The unnamed outsider   94

Luke

Finding the lost   96
Healing the sick   98
The Holy Spirit   100
A gospel for the whole world   102
Lifting up the lowly   104

John

The light of the world   106
The living Word   108
The body of Christ   110
The *ego eimi*   112
The way of love   114

Walking in the light (15 studies)   **117**

Justice   118
Mercy   120

Bearing witness   122

Humility   124

Honesty and transparency   126

Kindness   128

Accountability   130

Simplicity   132

Discipline   134

Chastity   136

Joy   138

Compassion   140

Courage   142

Fidelity   144

Stewardship   146

Tracing the circle of the church's year (15 studies)   149

Three Advent studies (there are four weeks in Advent
– three studies leave space for a Christmas party)   150

Five Lent studies (there are six weeks in Lent
– five studies leave space for an Easter party)   156

A study for Ascension   166

A study for Pentecost   168

A study for the Holy Trinity   170

Two studies for Ordinary Time   172

A study for Harvest Thanksgiving   176

A study for All Saints   178

Learning from the life of Jesus (20 studies)   181

His birth at Bethlehem   182

His home at Nazareth   184

His fasting in the wilderness   186

His healing work   188

His teaching work   190

His prophetic spirit   192

His servant spirit   194

His attitude to authority   196

His attitude to women   198

His emphasis on forgiveness   200

His emphasis on personal faith and choice   202

His emphasis on thanksgiving   204

His proclamation of the kingdom   206

His teaching about freedom   208

His relationship with creation   210

His path of simplicity   212

His faithfulness in prayer   214

His passion and death   216

His work of reconciliation   218

His resurrection and glorious ascension   220

Insights from the Law and the Prophets (5 studies)   223

Putting God first   224

The poor and needy   226

Choosing life   228

Keeping faith with a faithful God   230

To do justice, to love mercy and to walk humbly
with thy God   232

About this book

Why do we have house groups?

House groups offer a chance for existing relationships to deepen and new friendships to form. In a small group, new perspectives enrich our thinking, and we are encouraged to find ourselves not alone in our struggles and human weakness. In the small group we see the power of prayer most wonderfully, as we share our needs and concerns and then watch in amazement as the group gets praying and (time after time) things change, exceeding our timid hopes and building our faith.

The small group is the easiest place for newcomers in church to "taste and see", and the best context for shy and anxious people to sense that they are loved and accepted, so they can begin to gain in confidence. The small group is the seedbed for vocation and ministry, and the best place for our first tentative exploration of the gifts of the Holy Spirit.

In the small group, as people open up and begin to trust one another, deeper problems behind veneers of cheerfulness and self-sufficiency are slowly revealed. A young mother at the end of her tether after two years of sleepless nights; a woman who had an abortion a decade ago and has never been able to forgive herself; a man who is struggling desperately with increased responsibilities after staff cutbacks at his workplace in the recession; someone facing a diagnostic procedure at the hospital and dreading the outcome; someone who fears a loved daughter may be bulimic; someone facing the choice between redundancy or relocation – it is in the small group that these ordinary but profound life experiences will be uncovered and prayed through, so that individual believers are strengthened and sustained to continue living with courage and grace.

All of this is why almost every church runs small groups. They nurture, sustain, and strengthen faith.

Identity and spirituality have their roots in the same earth. The Genesis stories paint pictures of God creating not "humanity" but Adam and Eve. Right there at the start of things, at the place of our making, personhood and individuality are intrinsically involved in our existential nature and our relationship with God.

Human beings are social creatures too, and flourish in community. Oftentimes commandments or expectations are laid upon the community rather than the individual – and when we understand this, it is such a relief. It is interesting from time to time to read the New Testament in the King James Version of the Bible, because it makes the distinction between "thou" ("you" in the singular) and "you" (plural). Many of the charisms of the church – hospitality, healing, mercy, prophetic lifestyle – are meant to be job-shared, not to burn us out. We begin to see that no one of us is expected to be able to do it all, or to do any of it all the time.

The meeting of the whole church for prayer and praise, for ministry and preaching and witness and celebration and Eucharist, usually on a Sunday morning, is the focus of the church's common life. But by itself it is not enough to train and nourish and encourage the individual disciple in the faith. For that we need the small group – still a community, but where the individual can be personally known.

Resourcing the small group

The great virtue of the small group is not so much the input as the chance to explore, experiment, and share, to move on from being acquaintances or strangers to becoming fast friends and family in Christ.

So the two most vital resources for the small group are time and sensitive leadership. Without these, it cannot fulfil its vital role in the church community.

It is important for every member of the group to be welcomed, and to have a chance to be really heard. Discussion in the small group often takes us into areas of personal challenge and sensitivity, and if a painful story begins to pour out it may bring tears as very deep emotional matter emerges from its compressed and hidden state. To hurry this compounds pain and hints that the schedule takes precedence over the people, that everything has to be stuffed back down inside because it's time for the Bible study to begin. If you want your small-group members to grow and flourish, you have to make space for their stories, and for their unexpected crises when everything goes into overwhelm.

On many occasions I have searched for resource materials for small groups in my care. Though I have found excellent group studies with brilliant ideas and illustrations, interesting questions, and very helpful engagement with the biblical text, without exception every collection of study notes I have ever seen has had the same problem for me: too much input.

Most house-group resources assume the same pattern:

- A short welcome time when the group settles in and is offered drinks and biscuits – introductions are made and the leader encourages chat about how the week has gone and who has interesting news, etc.

- An icebreaker – something funny or thought-provoking to encourage personal sharing. It can be something a bit random, such as: "If you were a house/shoe/animal/car, what kind would you be?" This gives a glimpse of each person's individuality, and provides a bit of fun, gets people talking. Other icebreakers include games such as tossing a ball across the group or building a house of cards together – anything to loosen things up, break down inhibitions, and increase awareness of each other.

- Settling down to the main study material. This is often presented in sections – so section one might be a portion of Scripture, section two a story from contemporary life, section three a "case history" of a dilemma. Each section might be followed by a chance for discussion.

- There usually follows a series of questions that take the theme deeper into the lives of the participants – "How did you feel when you read… ?" or "Which character did you most identify with?" or "Have you ever been in a similar situation?" or "What most surprised you in the story?" – questions to encourage the participants to own the biblical material, to engage with the theme, to see the relevance of what they have read to their own daily lives.
- Then there is usually a suggestion about a prayer time, sometimes with themes or ready-made prayers as helps and guides.
- And quite often the notes include a "homework" item – some nugget for challenge or reflection for everyone to take home and work with during the week until next time. It follows of course that when next time comes around, feedback from the group about how they got on with their homework should be built in.

To get the most out of these resource materials, the group really does have to work over the whole territory. The welcome settles everyone in and makes them feel loved and wanted, the icebreaker creates some lighthearted effervescence that gets a good buzz going, the biblical material is the core discipling input, and the additional input material creates the vital link between the eternal gospel and the contemporary context of daily life. The questions allow for reflection; the prayer time is a chance for the Spirit to move and work directly with people, and for the group members to open themselves to the Spirit's conviction, or bring their response of thanksgiving, intercession or penitence following on naturally from the discussion. And the homework creates continuity as well as stretching and challenging the group to test the validity of their insights in the tough arena of daily life.

When I read the study notes, I find myself thinking, "Ooh, this is so interesting! This is such fun! I wonder what we'll make of this? This is so challenging!"

Hitting problems

But… every time without fail, in every group I have ever led, the whole thing comes completely unstitched, because the resource materials rely on the session being as tightly chaired as a business meeting.

Perhaps the study notes suggest breaking up into pairs for eight minutes to exchange stories of, say, an early childhood memory. We do this, and after four minutes the leader claps her hands and tells us to swap over, then after eight minutes she claps her hands again and insists we all come back into full group for each member to recount the story they heard.

Well, in the groups I've known, it never works like that. Either the person feeding back is interested only in telling her own story or the first of the pair took up the entire eight minutes on his own story and the second person never got a chance, or else the group members get very interested in the feedback and start chipping in with suggestions and related stories of their own.

I mean, you can *train* your group like a dog pack, making them wait their turn and stick to your timetable and not wander off topic and never interrupt and not ramble on – but that fosters compliance and conformity, not confidence and reflection and the ability to make their own decisions.

Exactly because their contributions were always affirmed and respected, because they were really welcomed and really heard, prayed for properly and encouraged to share in depth, the members of groups where I've borne responsibility arrive expecting to talk.

They also want to pray and sing, and to be offered some discussion starter they can really get their teeth into.

The reason study notes have never worked for me is that they seem to assume the group is the necessary resource for the marvellous study notes, whereas I'd been hoping that the notes would be a resource for my marvellous group.

But if I tried being completely non-directive and not preparing anything at all, just letting them chat on and direct themselves, that didn't work either. The talk came back to the same old issues, dominated by the obsessions and preoccupations of the same few members. People struck up private conversations with their neighbour, or allowed the conversation to drift on into pointless chit-chat.

And I found that, although I didn't want the evening to become a kind of relay race as we panted hastily from one section of the booklet to the next if we were to have an outside chance of being done by 9.30 in time for folk to hurry home and relieve the babysitter, I did still need some sense of purpose, direction, and continuity.

Then I have to admit that too often my house-group preparation involved the awful realization: "Oh, cripes, it's half past six, they'll be here in an hour and the supper still isn't cooked and what the dickens are we going to talk about tonight in any case?"

My groups used to go like this:

They arrive and take off their coats and I offer them drinks. They all want something different. Only one person still drinks coffee; there are two tea drinkers and one of them wants Earl Grey. The rest like fruit teas – except the lady who can't stand them and has brought her own peppermint teabag, and the two who only want a glass of water. Someone has no babysitter so has brought her two-year-old, who needs a spout cup.

Got that? OK. They all like biscuits but two of them are vegan and one is a diabetic.

I come puffing in ten minutes later like a newbie barista laden with everyone's complicated choices. They are all chatting happily.

I begin by going round the group encouraging each person to say something about their week since we last met. Forty-five minutes later we still haven't heard three of the people. While nodding in apparently rapt attention I am mentally revising our programme for the evening, wondering whether to keep the biblical material as it's our core item even though it's a bit boring by itself, or move straight on to the supplementary story and just refer to the Bible passage in introducing it.

I ditch the icebreaker completely with real regret, as it promised to be the most interesting and fun part of the evening. Or else I decide to do the icebreaker anyway, in which case that takes another forty-five minutes and then the Bible passage and supplementary story have to be morphed into introductory material for a time of prayer and the Challenging Question section becomes so much ballast overboard.

And, if we sing, they all want to choose a song and start saying to each other, "But what about you, Sharon – did you have a favourite?" while I'm squinting at the clock and mentally calculating what we can still squeeze in.

These nightmares have afflicted me when I have been on the receiving end of someone else's leadership too. I remember attending a group where we were trying the "Swedish Method" of Bible study, which involved reading a passage of about ten to fifteen verses in search of three specifics:

✹   A light bulb – something in the text that has resulted in an "Aha!" moment of realization.

?   A question mark – something that seems puzzling or hard to understand.

➔   An arrow – something that strikes home for personal application.

This exercise was done in silence and supposed to take about ten minutes. Haha! It took ages. At the end of ten minutes some people hadn't even finished their light bulbs.

After we were all done – or not really *all* done, but the leader got bored with waiting – we went round and shared our findings. I was burning to share my **?** but the leader said I wasn't allowed to – that would have to wait until we'd all done the ✹ s – and went round again. I felt bitterly disappointed and very frustrated because I did actually want the group to help me shed some light on my **?**.

The ✹ s took for ever, and by the time we were halfway round the group for the **?**s, it was ten o'clock and we had to stop, and never mind the ➔s. To be honest, I hadn't really had a ✹; I just made one up to fit in and be helpful, and I never did get to ask my puzzling question. And, if you notice, *I haven't forgotten*! That is, I've long since forgotten the question, but not the frustration.

Do these scenarios sound all too familiar to you?

With all this in mind, it occurred to me that it might help to have a book of outlines that will offer themes, Bible passages, supplementary material, questions and prayer starters, but in so minimalist a format that there is space and to spare for the sharing and discussing that allow a house group to listen respectfully and empathetically, giving each individual enough time to contribute, and for the affirmation that will offer comfort and build confidence.

Then, if someone has shared at length about the horrendous week they've just had, instead of looking at my watch and saying, "OK, thank you. Well, moving on…" there is time to look at the person and ask, "So what will you do about the car?" or "Did he actually call back, then?" This signals to the entire group that their stories, their lives, really *matter*; they are not just the meat for my industrial spiritual sausage machine.

I am assuming that a house group should ideally have the following ingredients:

- Welcome and drinks.
- Sharing: "How was your week?"
- A time of praise songs and worship – or, if singing seems too big an ask, then a time to come consciously into God's presence, focusing and centring ourselves on his loving-kindness and grace.
- Scripture passage and supplementary notes to help us build the bridge between the Bible and the present day.
- Group discussion.
- Prayer time to gather up what we have heard and said, and to bring before God any concerns and burdens currently on our hearts. NB: this prayer time, if your house group is as keen to share as mine always have been, should never be preceded by asking people if they have anything they want to pray about tonight – either you'll be there until dawn or all the praying will be squodged into two minutes. Just start.

The importance of sensitive leadership

The outlines in this book will be too scanty for the Silent House Group, and are unsuitable for the Dominant Leader. These are not the kind of house-group materials that offer instructions like: "First get your group to…" or "Split your group into two halves and do not allow married couples and friends to be in the same subgroup…" or "Allow two minutes per person for this sharing…"

These materials are for the house group in which people feel confident enough to question and object and express a preference, and want to do things differently, to share a ➤ when you'd asked for a **?**.

But you don't want it to degenerate into mere social chit-chat, you do have ground to cover, and you don't want strong personalities to take the ball and keep running with it, leaving quieter people's stories unheard.

Sensitive leadership means waiting patiently for the end of a paragraph when someone is just running on too long, to say, "Thank you so much! Gosh, what an amazing time you had when you were living in Africa. It would be brilliant to hear some more about that **some other time**! Anyone else had a similar experience? How about you, Dave? You've been very quiet tonight. Did anything in the passage especially speak to you?"

In a house group where people are heard – really listened to – they often cry. Have tissues handy, in case. But when someone begins to cry, just let it happen. If someone near them wants to put an arm round their shoulder or a hand on their knee, that's fine. But you the leader shouldn't soar to your feet and surge across the room to enfold them in a five-minute bear hug. Just as they laugh, people also cry. That's OK. It can be affirmed – "Yes, I can see how very painful that parting was for you… take your time … " But don't make a big deal of it.

Create a habit of saying "Yes" to everything, affirming every person, like this:

✔ "Wow, that provoked some discussion, didn't it? OK, let's see if the next question can give us just as much food for thought!"

✖ "Right! One more minute! Finish your sentence! Time to move on! Are you listening, Brian?"

✔ "Oh, man, I can see you've had one heck of a week. Thank you so much for sharing that with us. Have another cookie! Let's hope you feel a bit better by the end of the evening."

✖ "Well, that's very interesting, but I think we'd better move on now because time's getting a bit short."

As a preacher, my biggest routine discouragement has always been the people, in every church, whose stock of small talk obliges them to greet me with a jocular, "Keep it short!" In more than one church, I have been urged by the steward on duty to keep the sermon short because he was hoping to be home in time for the start of the ball game on TV.

Not many things are a bigger turn-off than being *required* to speak to someone who clearly has no interest in what you have to say.

The sensitive leader will position any clock where s/he can keep tabs on the time without her/his eyes ever appearing to leave whomever is speaking.

As someone once said:

"One of the most useful things you can learn is to yawn with your mouth closed, or in such a way that people think you are smiling at them."[1]

Preparing for your house-group meeting

Once your house-group members are all out of their shells and friends with each other, looking forward eagerly to the meeting, most of the work is done by the group members, not by the leader. They are no longer the rank and file, waiting meekly to be told what to do and what to think; the meeting is a circle of energy and ideas, self-stimulating.

This means that the leader doesn't have to spend two hours holed up in the study preparing input and reading up Leaders' Notes, which is good news if the house-group leader is a busy person with a heavy schedule (as is usually the case). These outlines are simple and minimalist, and do not require a big wodge of time for assimilation.

But, though the house-group leader need not spend a long session poring over my notes, preparation is still essential. The difference is that the leader will not be preparing the session or the input or figuring out how to rig the meeting and direct the members; the leader will take time to prepare her/himself.

Sensitive leadership is about attunement to the Holy Spirit, listening to people and listening to God (which is why we have two ears). In the meeting, the leader will listen with complete attention to the stories and ideas of the group members, alert to what the Holy Spirit is saying to and through the participants.

To lead well, one must become spacious and calm. Harassed, preoccupied people, who have given away too much of their time, exude resentment and lose their sense of humour. To lead your house group well it helps if you can find fifteen minutes during the day to sit quietly with your feet up, enjoying a cup of tea and listening to the birds sing, lovingly holding into the radiance of God's presence each individual expected at the meeting… their circumstances… their home… their families… their work… their church commitments… their hopes and dreams and struggles. The leader will put his/her head together with that of God who is our Father and our Friend, looking intently and affectionately into the wonderful herbaceous border of the house group, taking note of its growth, its state of health, and the condition of each individual who blooms there.

---

1   Source unknown; found at this website: http://www.users.globalnet.co.uk/~sstm/advice.htm

And the leader will watch and listen for the movement of the Spirit, the prompting whisper of the still small voice – suggesting, directing, reminding.

Early in the week, some days before the meeting, the leader will have read through the Bible passage, the supporting material, and the questions (which will not take long, just a few minutes), so that the thought seeds they contain can have the chance to germinate before the actual day of the meeting – worthwhile thoughts take time; they don't usually come in a flash.

So when the time comes to open the door and say, "Welcome! Come on in!", the leader's heart and mind will be properly prepared, focused on the evening ahead, centred in the overflowing love with which God regards the people gathering. The notes will have been absorbed and considered, so there will be no business of frowningly consulting, "What does it say to do next?" The leader will be ready to flex with the flow of the meeting and to encourage the exploration that arises from the interaction of the group members, holding in awareness the themes and questions offered to help this circle of pilgrims to grow in their discipleship.

Approached like this, the house group becomes neither a burden nor a chore, nor yet an event to be managed, but an opportunity to marvel at what God is doing in the lives of these individuals as they join in conversation, fellowship, song, and prayer.

How to work with the outlines

These Bible-study outlines have the purpose of making strong links between our own lives and the biblical text, rooting our everyday experiences in the nourishing earth of the Scriptures. Each outline has a Bible passage, some supporting commentary, a series of questions, and a prayer. The short commentaries and the questions are all written to encourage us to find clear relevance to daily life in the Scripture, and to identify with the people of the Bible as we discuss their stories and characters. The emphasis is on inspiring a sense of living connection with the biblical texts, finding our own story in the Scriptures, and teasing out the relevance of the theme and study passages for twenty-first-century life.

Each study outline is intended to act as a focus for the group, a central discussion item to support the serious purpose of growth in discipleship that will make the group feel worthwhile.

For the house group to be more than merely friendly fellowship, it is essential to have a deep, thoroughgoing time of prayer, allowing space for the Spirit to speak and work with the group as a group and its members as individuals, and it is also essential to have an honest engagement with the Scriptures. No opinion should be off-limits; no questioning should be discouraged. For people to really grow and deepen in faith, they must feel that *whatever* they think can be heard, without little frissons of shock or disapproval. Neither the group nor the leader is there to "get them to" think or believe this or that. The combination of the biblical text, the invited presence of the Holy Spirit, and the chance to share honestly and deeply will provide the opportunity to journey into truth. It is important to trust and respect the faith journey of each group member, even if it does not match your own perspective.

The questions that are given with each of the study outlines encourage group members to share from their own faith journey, and explore how the theme connects with their own life. The questions are phrased to build confidence and encourage positive attitudes.

A question in the study on the Bible character Eve reads: "Do you have a story to tell of a time when you, or someone you know, made a really disastrous choice and regretted it afterwards? What did you learn from that?"

So the emphasis remains on the positive – what we can learn from our mistakes – rather than on what went wrong.

I would suggest that, after the welcoming, the sharing of how the week has gone since the group last met, and a time of praise and worship, the leader (having earlier in the week read the material to give it time to sink in and ignite thoughts) should present to the group the themes and Bible passage or passages – probably asking the members to read the scriptural material aloud. There's a choice then. Here are the options:

1. Wait for comments and responses to the passage from the group, perhaps after asking: "Did anything strike you especially? Did you find anything weird or puzzling or particularly challenging? Did the Spirit speak to you as we read?" These questions should not be rattled off like machine-gun fire but asked thoughtfully, with pauses to allow responses, letting conversation be sparked across the group by both the question and any response. When this time or response has run its course, move on to the supplementary material, and repeat the process with that. Visit the questions provided in the outlines one by one – in any order – each time leaving space for responses and developing conversation.

2. Present the supplementary material at the beginning, right after the Bible text, and let the conversation develop from any points the group members pick out from either the passage or the supporting commentary.

3. Have the whole page copied so that the group members can see in advance what the Scripture passages, commentary, and questions are. Allow the choice of where to start and how to work with it to come from the group.

4. Having read through the materials earlier in the week and given your own mind time to play around with it, start the ball rolling by sharing your own thoughts.

Trust the group; don't be afraid of thoughtful silences; give space for conversation to develop.

If on one occasion there seems little to say and the group does *not* engage in discussion very readily, you have the option of either moving on to one of the related studies in the same section, or giving yourself extra time at that particular meeting for prayer and ministry towards the end – maybe offering prayer for healing, or time to sit quietly and wait on the Lord, or an opportunity to offer up to God those things we are finding difficult in life just at the moment... those things that have especially blessed us this week... those people whose troubles weigh heavily on our hearts... world issues for which we want to cry out to God for his help...

Each meeting should leave loads of space for thoughts and ministry to develop, the outlines being offered only for you to guide with a light touch so that the experience feels satisfying for the group. Be ready with your own questions and responses to the materials, but be ready also to step back – not determined to have your say at all costs.

In allowing the house group to grow in confidence, trust, and fellowship, it is impossible to overstate the importance of refraining from any **d**idactic attitude, from **d**isapproval to **d**irectiveness (**D**on't **D**o anything that begins with **D**!). These are *open* questions, encouraging open conversations for taking faith to a profounder level. In any given session, the idea is not that the leader attempts to shepherd the group towards a predetermined undisclosed correct conclusion, signalling by body language and tone of voice which perspectives are or are not acceptable. The leader is there to encourage and affirm, to allow the group to proceed at its own pace through the interactions of its own conversation to truth it can really own, with the Spirit's inspiration and help. If any offensive views are expressed, or if any simply incorrect statements are made, the leader should feel free to challenge – but as an equal, not as a disapproving parent.

So, for example, if in the study "The poor and needy" (in the section of studies on the Law and the Prophets) someone expresses the view that there aren't any poor people in our country nowadays or, if there are, it's their own fault because they should be more enterprising, the leader might well want to challenge this idea. But not by saying, "I think you'll find... " and proceeding to put down their point of view. Pick up the point, and probe it gently, perhaps like this: "I was very interested in your comment that poverty really comes from lack of enterprise, rather than simple misfortune. I guess that must be true sometimes. But I wonder if it always is? I wonder if there are some people struggling with poverty in our country that we maybe haven't noticed? And if there might be a variety of causes... and what those might be... Has anyone got any ideas or thoughts about that?"

If you say "we" not "you", the challenge feels less threatening and the challenged group member less daunted. If you challenge in this gentle way (rather than saying,

"Oh, come on, Dave! That's absolute tosh", even though it obviously is), you offer the challenged person a graceful opportunity to modify an extreme viewpoint and think again. But disapproval or domination will not loosen prejudiced, bigoted, or faulty thinking – it will merely drive it underground.

Where something has been expressed that is simply incorrect, try if you can to align yourself with the mistake. Example: suppose someone says, "I can't see why it says 'after three days he rose again' because he died on Friday afternoon and rose early on Sunday morning – that's not even two days!" Don't jump in quickly to defend the tradition of the church and step down hard on heresy. Allow openness: "Gosh, yes, I see what you mean! I wonder why we have always thought of it as 'three days'?" – and let the group offer the corrective. Or maybe: "Yes, I see what you mean. I always used to feel uneasy about that too – when I looked it up, the Bible commentary said… [explain]… but I agree with you that it only seems like three days if you look at it that way."

Always affirm, always encourage, always be understanding – never disapproving or shocked.

Have fun with these outlines – may your home be a place of friendship, somewhere people learn to love the Lord Jesus, and a safe place to become more self-aware and awake to the needs and the beauty and the vulnerability of their fellow pilgrims.

"Tell me about it!"

(25 Studies)

Bible characters in moments we can identify with

Adam
Eve
Abraham
Ruth
Cain
Elijah
Esther
The widow of Zarephath
David
Jeremiah
Peter
Dorcas
Paul
Martha
Judas
Barnabas
Mary the mother of Jesus
John the Baptist
Andrew
The boy with five loaves and two fishes
Pontius Pilate
Zacchaeus
Deborah
Joseph
Jacob

Adam

Bible passage – Genesis 3:8–12

Then the man and his wife heard the sound of the Lord God as he was walking in the garden in the cool of the day, and they hid from the Lord God among the trees of the garden. But the Lord God called to the man, "Where are you?"

He answered, "I heard you in the garden, and I was afraid because I was naked; so I hid."

And he said, "Who told you that you were naked? Have you eaten from the tree from which I commanded you not to eat?"

The man said, "The woman you put here with me – she gave me some fruit from the tree, and I ate it."

Commentary

How the stories of the Bible manage to fly like an arrow straight to the heart of the human condition!

The description of God "walking in the garden in the cool of the day" is so evocative. If you ask most people where they experience God most deeply, they rarely say "in church", "at a meeting", or even "reading the Bible". Their first response is usually something like: "walking in the hills", "by the seashore", "in the woods", "at the lakeside", or "sitting quietly in my favourite spot in the garden". In a quiet moment, surrounded by the wonder and beauty of nature, the presence of the Lord can be felt so profoundly.

In this particular story, it was unwelcome. Scared of being found out, guilty because he'd done something wrong, Adam hid from God.

It seems so daft to try to hide from God, but we do it. Running away from ourselves, dodging reality, refusing to face the truth – these are all different names for the thing Adam did.

And God calls: "Adam! Where are you?"

It is a heartbreaking moment; losing touch with love, drifting out of reach of the one who can make us whole, turning away from hope and peace – this is what it means to lose our integrity. This is how humanity starts to disintegrate.

And when God finally catches up with Adam, and reality confronts him in the shape of some very unwelcome questions, what does he do? He blames his wife.

Questions

- Can you think of a moment in your life when you felt very close to God – so close that you could actually feel him there? Where were you? What happened?
- Can you think of any instances in the lives of people you know, or in the lives

of public figures (politicians, celebrities), where you have seen them evading responsibility instead of being willing to face the music?

• Is there anything in your own life, just at the moment, that you wish was not happening, would go away? Is there anything that it might help to talk through, that you know you need to face squarely but you have been trying to avoid thinking about?

Prayer

O loving Lord, you see us and you know us. You, the God who made us, search us out and find us. You see through our pretences; our evasions mean nothing to you. You understand us, because you see and know who we really are. There is no need to put on an act for you – and no point in trying to. You are the only one in the whole of our lives who will never be taken in, who will always see the heart of us, who will always understand. Thank you for loving us, thank you for coming to find us, thank you for really seeing us. As we sit quietly here with you now, may the truth of who you are touch the truth of who we are and, in making the connection, make us whole. In Jesus' holy name; Amen.

Eve

Bible passage – Genesis 3:1–6

Now the snake was more crafty than any of the wild animals the Lord God had made. He said to the woman, "Did God really say, 'You must not eat from any tree in the garden'?"

The woman said to the snake, "We may eat fruit from the trees in the garden, but God did say, 'You must not eat fruit from the tree that is in the middle of the garden, and you must not touch it, or you will die.'"

"You will not certainly die," the snake said to the woman. "For God knows that when you eat from it your eyes will be opened, and you will be like God, knowing good and evil."

When the woman saw that the fruit of the tree was good for food and pleasing to the eye, and also desirable for gaining wisdom, she took some and ate it. She also gave some to her husband, who was with her, and he ate it.

Commentary

This is the story of the ultimate consumer. It reminds me of every shopping trip I wish I hadn't made.

Relocate to the mall. You have wandered into a hardware store where a salesman is doing a promotional demonstration of a kitchen gadget you never knew you wanted – until now! Somewhere underneath it all, you have left behind the frank reality that a kitchen knife, a wooden spoon, or a vegetable peeler will supply everything you need for the job in hand. The salesman convinces you that what you already have can't really be good enough – look: this is so much better!

Think of the time you will save. Think how much more economically you can use every scrap of fruit/vegetable/flour/whatever-it-is if you use this gadget to prepare it. Think how neat and pleasing it is – much more elegant than your tatty old implements tossing around in the drawer. And so much easier to clean! Why, it would be irresponsible, wasteful, and slovenly to try to keep house without it.

You call your husband over to have a look. You put it into his mind that, if only you had this, you'd probably have time to make apple dumplings again. And plum pie. With cream. And maybe ice cream as well. If he doesn't think you're being a bit extravagant, of course…

Six months later it's another useless lump of rusty dusty junk in the landfill site, and there you are back with your kitchen knife, your wooden spoon, and your vegetable peeler.

Questions

- Do you have a story to tell of a time when you, or someone you know, made a really disastrous choice and regretted it afterwards? What did you learn from that?

- Is there a temptation you always fall for – something you can never resist? Is cheesecake your downfall, or shoes? Or computer games? Some people find it hard to walk away from a stationer's without a bagful of Absolutely Indispensable Purchases, just as some people can see how all their problems could be solved with one more little bet on a horse… And what about sales patter? Is there a line that will always pull you in? Is there a particular bait that will always be sure to make you swallow the hook?

- Do you have any tips to share for helping us take a step back from temptation, helping us claw our way back to the truth we really know?

Prayer

Wise and loving God, you know what is good for us better than we know ourselves. You know how easily we are taken in, how readily we are tempted and persuaded. Please help us to put in place in our lives the firebreaks that will protect us from the consequences of temptation. May we learn to know ourselves and our vulnerabilities so well that we know when to walk away, take a breather, give ourselves twenty-four hours to think things over. And as we go about this world where the serpents, craftier than any other wild animals, are just waiting for suckers like us to come walking by, please travel with us, please remind and recall us – for you, God of love, know us better than we know ourselves. In Jesus' holy name; Amen.

Abraham

Bible passage – James 2:14–24

What good is it, my brothers and sisters, if someone claims to have faith but has no deeds? Can such faith save them? Suppose a brother or a sister is without clothes and daily food. If one of you says to them, "Go in peace; keep warm and well fed," but does nothing about their physical needs, what good is it? In the same way, faith by itself, if it is not accompanied by action, is dead.

But someone will say, "You have faith; I have deeds."

Show me your faith without deeds, and I will show you my faith by my deeds. You believe that there is one God. Good! Even the demons believe that – and shudder.

You foolish person, do you want evidence that faith without deeds is useless? Was not our father Abraham considered righteous for what he did when he offered his son Isaac on the altar? You see that his faith and his actions were working together, and his faith was made complete by what he did. And the scripture was fulfilled that says, "Abraham believed God, and it was credited to him as righteousness," and he was called God's friend. You see that a person is considered righteous by what they do and not by faith alone.

Commentary

Paul, in his letters to churches, is concerned to ensure that they understand that the love and grace of God cannot be earned; they are unconditional. No matter who we are or what we have done, it is as we put our trust in God and enter the wonder of a personal relationship with Jesus, knowing the life-giving joy of his presence in our hearts, that we discover for ourselves what salvation is. As the letter to the Ephesians says: "For it is by grace you have been saved, through faith – and this is not from yourselves, it is the gift of God – not by works, so that no one can boast" (Ephesians 2:8–9). So we cannot earn salvation; it is not deserved. It is the gift of God's love that blooms in our lives as we put our trust in him.

But James balances up that teaching by pointing out that once a person has found faith in God, the evidence of faith will be clearly apparent in that person's life. If we really have entered into a personal relationship with the living God, the transformation will surely be seen in our choices and actions.

Abraham, man of faith and great intercessor, put his trust in God so completely that he left behind everything he knew to travel into the uncharted territory of the desert – because that was what God called him to do. Perhaps he was called God's friend because the hallmark of friendship is trust.

Our Bible passage refers to Abraham's willingness to offer his own child in sacrifice if that was what God asked (the story is in Genesis 22). If you imagine the ancient nomadic Hebrews hearing tales of their people's faith around the evening campfires, you can see that this story has great power. Sacrificing children was part of the old Canaanite religion; when crops failed or disaster threatened it would have been easy to slip back into old ways. In this exciting story the whole future of the people of Israel is jeopardized as Isaac is bound and laid on the altar. God's provision of a ram instead of a child must have made an indelible impression on their understanding. For Christians, the only son carrying the wood on his back to the place of sacrifice has other overtones. The story of Christ who was the Lamb of God as well as God's only Son develops further our insight into the mystery of sacrifice – the acknowledgment that at a very deep place we are all one. Jesus took upon himself the lostness and suffering of all humanity.

Questions

- Can you trace in your own life the difference made by believing in God and knowing him? Can you identify times when that has made the difference to your choices and actions – or those of someone you know?
- Thinking back to people you have known who had real, deep, authentic faith in God – how could you tell?
- What does it mean to you, to be someone's friend? What are the essentials of friendship? Would you describe your relationship with God as friendship? Or does that not express the way you personally feel about God?

Prayer

Lord God, as far above us as the stars, as close as our heartbeats and our breath, make yourself real to us. Draw near to us; make your home in our hearts. Just as Abraham, travelling out into the unknown vastness of the desert, walked so closely with you that people said you and he were friends, so may we also enter the mystery of that relationship, and find your living reality in the intimate chamber of our hearts. For we ask it in Jesus' holy name; Amen.

Ruth

Bible passage – Ruth 1:8–19

Naomi said to her two daughters-in-law, "Go back, each of you, to your mother's home. May the Lord show you kindness, as you have shown kindness to your dead husbands and to me. May the Lord grant that each of you will find rest in the home of another husband."

Then she kissed them goodbye and they wept aloud and said to her, "We will go back with you to your people."

But Naomi said, "Return home, my daughters. Why would you come with me? Am I going to have any more sons, who could become your husbands? Return home, my daughters; I am too old to have another husband. Even if I thought there was still hope for me – even if I had a husband tonight and then gave birth to sons – would you wait until they grew up? Would you remain unmarried for them? No, my daughters. It is more bitter for me than for you, because the Lord's hand has turned against me!"

At this they wept aloud again. Then Orpah kissed her mother-in-law goodbye, but Ruth clung to her.

"Look," said Naomi, "your sister-in-law is going back to her people and her gods. Go back with her."

But Ruth replied, "Don't urge me to leave you or to turn back from you. Where you go I will go, and where you stay I will stay. Your people will be my people and your God my God. Where you die I will die, and there I will be buried. May the Lord deal with me, be it ever so severely, if even death separates you and me." When Naomi realised that Ruth was determined to go with her, she stopped urging her.

So the two women went on until they came to Bethlehem.

Commentary

Can you imagine what life must have felt like for Naomi, Ruth, and Orpah, standing at the graveside of their husbands? What now? For a woman in their society, all economic security and social well-being were bound up with marriage. They were facing ruin as well as personal loss. Their lives were devastated. Married out of their own culture, the practical option for the younger women is to return to their families of origin where traditional obligations may offer protection. A widow might be less attractive than a virgin, but she can hope to marry again, and so find shelter from the unforgiving climate of economic isolation. Orpah sees the sense of this option. Dazed and stupefied with grief (and no doubt numb with fear) though they all are, she turns away from the place of death and begins to make her way back home. But another question has arisen in Ruth's mind. She turns to Naomi, wondering, "And what about you?"

People in the shocked state of recent bereavement often display a characteristic introspection that can look like selfishness. Ruth's inability to forget the concerns of others marks her out as an extraordinary woman. She is part of the line of ancestry that leads to Jesus. Why are we not surprised?

Questions

- A friend of mine returning from a conference reported that the most memorable moment for her had been the wisdom: "If you want to travel fast, go alone; if you want to travel far, stick together." In the film *Gladiator* (2000), Russell Crowe's character Maximus speaks the memorable lines: "Whatever comes out of these gates, we've got a better chance of survival if we work together. Do you understand? If we stay together, we survive." How does this line of thinking resonate for your own life? Are you an essentially tribal person, or a cat that walks alone?

- Have there been moments of loss or bereavement in your own life when you really didn't know what to do or where to turn? What were the things and people that helped you start again?

- Did you notice how our passage ended: "So the two women went on until they came to Bethlehem"? Can you identify points in this passage or your wider reading of the book of Ruth that begin to speak to us of the life of Jesus, even though she lived so long before he was born?

Prayer

O Father of Israel, protector of the people of God, our refuge and our eternal home, may we, like Ruth, grasp the essential truth that we belong together, that if we stick together we are strong, that whatever befalls my brother, my sister, is in the end my future too. In Jesus' holy name; Amen.

Cain

Bible passage Genesis 4:2–9

Now Abel kept flocks, and Cain worked the soil. In the course of time Cain brought some of the fruits of the soil as an offering to the Lord. But Abel also brought an offering – fat portions from some of the firstborn of his flock. The Lord looked with favour on Abel and his offering, but on Cain and his offering he did not look with favour. So Cain was very angry, and his face was downcast.

Then the Lord said to Cain, "Why are you angry? Why is your face downcast? If you do what is right, will you not be accepted? But if you do not do what is right, sin is crouching at your door; it desires to have you, but you must rule over it."

Now Cain said to his brother Abel, "Let's go out to the field." While they were in the field, Cain attacked his brother Abel and killed him.

Then the Lord said to Cain, "Where is your brother Abel?"

"I don't know," he replied. "Am I my brother's keeper?"

Commentary

This story doesn't explain why Abel's offering pleased God and Cain's didn't; that remains a mystery to us. What is less puzzling is what happens next. Jealous, embarrassed, and resentful, Cain brews up such anger against his brother that he murders him. Interesting. Maybe the root of the problem is Cain's shame and rejection – so painfully uncomfortable, so hard to bear. Instead of facing the cause in his own life that he could work on and change, he turns his wretchedness outwards: "It's your fault!"

It's always tempting, if something has happened to make us feel inadequate, to begin to really dislike the person who has done well and whom everyone admires, while our own work is ignored or passed over or dismissed. Angry shame and jealousy gather into a focus as comparisons reinforce our sense of rejection.

Questions

• Can you think of a time when someone else came first in a competition you badly wanted to win and thought you deserved to? How did you feel? What were your feelings about the person who won?

• God said to Cain, "Where is your brother Abel?"
Cain – angry, guilty, and frightened, answered God: "I don't know. Am I my brother's keeper?" As we look at the modern world – our clothes made in sweatshops to keep the prices down, poor people pushed off their homelands to make way for farms where big corporations will grow our food – we maybe

hear God asking us, "But what about your brother, your sister?" Feeling guilty and overwhelmed, we come back with the same answer: "I don't know. Am I my brother's keeper?" What changes could we make in our lives to take better care of one another? In our global village, how far are we responsible for the way our commodities are produced, and to what extent is that the responsibility of the producers?

- Can you think of any instances in your own life where you felt you had let someone down but it was too late to go back and put it right? What did you do about that? Is there anything you would like to change about it still?

Prayer

When we call you "Father", we are saying we belong to one another as family. Reaching out for your love and mercy, we remember that you expect us to begin the costly work of compassion and reconciliation in our own lives. Breathe into our hearts, Spirit of God, your loving-kindness and humility. Speak quietly to us about anything we need to put right. Give us the necessary courage to face our own shortcomings, without blaming anybody else, or passing on the responsibility. For we ask it in Jesus' name; Amen.

Elijah

Bible passage – 1 Kings 19:9–13

And the word of the Lord came to him: "What are you doing here, Elijah?"

He replied, "I have been very zealous for the Lord God Almighty. The Israelites have rejected your covenant, torn down your altars, and put your prophets to death with the sword. I am the only one left, and now they are trying to kill me too."

The Lord said, "Go out and stand on the mountain in the presence of the Lord, for the Lord is about to pass by."

Then a great and powerful wind tore the mountains apart and shattered the rocks before the Lord, but the Lord was not in the wind. After the wind there was an earthquake, but the Lord was not in the earthquake. After the earthquake came a fire, but the Lord was not in the fire. And after the fire came a gentle whisper. When Elijah heard it, he pulled his cloak over his face and went out and stood at the mouth of the cave.

Then a voice said to him, "What are you doing here, Elijah?"

Commentary

Elijah's boldness and faith in confronting the prophets of Baal resulted in resounding success and mighty signs and wonders, and we see him here in a fit of post-miracle depression, hiding from the enemies his audacity has won him, feeling vulnerable and lonely. The Lord seeks him out, demonstrating to him that God's presence does not always require a dazzling and spectacular display or accomplishment, but is there in quietness too, in the silent whisper of the heart.

And God prompts Elijah to reflect and evaluate: "What are you doing here, Elijah?"

You might say God did not indulge Elijah but put him on the spot! This is the God who knows your name and knows where you live! There's no escape, then – and that can be challenging. But it's comforting too, because God loves us, and we belong to him.

Questions

- Have there been times in your life when you felt very flat and tired after a difficult, dangerous, demanding, or very exciting time? If you felt an encounter with God then, or if you prayed during that time, can you remember how it all felt? Did God seem near to you or far away?

- Elijah said to God, "I am the only one left, and now they are trying to kill me too." Can you remember a time when you felt very lonely and beleaguered – or maybe you feel that way at the moment! How did you find your way out of that state of mind?

- In John's Gospel (chapter 9) there's a story about a man who was born blind. Jesus healed him, and he seriously annoyed the Temple authorities by standing up for Jesus when they questioned him. So after a few choice words they threw him out. The story says, "Jesus heard that they had thrown him out, and when he found him, he said, 'Do you believe in the Son of Man?'" (John 9:35). Can you find similarities and connection between Jesus seeking out the man who had been blind, and God seeking out Elijah?

Prayer

Faithful God, you come looking for us. You know our story and you see how we feel. You never abandon us. When we are lonely and desolate, when we are rejected, when we are afraid, you come to find us. You bring us a new challenge, new hope, and the comfort of your company. Help us to reach deep inside at times like this, to find the faith to respond to all that your love asks of us today. In Jesus' holy name; Amen.

Esther

Bible passage – Esther 2:7–11, 17

Mordecai had a cousin named Hadassah, whom he had brought up because she had neither father nor mother. This young woman, who was also known as Esther, had a lovely figure and was beautiful. Mordecai had taken her as his own daughter when her father and mother died.

When the king's order and edict had been proclaimed, many young women were brought to the citadel of Susa and put under the care of Hegai. Esther also was taken to the king's palace and entrusted to Hegai, who had charge of the harem. She pleased him and won his favour. Immediately he provided her with her beauty treatments and special food. He assigned to her seven female attendants selected from the king's palace and moved her and her attendants into the best place in the harem.

Esther had not revealed her nationality and family background, because Mordecai had forbidden her to do so. Every day he walked to and fro near the courtyard of the harem to find out how Esther was and what was happening to her...

... Now the king was attracted to Esther more than to any of the other women, and she won his favour and approval more than any of the other virgins. So he set a royal crown on her head and made her queen instead of Vashti.

Commentary

Look well. This is the first and last time you will see a beauty queen taken seriously by the church. In fact, the members of the group will probably need the leader to go through the story with them, because the book of Esther is a Place We Don't Often Go in the church, so they might never have read it at all.

The book of Esther raises big questions for modern women. It does not question the right of a man to order his wife about and get rid of her if she does not comply at once with his wishes and demands. It assumes the normality of a harem – and trawling the country for beautiful virgins to put in it for the king's pleasure. It accepts as a matter of course the necessity for a woman to be shapely of form and beautiful of face to get anywhere in life. We are, of course, all familiar with these depressing realities – but we might have hoped they would not be rammed home by the Bible.

As the story of Esther unfolds, we see how her womanly qualities of patience, lowliness, beauty, shapeliness, and respect can be converted into weapons for use in the war between the Jews and their enemies. Not only does she save her people from destruction with her careful feminine diplomacy, but she sees to it that those who wished to harm them are executed by being impaled on poles, as was the custom in the culture she had married into.

Questions

- How do you feel about social traditions of feminine beauty – high heels, make-up, dressed hair? Should we affirm these as a celebration of femininity? Are they worldly fashions to be avoided, as many Christian teachers have asserted? Or are they just matters of self-expression and personal preference?

- How do you feel about the so-called womanly attributes of beauty, docility, and a gentle and yielding spirit being stepping stones to advancement and preferment? Is this simply the way of nature, is it obnoxious gender discrimination, or does it express the God-ordained difference between men and women?

- Can you put into words how you feel men and women should relate to one another, in marriage and the home and also in wider society? Should a woman defer to her husband, or do you feel that they should offer one another the respect of equals? You may like to explore such Scriptures as Galatians 3:26–29, Ephesians 5, and 1 Peter 3:1–7 for New Testament perspectives on the same theme.

Prayer

Creator God, you made us as we are, breathed your Spirit into us to give us life, and redeemed each one of us when we were lost and broken in sin. To each of us you hold out your gift of freedom and belonging – the love of your heart. Help us to see ourselves as you see us, to look at one another through your eyes of love. May the beauty that pleases you shine forth in our lives, may the humility of your reconciling and redeeming love be apparent in the way we respect each other, and may the honour you accord us in setting us free be mirrored in the societies we shape and build. For we ask it in Jesus' holy name; Amen.

The widow of Zarephath

Bible passage – 1 Kings 17:8–16, NKJV

Then the word of the Lord came to [Elijah], saying, "Arise, go to Zarephath, which belongs to Sidon, and dwell there. See, I have commanded a widow there to provide for you." So he arose and went to Zarephath. And when he came to the gate of the city, indeed a widow was there gathering sticks. And he called to her and said, "Please bring me a little water in a cup, that I may drink." And as she was going to get it, he called to her and said, "Please bring me a morsel of bread in your hand."

So she said, "As the Lord your God lives, I do not have bread, only a handful of flour in a bin, and a little oil in a jar; and see, I am gathering a couple of sticks that I may go in and prepare it for myself and my son, that we may eat it, and die."

And Elijah said to her, "Do not fear; go and do as you have said, but make me a small cake from it first, and bring it to me; and afterward make some for yourself and your son. For thus says the Lord God of Israel: 'The bin of flour shall not be used up, nor shall the jar of oil run dry, until the day the Lord sends rain on the earth.'"

So she went away and did according to the word of Elijah; and she and he and her household ate for many days. The bin of flour was not used up, nor did the jar of oil run dry, according to the word of the Lord which He spoke by Elijah.

Commentary

Just as creeping buttercup grows in acidic earth, so secularism flourishes in times of peace and plenty, as the warning in Deuteronomy 8:12–14 suggests: "… when you build fine houses and settle down, and when your herds and flocks grow large and your silver and gold increase and all you have is multiplied, then your heart will become proud and you will forget the Lord your God, who brought you out of Egypt."

So with the growth of mass production and a gradual dislocation from the processes of nature has come into our hearts a sense of self-reliance.

The widow of Zarephath lived with no such luxuries. Like the poor everywhere, she eked out a hand-to-mouth existence, never sure if there would be anything for tomorrow. Even so, despite the anxieties of hard times as a single mother with nothing to spare, a lifelong habit of hospitality compelled her to share what she had with the stranger who begged for her help.

Poverty and adversity are not conditions we embrace with enthusiasm, but they do have this to commend them: it is when we are between a rock and a hard place that we are best situated to experience for ourselves the God of miracles. Almost every testimony of answered prayer and the wonders of God's mighty power is also a testimony of hard times.

Questions

- Have you ever experienced first-hand a miracle of God's provision or an astonishing answer to prayer? What happened?
- In your own life, can you notice any correlation between material prosperity or hardship and spiritual dryness or depth? What have been, for you, the conditions or experiences that deepened faith and inspired a sense of real connection to the living God?
- Where we see people suffering through poverty, compassion moves us to help and rescue them. It is a terrible thing that children should die from starvation or easily preventable diseases. What sort of a balance do you think we might aim for in our personal lives and society in general, in alleviating suffering yet living simply enough and close enough to nature that we do not lose our sense of wonder or cease to turn to God for daily help?

Prayer

God of love and compassion, you care about every single person, from the poorest beggars in the streets to directors of giant corporations who can pull the strings of nation states. Help us to live wisely, choosing the freedom of simplicity and the kindness of hospitality. Help us to remember, whatever circumstances life holds out to us, that you are our God and our hope is in you. Whatever happens to us as we go along the unknown way of life's journey, may we always keep faith with you, never lose our trust in you, and never let go of your hand. In Jesus' name; Amen.

David

Bible passage – 2 Samuel 18:33 – 19:8

The king was shaken. He went up to the room over the gateway and wept. As he went, he said: "O my son Absalom! My son, my son Absalom! If only I had died instead of you – O Absalom, my son, my son!"

Joab was told, "The king is weeping and mourning for Absalom." And for the whole army the victory that day was turned into mourning, because on that day the troops heard it said, "The king is grieving for his son." The men stole into the city that day as men steal in who are ashamed when they flee from battle. The king covered his face and cried aloud, "O my son Absalom! O Absalom, my son, my son!"

Then Joab went into the house to the king and said, "Today you have humiliated all your men, who have just saved your life and the lives of your sons and daughters and the lives of your wives and concubines. You love those who hate you and hate those who love you. You have made it clear today that the commanders and their men mean nothing to you. I see that you would be pleased if Absalom were alive today and all of us were dead. Now go out and encourage your men. I swear by the Lord that if you don't go out, not a man will be left with you by nightfall. This will be worse for you than all the calamities that have come on you from your youth till now."

So the king got up and took his seat in the gateway. When the men were told, "The king is sitting in the gateway," they all came before him.

Meanwhile, the Israelites had fled to their homes.

Commentary

King David – poet, soldier, shepherd, lover, musician, statesman – is a central figure in the history of Israel, so important that Jesus is sometimes called the Son of David and his kingdom likened to a perfecting and fulfilling of the golden era of King David's reign.

In this story we see David's strength of character and sense of responsibility in turning aside from heart-rending personal grief to attend to the affairs of state. We might notice his willingness to listen to his advisors and to put first the well-being of his people, his self-control, and his sense of priorities – but also the passion and depth of the love he brought to his personal relationships.

Questions

- The Bible describes King David as "a man after God's own heart" (1 Samuel 13:13–14; Acts 13:22). Why do you think this was? Because of his courage? Because of his honesty? Because he was a 100-per-cent man – all passion?

Because of his willingness to repent and his ability to have mercy? Thinking about people you have known in your own life, who would you pick out as a man or woman after God's own heart?

- The story about King David chosen for our study of him shows a moment of tremendous self-discipline, as he puts aside his personal concerns to honour the people in line with his state duty. Thinking about our own national leaders, what comment do you have to make about getting the balance right between private and public life?

- Can you look back to a time in your own life, or the life of someone you know, when big personal stuff had to be set aside while you met the expectations and requirements of your job or social position?

For more wonderful stories about David's passionate nature and colourful life, you might like to look at 2 Samuel 11:1 – 12:24 (David and Bathsheba), 2 Samuel 6:12–22 (David dancing before the Lord), 1 Samuel 16:23 (David's gift of music), 1 Samuel 24 (David spares Saul's life), and 1 Samuel 17 (David and Goliath), or read one of his songs – perhaps Psalm 51, 55, or 139.

Prayer

Examine us, O God, and look deeply into our hearts and minds. What do you find there? If we are half-hearted, breathe upon the flame of life ebbing and guttering within us, and kindle it again. If we have been selfish, always putting our own interests above those of our family or community, ignite in us your vision of what it means to serve and to belong to the whole people of God, the household of faith. In this, our time on earth, may we grasp and appreciate the opportunity we have been given to really live and really love; for we ask it in Jesus' holy name. Amen.

Jeremiah

Bible passages

Jeremiah 1:4–8

The word of the Lord came to me, saying,

"Before I formed you in the womb I knew you, before you were born I set you apart; I appointed you as a prophet to the nations."

"Alas, Sovereign Lord," I said, "I do not know how to speak; I am too young."

But the Lord said to me, "Do not say, 'I am too young.' You must go to everyone I send you to and say whatever I command you. Do not be afraid of them, for I am with you and will rescue you," declares the Lord.

Jeremiah 20:8–9

So the word of the Lord has brought me insult and reproach all day long. But if I say, "I will not mention his word or speak any more in his name," his word is in my heart like a fire, a fire shut up in my bones. I am weary of holding it in; indeed, I cannot.

Commentary

Jeremiah was a reluctant prophet who didn't like what he saw, correctly anticipated that speaking out would make him seriously unpopular, and tried his best to dodge the responsibility of what the Quakers call "speaking Truth to Power".

But there is something about God's truth that simply won't let him alone. Maybe that's what it means to be a prophet, someone who can't just be content to do what everyone else does – turn a blind eye to injustice and wrongdoing, choose what is convenient, expedient, and comfortable over what we really know deep inside is responsible and good.

Jeremiah's prophetic career started early. One of the first objections he made to God's call on his life was that he was way too young – nobody would listen to him. God promised he would be with him. That may not have been entirely reassuring. I remember the great preacher John Wimber commenting that God's way is never easy. What he actually said was, "Get filled with the Holy Spirit and spend the rest of your life desperate!" John Wimber said he knew three prayers: "Help!", "Oh God!", and "Oh God, help!"

I guess Jeremiah knew what he meant.

Questions

- Any day of the week you can hear the old folks complaining about "young people today"; they seem to be held in no higher regard than they were in Jeremiah's day. What do you think? Does the church community take its young people seriously? Do the lives of the older church members offer enough of a prophetic example and ethical challenge to inspire the younger ones? Can you remember a time when someone who you assumed was too young to have a worthwhile opinion surprised you by their insight and sagacity?

- The prophetic life is not easy. Can you think of issues of importance in our day where doing the right thing seems too large and complicated to tackle? What would it mean to live a prophetic life in the modern world? On what topics would you want to speak out and try to make a difference?

- Jeremiah's ministry meant accepting unpopularity and loneliness as an everyday way of life. Have there been times when you (or someone you know) have lost friends and encountered antagonism and disapproval by standing up for truth and goodness?

Prayer

O God of truth, whose word burns like fire, whose light exposes what is hidden away, who calls us to live as the prophets of our day – give us wisdom and courage, give us honesty and determination, and with that give us graciousness, gentleness, and kindness, so that we may witness to both your truth and your love to the people of our own day. In Jesus' holy name; Amen.

Peter

Bible passage – Luke 22:54–62

Then seizing him, they led him away and took him into the house of the high priest. Peter followed at a distance. And when some there had kindled a fire in the middle of the courtyard and had sat down together, Peter sat down with them. A servant-girl saw him seated there in the firelight. She looked closely at him and said, "This man was with him."

But he denied it. "Woman, I don't know him," he said.

A little later someone else saw him and said, "You also are one of them."

"Man, I am not!" Peter replied.

About an hour later another asserted, "Certainly this fellow was with him, for he is a Galilean."

Peter replied, "Man, I don't know what you're talking about!" Just as he was speaking, the cock crowed. The Lord turned and looked straight at Peter. Then Peter remembered the word the Lord had spoken to him: "Before the cock crows today, you will disown me three times." And he went outside and wept bitterly.

Commentary

Who could not love Peter? Reading the Gospel story, we recognize our own humanity in him – the moments of insight and audacity, the situations when blind panic sets in, love and fear jostling together. One minute he and Jesus are on the same wavelength; the next minute Peter gets the wrong end of the stick and is demoted from "this was not revealed to you by flesh and blood, but by my Father in heaven" to "Get behind me, Satan!" (Matthew 16:13–23). In the book of Acts he is revered as a great leader – and has to endure a severe ear-bashing from Paul on the subject of his hypocrisy. We hear about this in Paul's letter to the Galatians – Luke is more discreet in his account of the matter in Acts! (Acts 15; Galatians 2:11–14).

Our passage here has a corresponding one in John 21:15–19, where the risen Jesus asks Peter three times, "Do you love me?" We feel the gentle touch of the Master on Peter's triple denial in this passage.

Peter comes across as a man of immense potential continually undermined by ordinary human failings – and of which of us is that not true?

He is on the one hand the man whose faith failed him and left him floundering in the lake, reaching out in panic to Jesus, but that's because on the other hand he was the only man other than Jesus Christ to have successfully attempted to walk on water – even if only for a few steps (Matthew 14:22–31). And in the Gospels Peter's story contrasts starkly with that of Judas – for they both betrayed Jesus, but Peter had the humility to say sorry and start again, whereas Judas succumbed to despair.

Questions

- Can you think of areas of contrast – in yourself or in others – where you can be strong one minute and fall the next? What helps you to be strong? What tends to trip you up?
- Do you find it easy to identify with Peter when you read the Gospel story? Which of the other Bible characters specially strike a chord with you? Are there some who simply don't resonate with you at all?
- Our passage shows the immense risk the friends of Jesus took in being his followers. Have there been times in your own life when doing the right thing or speaking up for your faith has been costly and sacrificial?

Prayer

O God of life and power, who made yourself known to us in Jesus, may his courage, faith, and love so take root in us that we cannot help but follow him. Thank you for the example of his disciple Peter, who shows us how to start again and never give up. May we too quietly align ourselves with the great company of witnesses to the gospel, so that at the last we may hear Jesus speak over our lives the words we long for: "Well done, thou good and faithful servant." In Jesus' holy name; Amen.

Dorcas

Bible passage – Acts 9:36–42

In Joppa there was a disciple named Tabitha (in Greek her name is Dorcas); she was always doing good and helping the poor. About that time she became ill and died, and her body was washed and placed in an upstairs room. Lydda was near Joppa; so when the disciples heard that Peter was in Lydda, they sent two men to him and urged him, "Please come at once!"

Peter went with them, and when he arrived he was taken upstairs to the room. All the widows stood round him, crying and showing him the robes and other clothing that Dorcas had made while she was still with them.

Peter sent them all out of the room; then he got down on his knees and prayed. Turning towards the dead woman, he said, "Tabitha, get up." She opened her eyes, and seeing Peter she sat up. He took her by the hand and helped her to her feet. Then he called for the believers, especially the widows, and presented her to them alive. This became known all over Joppa, and many people believed in the Lord.

Commentary

I wonder why Peter sent all those women out of the room. There's something about the way this story is told – "Peter sent them all out of the room; then he got down on his knees and prayed" – that causes me to suspect Peter wasn't 100 per cent sure this was going to work, but he thought he'd give it his best shot. The ministry of signs and wonders is exciting and faith-building – but it has nothing certain or predictable about it. It always means going out on a limb.

Can you imagine Dorcas? She sounds like a practical, capable, peaceable, gentle woman; a seamstress, sitting quietly in her Mediterranean seaside home sewing tunics and robes. A loving, kindly woman who cared about other people and would always help when she could. We don't know much about Dorcas, but enough to find a role model for our imagination.

What a strange thing, for her to be called back into this life by a miracle, after she had found her way out through the great doorway of death into the world of light. This is a story that, if we look deeply into it, probably leaves us with more questions than answers. We would expect a believer to leave this life when her work is done and God calls her home, but God had one more blessing-task for Dorcas – to turn back to her sisters in this world and show them what power and glory can be. Without arrogance, without a single word, just by being alive, Dorcas witnesses to the power of God.

Questions

- Has there been someone in your life whose death has made a really big hole? If you could choose one person to be miraculously raised from the dead, who would that be?

- Have you ever come close to a miracle, or seen the power of God at work in a special and unusual way? What happened?

- Without saying or doing anything, Dorcas was living proof of God's mighty power and healing love. Can you think of ways in which, even without a startling miracle like this, we might be able to fulfil the words of Jesus to "let your light shine before others, that they may see your good deeds and glorify your Father in heaven"? (Matthew 5:16).

Prayer

Wonder-working God, we stand amazed when we come close to the signs of your power, the lives your glory has touched and healed. May we be filled with faith and trust in you, as Peter was, to act in your name for healing and fullness of life. May our lives radiate the sweet fragrance of kindness that Dorcas showed, to care for the poor and needy and work quietly and faithfully in the everyday calling of our lives. In Jesus' holy name; Amen.

48

Paul

Bible passage – Philippians 3:1–14

Further, my brothers and sisters, rejoice in the Lord! It is no trouble for me to write the same things to you again, and it is a safeguard for you.

Watch out for those dogs, those evildoers, those mutilators of the flesh. For it is we who are the circumcision, we who serve God by his Spirit, who boast in Christ Jesus, and who put no confidence in the flesh – though I myself have reasons for such confidence.

If someone else thinks they have reasons to put confidence in the flesh, I have more: circumcised on the eighth day, of the people of Israel, of the tribe of Benjamin, a Hebrew of Hebrews; in regard to the law, a Pharisee; as for zeal, persecuting the church; as for righteousness based on the law, faultless.

But whatever were gains to me I now consider loss for the sake of Christ. What is more, I consider everything a loss because of the surpassing worth of knowing Christ Jesus my Lord, for whose sake I have lost all things. I consider them garbage, that I may gain Christ and be found in him, not having a righteousness of my own that comes from the law, but that which is through faith in Christ – the righteousness that comes from God on the basis of faith. I want to know Christ – yes, to know the power of his resurrection and participation in his sufferings, becoming like him in his death, and so, somehow, attaining to the resurrection from the dead.

Not that I have already obtained all this, or have already arrived at my goal, but I press on to take hold of that for which Christ Jesus took hold of me. Brothers and sisters, I do not consider myself yet to have taken hold of it. But one thing I do: forgetting what is behind and straining towards what is ahead, I press on towards the goal to win the prize for which God has called me heavenwards in Christ Jesus.

Commentary

In our Bible passage we can see how passionate Paul was, and how strongly he expressed himself – he was a man who made loyal friends but also a lot of enemies! The passage tells us about his high status as a Pharisee in his faith community of origin. Once meticulously observant of the Jewish Law, he came to believe that it had no power to save his soul at all, that salvation was freely given by God, grace received by faith.

The passage refers to Paul's valiant struggle to keep the faith from becoming just another Jewish sect. He became known as "the apostle of the Gentiles". If he had not argued and insisted that Gentiles did not have to embrace Jewish ways to be accepted by God, Christianity might never have come to those of us not of Jewish descent. We have a lot to thank him for.

Much of the New Testament is by or about Paul. Here are two more quotations from his letters:

"For it is by grace you have been saved, through faith – and this is not from yourselves, it is the gift of God – not by works, so that no one can boast" (Ephesians 2:8–9);

... "he said to me, 'My grace is sufficient for you, for my power is made perfect in weakness.' Therefore I will boast all the more gladly about my weaknesses, so that Christ's power may rest on me" (2 Corinthians 12:9).

Questions

- Are you an all-or-nothing person, like Paul, impetuous and passionate, or are you a more cautious person, inclined to think things through and express yourself mildly? Did you come to faith suddenly and dramatically, as Paul did (Acts 9:1–7), or has your faith grown more gradually and quietly?

- Our passage says, "But whatever were gains to me I now consider loss for the sake of Christ." Can you think of anything in our modern life that is something to be proud of in the eyes of the world, but comes to seem pointless and cumbersome when seen with the eyes of faith? For example, might faith change our attitude to awards or status or money or success in exams?

- Paul says it is in our areas of weakness that we can really discover God's power. Have you found this to be true in your own experience, or can you think of someone's life that is an example of God's power shining through their weakness?

Prayer

O God, your grace to us is wonderful. Your strength lifts us up and carries us in our weakness; your love finds and saves us when we are broken and lost. We thank you for the great apostle Paul, for his passionate spirit and his faith in Jesus that came to him with such overwhelming power. Please help us to find, as Paul did, so real a vision of Jesus that our lives are transformed until we too can say – and really mean it – "for me to live is Christ, to die is gain". For we ask it in Jesus' holy name; Amen.

Martha

Bible passage – Luke 10:38–42

As Jesus and his disciples were on their way, he came to a village where a woman named Martha opened her home to him. She had a sister called Mary, who sat at the Lord's feet listening to what he said. But Martha was distracted by all the preparations that had to be made. She came to him and asked, "Lord, don't you care that my sister has left me to do the work by myself? Tell her to help me!"

"Martha, Martha," the Lord answered, "you are worried and upset about many things, but few things are needed – or indeed only one. Mary has chosen what is better, and it will not be taken away from her."

Commentary

Jesus challenges the status quo in several radical ways here. In a segregated society it is likely that Mary was not even supposed to be sitting where she was – the women would probably have a separate room. Certainly it was not a woman's place to be sitting at the feet of the Master studying theology. It was a woman's place to serve and to ensure that the domestic sphere ran smoothly, yet Jesus does not insist that these traditions are upheld.

But perhaps the most radical proposal of all implied here is that to follow social tradition *is a choice*. Martha was overwhelmed by the pressures and demands of domestic responsibility. Simply to put it down, and walk away from it, was unthinkable to her. This is the housewife's equivalent of Christ's words to the rich young man: "Go, sell all that you have, and then come, follow me" (Mark 10:17–22).

There is a danger of missing some of the best opportunities life holds for us if we assume that what is already in place in our routines and circumstances cannot be changed. "My husband would never allow it"; "I couldn't possibly because I have a family"; "I have a mortgage on my house so I have to stay in this job" are the kind of reasons given for making no change. And they are offered in all sincerity; they seem as immoveable as mountains.

But we are talking about the same Jesus who said, "Truly I tell you, if you have faith as small as a mustard seed, you can say to this mountain, 'Move from here to there,' and it will move. Nothing will be impossible for you" (Matthew 17:20).

Questions

• What would you say are the non-negotiable obligations in your life, the responsibilities you could not possibly consider leaving?

- When we read this passage, we often identify most readily with either Martha or Mary. Which one seems most like you, and why?
- Imagine you had been in Mary and Martha's house that night. They had a bunch of guests to feed, and the opportunity to hear Jesus teaching. Suppose you were there and didn't want to miss what he had to say. How would you go about sorting out the supper?

Prayer

Hospitable and generous God, you make us welcome with unquestioning love. May your Holy Spirit so fill our hearts and minds that we find the wise balance between the prayerful and the practical, serving with gladness and knowing when to withdraw to be quiet with you. As we think about Mary and Martha, please whisper into our hearts, you who know us so well, if there is any area of challenge and change we too should be facing. If there is any area where we have become the prisoners of our own assumptions, by your grace may we not be conformed to the same old ways, but transformed by the renewing of our minds. For we ask it in Jesus' holy name; Amen.

Judas

Bible passages

Matthew 26:20–23

When evening came, Jesus was reclining at the table with the Twelve. And while they were eating, he said, "Truly I tell you, one of you will betray me."

They were very sad and began to say to him one after the other, "Surely you don't mean me, Lord?"

Jesus replied, "The one who has dipped his hand into the bowl with me will betray me."

Matthew 27:1–5

Early in the morning, all the chief priests and the elders of the people made their plans how to have Jesus executed. So they bound him, led him away and handed him over to Pilate the governor.

When Judas, who had betrayed him, saw that Jesus was condemned, he was seized with remorse and returned the thirty pieces of silver to the chief priests and the elders.

"I have sinned," he said, "for I have betrayed innocent blood."

"What is that to us?" they replied. "That's your responsibility."

So Judas threw the money into the temple and left. Then he went away and hanged himself.

Commentary

The Last Supper is the beginning of the Christian Eucharist. Throughout the centuries since then Christians have done as Jesus asked, and broken bread and shared wine in memory of him. It was most probably a Passover meal, at which by tradition the host would dip into the blessing cup a piece of bread, and offer the sop of bread-soaked wine to his honoured guest.

At the Last Supper, when Jesus celebrated with his friends the Passover, that momentous occasion when the people of God were protected from death's angel by the blood of the sacrificial lamb smeared on the lintels of their houses, he the host offered the sop to the guest who that night stood most in need of his love, Judas, who would betray him.

From that moment on Judas' life began to unravel, and his choices ended in unendurable remorse and death at his own hand. He became unbearable to himself. But it did not stop there. God does not give up that easily.

At every Eucharist in the course of 2,000 years, one by one by one, millions of believers have stood in the place of Judas and humbly received the bread and wine held out by the divine host for the transformation of souls and the healing of the world. God has never given up on Judas. We are all one in Jesus. In each one of us Judas the betrayer is sought, beheld, and forgiven. The Judas in us is touched and cleansed by the Jesus we meet in bread and wine.

Questions

- For many believers, the story of Judas is one of the most sombre and disquieting in the whole Bible. How do you feel about Judas?

- Peter also betrayed Jesus but, though he was also overwhelmed with remorse, he did not end his life in despair but lived with what he had done. And the risen Jesus came and found him, and forgave him. Can you think of examples from your own life of seeing things through, not giving up, seeing sunrise again after impossible darkness?

- The phrase "toxic shame" is very accurate. People live through some terrible circumstances, but living with the shame of having done something terribly wrong can be unendurable. The greatest gift of God is forgiveness, the grace of a new beginning. Are there people in your life whom you would like to forgive? Is there something for which you need to be forgiven? Is this the time to lay these matters quietly before God, and allow the new to begin?

Prayer

O God of love, your kindness and mercy are inexhaustible. You never give up on us, never abandon us, and never turn anybody away. In the quietness now, we open our hearts to you. We ask you to look well, and begin to heal and transform any shadows of resentment, any old grudges, any scars of toxic shame. Forgive us, loving Father, for the things we are ashamed of, the things we have done wrong, and give us grace, in our turn, to forgive. For we ask it in Jesus' holy name; Amen.

Barnabas

Bible passages

Acts 9:26–28

> When [Saul] came to Jerusalem, he tried to join the disciples, but they were all afraid of him, not believing that he really was a disciple. But Barnabas took him and brought him to the apostles. He told them how Saul on his journey had seen the Lord and that the Lord had spoken to him, and how in Damascus he had preached fearlessly in the name of Jesus. So Saul stayed with them and moved about freely in Jerusalem, speaking boldly in the name of the Lord.

Acts 11:19–26

> Now those who had been scattered by the persecution that broke out when Stephen was killed travelled as far as Phoenicia, Cyprus and Antioch, spreading the word only among Jews. Some of them, however, men from Cyprus and Cyrene, went to Antioch and began to speak to Greeks also, telling them the good news about the Lord Jesus. The Lord's hand was with them, and a great number of people believed and turned to the Lord.
>
> News of this reached the church in Jerusalem, and they sent Barnabas to Antioch. When he arrived and saw what the grace of God had done, he was glad and encouraged them all to remain true to the Lord with all their hearts. He was a good man, full of the Holy Spirit and faith, and a great number of people were brought to the Lord.
>
> Then Barnabas went to Tarsus to look for Saul, and when he found him, he brought him to Antioch. So for a whole year Barnabas and Saul met with the church and taught great numbers of people. The disciples were called Christians first at Antioch.

Commentary

Barnabas does not have the biggest part to play in the unfolding story of the spread of the gospel, but everyone notices him and everyone loves him. We first come across him in Acts 4, when he sells a field he owns and donates the money to the church. We learn that he is a Levite whose real name is Joseph, but he has earned the nickname "Barnabas" because it means "Son of Encouragement". Everybody – but everybody – needs encouragement, and it turns out that Barnabas is not only generous but also trusting and kind.

He is the one man willing to take a chance on Paul after his spectacular conversion ("Saul" and "Paul" are the same person – he changed his name from Saul to Paul to show he had been born again), a courageous act that showed he had good judgment and wise insight. "Full of the Holy Spirit and faith", our passage says. Barnabas' faith and Holy Spirit discernment was evident in his trusting Paul, and also in his enthusiastic willingness to accept Gentiles into the faith community when he saw for himself the evidence of God's grace in their lives. As a Levite, he had been raised in the heartland of Jewish tradition, but his interest was not in preserving ritualized external forms of religion but in rising to the challenge of the new thing God was doing.

Ever since the book of Acts was written, Christians have been recognizing a wonderful role model in Barnabas. He was not rash – in each case we see him going to take a look for himself before making up his mind; he did not rely on hearsay – but he was trusting and optimistic, kind and full of faith. He had the lovely gift of being happy for other people.

Questions

- When you think about the modern-day church, do any circumstances come to mind that are similar to those in our passages? Can you think of any people traditionally beyond the pale in whose lives God's grace can be seen – individuals or groups – who could do with a Barnabas to help them get past prejudice and suspicion in the church?

- Have you had cause to give thanks for a Barnabas in your own life? If you had a Barnabas Award to hand out in your church, to whom would you give it?

- Barnabas took a chance on Paul when everyone else hesitated, and he welcomed in the Gentiles when no one had imagined they'd ever be part of the Jesus Movement. If you were asked to offer the hand of friendship to someone everybody considered seriously dodgy, how would you make up your mind what to do?

Prayer

O God of hope and love and kindness, we thank you so much for the Barnabas people in our lives – the ones who have encouraged and welcomed and accepted us when we were newcomers and strangers. Give us grace to develop in our own lives this lovely ministry of trust and acceptance, healing old wounds of rejection and helping the community to grow. For we ask it in Jesus' holy name; Amen.

Mary the mother of Jesus

Bible passage – Luke 1:46–55

And Mary said:
"My soul glorifies the Lord
and my spirit rejoices in God my Saviour,
for he has been mindful
of the humble state of his servant.
From now on all generations will call me blessed,
for the Mighty One has done great things for me –
holy is his name.
His mercy extends to those who fear him,
from generation to generation.
He has performed mighty deeds with his arm;
he has scattered those who are proud in their inmost thoughts.
He has brought down rulers from their thrones
but has lifted up the humble.
He has filled the hungry with good things
but has sent the rich away empty.
He has helped his servant Israel,
remembering to be merciful
to Abraham and his descendants for ever,
just as he promised our ancestors."

Commentary

There are so many statues of Mary the mother of Jesus in the world! In all of them (except the ones where her expression is full of sorrow) her face is soft, gentle, calm, and sweet-natured. How else would we imagine a young maiden of such purity of heart that to her out of all humanity was entrusted the baby Jesus? But though the gentleness is beautiful, it doesn't quite sit right with the Magnificat, the Song of Mary – which is highly political, gutsy, and revolutionary. If this is what she sang, Mary was more of a red-hot-radical than a blushing violet.

Near the beginning of his public ministry, Jesus preached at Nazareth (Luke 4:14–22) on the passage in Isaiah about the Lord's year of Jubilee, when the captives will go free and the sick be healed. "Today", he said, "this scripture is fulfilled in your hearing."

Jesus was the Son of God, sure enough, but never was he more his mother's son than in that moment. As Archbishop Desmond Tutu said, "I am not interested in picking up crumbs of compassion thrown from the table of someone who considers himself my master. I want the full menu of human rights."

When Mary sang her Magnificat, we should imagine not the soulful piping of a docile schoolgirl, but Malvina Reynolds, Joan Baez, and Buffy Sainte-Marie all rolled into one. "My soooooul doth *magnify* the Lord!!!" Alleluia! All right!!

Questions

- Many Christians have held the view that religion and politics don't mix – some Christian groups even refuse to vote because the kingdom of God is not of this world. Others hold passionately to the view that to mean anything the gospel must be worked out politically, changing society to eliminate poverty and alleviate inequality. What is your view on this?

- Mary's most famous words were spoken in response to the angel Gabriel announcing that she was chosen to be the mother of Jesus: "Be it unto me according to your word." This was a choice of great courage, as it brought her social disgrace in a culture where dishonour had very serious consequences indeed. Have there been times when you (or someone you know) have accepted something you believed to be the call of God, even though it meant tough times as a result? Or is there something like this you are trying to make your mind up about right now?

- Mary carried within her the baby Jesus. That is such a potent image for our own reflection! Can you think of ways in which we, too, can bear Jesus within us, and give birth to him in our day?

Prayer

O God of love, our imagination recoils from how hard it must have been for Mary to stand at the foot of the cross, and see Jesus crucified. Most of us would have found it unbearable, would have run away. May we be the kind of brave that Mary was – with the courage to stay with the ones we love and never abandon them, to accept disgrace and humiliation in the service of your calling, to hold bright the vision for a better world, to choose the way of miracles and amazing grace rather than shelter in what feels safe because it is normal. May we like Mary consent to receive the living Jesus, so that the grace of his salvation may be evident in our lives from day to day. For we ask it in Jesus' holy name; Amen.

John the Baptist

Bible passage – Matthew 11:2–14

When John, who was in prison, heard about the deeds of the Messiah, he sent his disciples to ask him, "Are you the one who is to come, or should we expect someone else?"

Jesus replied, "Go back and report to John what you hear and see: the blind receive sight, the lame walk, those who have leprosy are cleansed, the deaf hear, the dead are raised, and the good news is proclaimed to the poor. Blessed is anyone who does not stumble on account of me."

As John's disciples were leaving, Jesus began to speak to the crowd about John: "What did you go out into the wilderness to see? A reed swayed by the wind? If not, what did you go out to see? A man dressed in fine clothes? No, those who wear fine clothes are in kings' palaces. Then what did you go out to see? A prophet? Yes, I tell you, and more than a prophet. This is the one about whom it is written:

'I will send my messenger ahead of you,
  who will prepare your way before you.'

Truly I tell you, among those born of women there has not risen anyone greater than John the Baptist; yet whoever is least in the kingdom of heaven is greater than he. From the days of John the Baptist until now, the kingdom of heaven has been subjected to violence, and violent people have been raiding it. For all the Prophets and the Law prophesied until John. And if you are willing to accept it, he is the Elijah who was to come."

Commentary

John the Baptist comes across as such an extreme, uncompromising kind of man. To live rough in the desert, subsisting on foraged wild food, is a lifestyle demanding courage and perseverance and strong belief.

He recognized and identified Jesus as the messiah, yet, held captive in Herod's prison, his faith falters. It must have been exceptionally hard for John to endure prison life. Used to wandering and climbing, walking, eating wayside herbs, knowing which mushrooms and berries to pick safely and where to find wild honeycomb – this is not a soul who could ever accept confinement. And alone in the prison, doubts and uncertainty creep into his spirit like rising damp. Jesus… he wonders… is he really the one? Had that recognition been accurate? Was the great kingdom really at hand? Or was it all an embarrassing and costly mistake?

Jesus does not rebuke this uncertainty. He sends back the messengers with confirmation that the work of salvation really has begun. This is it, now. That's all John would need to know. The kind of man he was would have been able to bear the incarceration, the execution, just as long as he knew it wasn't all for nothing. He was, as Jesus said, a soul of great stature, a prophet of singular calibre.

But Jesus adds, "Among those born of women there has not risen anyone greater than John the Baptist; yet whoever is least in the kingdom of heaven is greater than he." For the greatness of the kingdom is not in the magnificence of its members, but in the love and truth and peace that constitute its reality. It is for anyone and everyone, and whoever partakes of it can draw freely and fully on its upwelling fountain of life.

Questions

- Does John the Baptist inspire you? Does his ministry and way of life strike a chord with you? Could you see him as a role model? Or does he seem too wild and dangerous to you – intimidating and alienating?

- When he was held in prison, John's certainty and vision came under attack. Can you think back to times in your life when you felt so sure and full of faith and conviction – and then a change of circumstances left you feeling wobbly and empty and unsure?

- Every strand of the Christian faith community has its spiritual giants – household names to be spoken with reverence in one church denomination while completely unknown in the others. Do you feel we ask too much of our Christian leaders? Are we inclined to admire and respect them excessively? Or do we take them for granted – should we respect their authority more than we do? And what place and recognition does our own church give to the ministry of prophets? How is it discerned and affirmed?

Prayer

O God of truth and power, mighty God, you called and anointed John the Baptist, that great and wild soul. May your fire and zeal inspire our souls too, so that like John we may have the courage to live and speak in simplicity and without compromise, bringing in your kingdom in the context of our everyday lives. For we ask it in Jesus' holy name; Amen.

Andrew

Bible passage – John 1:35–42

The next day John was there again with two of his disciples. When he saw Jesus passing by, he said, "Look, the Lamb of God!"

When the two disciples heard him say this, they followed Jesus. Turning round, Jesus saw them following and asked, "What do you want?"

They said, "Rabbi" (which means "Teacher"), "where are you staying?"

"Come," he replied, "and you will see."

So they went and saw where he was staying, and they spent that day with him. It was about four in the afternoon.

Andrew, Simon Peter's brother, was one of the two who heard what John had said and who had followed Jesus. The first thing Andrew did was to find his brother Simon and tell him, "We have found the Messiah" (that is, the Christ). And he brought him to Jesus.

Jesus looked at him and said, "You are Simon son of John. You will be called Cephas" (which, when translated, is Peter).

Commentary

This is a really important passage for our understanding of what evangelism is, as well as an encouragement to practise it.

In our post-modern, post-Christian era, a significant shift in our thinking is the movement away from seeing truth as objective to seeing truth as personal. Existential norms and core realities are increasingly seen in terms of personal viewpoints to be expressed rather than eternal truths to be discovered. Thus faith in God is increasingly seen as an attribute of a person ("I wish I had your faith") rather than as a response to an actual external reality.

In this passage from John's Gospel, we are reminded to think of evangelism as introducing somebody not to an idea but to a real person. Conversion to Christian faith is not complete without an actual personal encounter with the living Christ. Without directly meeting him, without personally knowing him, all we have is the random pieces of a religious jigsaw puzzle.

This passage makes that very clear. Jesus challenges the seekers first with the question, "What do you want?" (sometimes translated as "What are you looking for?").

We are to understand that this is a question to the wider church (i.e. us too) as well as a story of the call of the first disciples. When they ask him where they can find him, Jesus answers them, "Come and see." See for yourself, make the journey, settle for nothing less than personal experience.

Then Andrew (who also sets off the feeding of the five thousand by bringing the little boy with the bread and fish to Jesus) goes to find Simon Peter, and does not content himself with describing or discussing Jesus, but *brings him to meet Jesus*. How we go about this will vary according to personal style and circumstances, but what remains constant is that, for conversion to take place, we must have a direct personal encounter with Jesus, and for evangelism to be effective we must find a way of introducing those who seek him to the living Lord.

Questions

- Do you feel you could say you have met Jesus? Or do you feel your faith is more a matter of the philosophy you have developed or maybe had passed on to you – your outlook on life?

- While remaining respectful of someone else's personal beliefs, how might we go about suggesting to them that Jesus Christ is somebody they can actually meet and know? Is it helpful to consider strategies and methods? Do we need some ground rules in place for evangelism? Are some forms of evangelism more acceptable to us than others? Or do we mainly pray and wait upon the Holy Spirit to give us the right words at the right time?

- Have you met someone like Andrew, who has a ministry of bringing people to Jesus, and has the graceful art of naturally introducing those who are seeking him to the Lord?

Prayer

Living Lord Jesus, I open my heart's door to you. My heart is open to you. Please come in. Please make yourself known to me, as directly and personally as Andrew knew you, as Simon Peter knew you. Please forgive the sins and attitudes that block your entrance to my heart. I cannot shift them on my own, but please will you clear them away, and allow me to make a new start. There is so much to forgive, and so much that I need to learn, but please may I do that? Lord Jesus, please make yourself known to me. Please come into my heart. I need you; I cannot be whole without you. Amen.

The boy with five loaves and two fishes

Bible passage – John 6:5–12

When Jesus looked up and saw a great crowd coming toward him, he said to Philip, "Where shall we buy bread for these people to eat?" He asked this only to test him, for he already had in mind what he was going to do.

Philip answered him, "It would take more than half a year's wages to buy enough bread for each one to have a bite!"

Another of his disciples, Andrew, Simon Peter's brother, spoke up, "Here is a boy with five small barley loaves and two small fish, but how far will they go among so many?"

Jesus said, "Have the people sit down." There was plenty of grass in that place, and they sat down (about five thousand men were there). Jesus then took the loaves, gave thanks, and distributed to those who were seated as much as they wanted. He did the same with the fish.

When they had all had enough to eat, he said to his disciples, "Gather the pieces that are left over. Let nothing be wasted." So they gathered them and filled twelve baskets with the pieces of the five barley loaves left over by those who had eaten.

Commentary

Well, that child had something to talk about for the rest of his life, didn't he? People who go looking for Jesus find themselves taken up into his good purposes in surprising ways!

Philip came from the part of the country where this massive picnic happened, so when Jesus asked him where they could buy some bread, it was a bit like saying, "In the ordinary way of things, if I wasn't here, what would you do?" Philip's answer could be summarized as, "Panic."

There is one huge difference between the NIV translation (given above) of our passage, and the King James translation. In the KJV, verse 11 reads: "And Jesus took the loaves; and when he had given thanks, he distributed to the disciples, and the disciples to them that were set down; and likewise of the fishes as much as they would."

Do you see? In the NIV, Jesus feeds the multitude. In the KJV, the disciples feed the multitude. Though the different Greek–English translations turn up different results (maybe working from different manuscripts), the translators agree that the food was distributed via the disciples. We know, because the other evangelists include this miracle too (Matthew 14:13–21; Mark 6:30–44; Luke 9:10–17); it's the only miracle recorded in all four Gospels.

John, writing late, is showing the church how to find the presence of the ascended Jesus still in their midst. He is showing them that the body of Christ is found here and now in the people as they meet to break bread in his name. He has a special purpose as he records this miracle of drawing our attention to similarities with the Eucharist and the Last Supper: "he took bread… he broke it… he shared it…"

John is showing us how the Eucharistic presence of Christ knits into ordinary events and people as we gather, as we offer what we have, as we share. Even though Jesus is there through us, it is him and he is really there. It is Jesus himself, through his disciples, distributing the bread.

Questions

- Can you think of times in your life when what was asked of you just seemed impossible, beyond your capability? How did you get through? Here you are today, still standing! What was your miracle?

- When they had all eaten, Jesus said to his disciples, "Gather the pieces that are left over. Let nothing be wasted." These words apply well to every kind of aftermath – not just a picnic but also a tsunami, a divorce, an acrimonious church meeting. When have you had to do just that – pick up the pieces to make a new beginning? What were the fragments you used to build a new life, a new beginning?

- The boy with the loaves and fishes probably just came along with his family – he didn't know his packed lunch had the ingredients for a miracle. Can you think of times when God's presence and power has caught you unawares – found you when you were just trundling along in the ordinary business of everyday life?

Prayer

O God of love and power, Jesus showed us your presence in signs and wonders and also in sacrificial love. As we go about our daily lives, wake us up to your presence with us, for you are the same today as you always were. When we are worried or stuck, remind us to turn to you. When what we have seems too little to go round, remind us to offer it to you. When the needs of people around us seem overwhelming, help us to remember that sharing is Eucharist and help us to stay peaceful in simply sharing what we have. For the miracle is yours, not ours, to do. In Jesus' holy name; Amen.

Pontius Pilate

Bible passage – Matthew 27:19–26

While Pilate was sitting on the judge's seat, his wife sent him this message: "Don't have anything to do with that innocent man, for I have suffered a great deal today in a dream because of him."

But the chief priests and the elders persuaded the crowd to ask for Barabbas and to have Jesus executed.

"Which of the two do you want me to release to you?" asked the governor.

"Barabbas," they answered.

"What shall I do, then, with Jesus who is called the Messiah?" Pilate asked.

They all answered, "Crucify him!"

"Why? What crime has he committed?" asked Pilate.

But they shouted all the louder, "Crucify him!"

When Pilate saw that he was getting nowhere, but that instead an uproar was starting, he took water and washed his hands in front of the crowd. "I am innocent of this man's blood," he said. "It is your responsibility!"

All the people answered, "His blood is on us and on our children!"

Then he released Barabbas to them. But he had Jesus flogged, and handed him over to be crucified.

Commentary

This is probably one of the most depressing, and the most modern, passages in the entire Bible. The culture of blame and avoidance so evident in twenty-first-century commerce and politics started early, evidently – well, probably with Adam and Eve, but we see it here still going strong with Pontius Pilate. Fickle, sensationalist, and excitable, the crowd bays for blood. Then as now, mob thinking swings between adoring adulation and tearing their idol to pieces.

And Pilate, anxious to hold on to his position, pressured from every side, knowing full well that if he doesn't do what other people want him to, he'll be the next to go, bows to public opinion and hands Jesus over.

Questions

• Since the technological revolution, the internet has given us radically increased power to lobby and petition, and the weight of public opinion has been harnessed to effect social change. Sometimes a precious tract of forest may be saved from loggers, and sometimes a destructive riot may be planned and set in motion. How do you feel about this? Where have you seen public opinion and demand making a difference in our modern day?

- Have you (or someone you know) ever been trapped in a similar position to that of Pontius Pilate, pressurized into taking some action seriously against your conscience? What happened? What did you do?

- In modern times as in Bible times, people can be executed on very dodgy grounds in those places where capital punishment is still practised. Even if they are legally tried, flawed justice systems and inadequate legal representation result sometimes in innocent individuals being put to death. Do you have strong views about capital punishment – for or against it, or concerning the way it is carried out today?

Prayer

O God of love and mercy, our creator, our Lord and our judge, you see into the human heart, and humble yourself to stoop under that low lintel to make our hearts your dwelling place. You see our justice systems, our social organization, and the punishments we mete out when somebody is accused of doing something wrong. We acknowledge before you that truth does not always prevail, that the innocent sometimes bear the consequences of the crimes of others, and that shoddy investigation and indifference to truth result in tragedy more often than we like to admit. We ask for your forgiveness and the illumination of your Holy Spirit. Transform our hearts and lives until our legal systems reflect the justice and mercy of heaven, and our private faith shines more brightly in our public life, for we ask it in Jesus' holy name; Amen.

Zacchaeus

Bible passage – Luke 19:1–9

Jesus entered Jericho and was passing through. A man was there by the name of Zacchaeus; he was a chief tax collector and was wealthy. He wanted to see who Jesus was, but because he was short he could not see over the crowd. So he ran ahead and climbed a sycamore-fig-tree to see him, since Jesus was coming that way.

When Jesus reached the spot, he looked up and said to him, "Zacchaeus, come down immediately. I must stay at your house today." So he came down at once and welcomed him gladly.

All the people saw this and began to mutter, "He has gone to be the guest of a sinner."

But Zacchaeus stood up and said to the Lord, "Look, Lord! Here and now I give half of my possessions to the poor, and if I have cheated anybody out of anything, I will pay back four times the amount."

Jesus said to him, "Today salvation has come to this house, because this man, too, is a son of Abraham. For the Son of Man came to seek and to save the lost."

Commentary

This passage reads like a gospel psychology textbook! It's a lesson in how what goes around comes around. Reading between the lines, we can guess how Zacchaeus, short and geeky, was pushed to the edge, maybe laughed at and left out. Compensating with remarkable success he turned the tables on the community in which he grew up, and extorted in cash the well-being that was not on offer in the form of acceptance and affirmation. And eventually everyone hated him.

The phrase "at the top of the tree" comes into its own in the story of Zacchaeus. We see him perched at the top of the tree in every way – powerful, abundantly wealthy, and isolated on the perch to which he had scrambled, shoved as he was to the outskirts of the crowd who would make no place to let him in.

Jesus turns this around by loving him, choosing him, affirming him. That's all it takes.

Questions

- It's easy to be jealous of people who have great wealth, big houses, and a life of luxury – but who, reading this story, could possibly feel jealous of Zacchaeus? Of course it's natural to enjoy our creature comforts. Make a list of five things you would like to have if you could afford them, and five things you would love to have that money cannot buy. What would have to change in your life to bring them into reality?

- Zacchaeus was a lonely man, ostracized, and unloved. He had chosen wealth instead of human relationships – and maybe had taken refuge in money because he had lacked friends and the social skills to make them. Can you think of ways in which you have sometimes sought comfort in material things because you felt sad or inadequate or depressed? They don't call it "retail therapy" for nothing!

- Unlike the rich young man, Jesus did not ask or expect Zacchaeus to sell up, give away everything he had, and follow him. Zacchaeus' generous but realistic plan of giving away half of what he had, and repaying at huge interest money he had acquired unjustly, was enough to win Jesus' approval. We are called to live honestly and generously, but at different levels of relative wealth or simplicity. At what point do you think wealth might get in the way of a person's practising their faith? Do you think everybody should tithe at 10 per cent or do you think giving is a very individual matter? Do you feel that there are adjustments you would like to make in your own lifestyle, and what might make it easy or hard for you to do that?

Prayer

O God of generous love and abundant provision, we give thanks to you for your mercy and kindness poured out upon our own lives. Thank you for our friends, our homes and families, the hospitality we enjoy in the homes of others, and the chance to offer hospitality ourselves. Thank you for the material benefits of our lives, and the well-being we enjoy. By your grace at work in our hearts, make us generous and forgiving, eager to share, and sensitive to the loneliness and needs of others. May we so treat other people that injustice and greed cannot flourish easily in the environments we create, because love and acceptance are the keynotes of our communities. This we ask in Jesus' holy name; Amen.

Deborah

Bible passage – Judges 4:1–15

Again the Israelites did evil in the eyes of the Lord, now that Ehud was dead.
So the Lord sold them into the hands of Jabin king of Canaan, who reigned in
Hazor. Sisera, the commander of his army, was based in Harosheth Haggoyim.
Because he had nine hundred chariots fitted with iron and had cruelly
oppressed the Israelites for twenty years, they cried to the Lord for help.

Now Deborah, a prophet, the wife of Lappidoth, was leading Israel at that
time. She held court under the Palm of Deborah between Ramah and Bethel
in the hill country of Ephraim, and the Israelites went up to her to have their
disputes decided. She sent for Barak son of Abinoam from Kedesh in Naphtali
and said to him, "The Lord, the God of Israel, commands you: 'Go, take with you
ten thousand men of Naphtali and Zebulun and lead them up to Mount Tabor.
I will lead Sisera, the commander of Jabin's army, with his chariots and his
troops to the River Kishon and give him into your hands.'"

Barak said to her, "If you go with me, I will go; but if you don't go with me, I
won't go."

"Certainly I will go with you," said Deborah. "But because of the course you
are taking, the honour will not be yours, for the Lord will deliver Sisera into
the hands of a woman." So Deborah went with Barak to Kedesh. There Barak
summoned Zebulun and Naphtali, and ten thousand men went up under his
command. Deborah also went up with him.

Now Heber the Kenite had left the other Kenites, the descendants of Hobab,
Moses' brother-in-law, and pitched his tent by the great tree in Zaanannim
near Kedesh.

When they told Sisera that Barak son of Abinoam had gone up to Mount
Tabor, Sisera summoned from Harosheth Haggoyim to the River Kishon all his
men and his nine hundred chariots fitted with iron.

Then Deborah said to Barak, "Go! This is the day the Lord has given Sisera
into your hands. Has not the Lord gone ahead of you?" So Barak went down
Mount Tabor, with ten thousand men following him. At Barak's advance, the
Lord routed Sisera and all his chariots and army by the sword, and Sisera got
down from his chariot and fled on foot.

Commentary

If you fossick about a bit online searching on biblical womanhood, living as a
biblical woman, how the Bible intends women to be, sooner rather than later you
will come upon this quotation from 1 Peter 3:3–4: "Your beauty… should be
that of your inner self, the unfading beauty of a gentle and quiet spirit…" You'll
find a lot about modest dress and skirt lengths, about head coverings and gentle,

teachable behaviour. You're unlikely to come across anyone mentioning Deborah (or her friend Jael – see the unfolding story in the second half of Judges 4).

Can women be leaders? Are women designed to be under a man's authority? Are women by nature and vocation gentle and sweet, quiet and kind, called to submission? If the answer is an unequivocal "Yes", what are we to say about Deborah? A prophet, a judge, the leader of all Israel, decisive, courageous, warlike, bold.

Questions

- How do you see the role of women in the church, in the home and family, and in wider society? Just the same as that of men, or are there God-ordained gender differences?

- It is said that a prophet's primary, hidden calling is into the presence of God to hear his voice. Only secondary is the public face of the prophetic vocation – to declare the Lord's truth for the contemporary circumstances. Who can you identify as a prophet for our times, and why?

- Deborah says to Barak, when he pleads with her to accompany him, "Certainly I will go with you. But because of the course you are taking, the honour will not be yours, for the Lord will deliver Sisera into the hands of a woman." Why do you think her going with him would diminish his honour? It sounds from what she said as though Barak's dependence on the support of a woman would make him appear contemptible in the eyes of his fellow Israelites. What do you make of this socio-religious system that recognizes the anointing of a prophet in Deborah, chooses her as a leader fit to judge the disputes of the people, yet would regard her involvement in the victory as diminishing to Barak's manhood? Are there similar inconsistencies in our modern-day church and society – and in the workplace and the home?

Prayer

O God of strength and truth, who has called us to prophetic lives, declaring by our every word and action the gospel of your truth, give us insight, give us courage, give us discernment, so that – men and women together – we may stand firm for your kingdom and prove triumphant in the battle against all that would undermine and destroy the work of your Spirit in us. For we ask it in Jesus' holy name; Amen.

Joseph

Bible passage – Matthew 1:18–25

This is how the birth of Jesus the Messiah came about: his mother Mary was pledged to be married to Joseph, but before they came together, she was found to be pregnant through the Holy Spirit. Because Joseph her husband was faithful to the law, and yet did not want to expose her to public disgrace, he had in mind to divorce her quietly.

But after he had considered this, an angel of the Lord appeared to him in a dream and said, "Joseph son of David, do not be afraid to take Mary home as your wife, because what is conceived in her is from the Holy Spirit. She will give birth to a son, and you are to give him the name Jesus, because he will save his people from their sins."

All this took place to fulfil what the Lord had said through the prophet: "The virgin will conceive and give birth to a son, and they will call him Immanuel" (which means "God with us").

When Joseph woke up, he did what the angel of the Lord had commanded him and took Mary home as his wife. But he did not consummate their marriage until she gave birth to a son. And he gave him the name Jesus.

Commentary

This passage speaks volumes about the sort of man Joseph was. For starters, his initial reaction to Mary's pregnancy is unusual. Many men in this position would have been loud in their outrage and interested in public vengeance and vindication. Joseph's reaction is restrained, moderate, firm in purpose, and very kind.

Then he has his dream, and changes his course of action on the strength of it. This indicates both that he *wants* to believe Mary, whom he clearly loves and respects deeply, and that he is in the habit of listening to God. People who listen to God and act on what they hear become practised at discerning and noticing the Spirit's voice. People in the habit of ignoring and overriding the whisper of the Spirit, taking refuge in busyness and distraction, find their faith and spiritual discernment growing dull and dim and tired.

Joseph listens and takes action – but he does not speak. He passes through the pages of the Gospels without uttering a single word. We may learn from this the simple lesson that he was a quiet, modest man, but also the greater lesson that silence nurtures the word. As Jesus, the Word of God, was nurtured and protected by Joseph, so in our own lives will silence nourish and shelter our words towards graceful maturity.

The example of Joseph encourages us to see how moderation, kindness, quietness, and restraint save us from the regrets and false starts of impetuosity.

Questions

- Joseph was a carpenter, working responsibly at an honest trade. God entrusted to his care the infant Jesus, to grow to maturity in the shelter of his home and under his authority. Can you think of ways in which your home and family life are nurturing the growth of Christ in your midst? Or can you think of some small changes you could make to better nurture the word of life in your household?

- Can you think of examples of quiet, gentle people who have made a difference in your life, or in your church community? What would you say was their particular gift and contribution?

- Do you find it easy to be quiet, or are you someone who needs to think aloud? In a conversation, do you find it easy to listen, or do you tend to find yourself waiting impatiently to share your thoughts? How do you (or might you) nurture quietness and thoughtfulness in your own life?

Prayer

O God who sees and knows us all, you chose Joseph to be the man who would care for Mary and the baby Jesus, protecting them from persecution, and ordering their family life according to the ways of peace. As we, inspired by Joseph's example, seek to align our own homes with the gentle restraint and self-discipline of your kingdom, grant us strength and perseverance so that Christ may grow to maturity in the innermost sanctuary of our hearts and souls. For we ask it in Jesus' holy name; Amen.

Jacob

Bible passage – Genesis 32:7–12, 22–31

In great fear and distress Jacob divided the people who were with him into two groups, and the flocks and herds and camels as well. He thought, "If Esau comes and attacks one group, the group that is left may escape."

Then Jacob prayed, "O God of my father Abraham, God of my father Isaac, Lord, you who said to me, 'Go back to your country and your relatives, and I will make you prosper,' I am unworthy of all the kindness and faithfulness you have shown your servant. I had only my staff when I crossed this Jordan, but now I have become two camps. Save me, I pray, from the hand of my brother Esau, for I am afraid he will come and attack me, and also the mothers with their children. But you have said, 'I will surely make you prosper and will make your descendants like the sand of the sea, which cannot be counted.'"...

... That night Jacob got up and took his two wives, his two female servants and his eleven sons and crossed the ford of the Jabbok. After he had sent them across the stream, he sent over all his possessions. So Jacob was left alone, and a man wrestled with him till daybreak. When the man saw that he could not overpower him, he touched the socket of Jacob's hip so that his hip was wrenched as he wrestled with the man. Then the man said, "Let me go, for it is daybreak."

But Jacob replied, "I will not let you go unless you bless me."

The man asked him, "What is your name?"

"Jacob," he answered.

Then the man said, "Your name will no longer be Jacob, but Israel, because you have struggled with God and with humans and have overcome."

Jacob said, "Please tell me your name."

But he replied, "Why do you ask my name?" Then he blessed him there.

So Jacob called the place Peniel, saying, "It is because I saw God face to face, and yet my life was spared."

The sun rose above him as he passed Peniel, and he was limping because of his hip.

Commentary

This story of Jacob is an encouragement. In the first place, Jacob was an out-and-out rogue (see Genesis 27:1–41, the background to our study passage, and Genesis 30:25 – 31:2). If God was on his side, he is on your side too – whoever you are and whatever you've done!

Then, secondly, Jacob came away from his encounter with God limping. This is something to remember if ever you feel that you are not as shiny a Christian as you might be, that following Jesus seems difficult, and that your encounters with the people of God can be a little bruising at times. Jacob was blessed by God, but he couldn't get the blessing without the collateral damage. When he found himself between a rock and a hard place Jacob turned to God (he maybe didn't have too many other friends), and he met God face to face and that changed everything. And God kept his promises – but so did Jacob keep his limp. Maybe some of our personal vulnerabilities and the scars life has left us with are the medals we wear from our encounters with the living God.

Questions

- Can you think of decisions or events in your faith journey that have been both very costly and very rewarding?
- If you could choose for yourself a new name, representing that path you have travelled with God, what would it be? And if you could give a name to the place you live now, describing what it has meant for you spiritually, what would that name be?
- Can you think of moments in your life that changed everything, dividing your life into two parts – before that happened and afterwards?

Prayer

How strange and wonderful it is that you, Lord God, who made the heavens and the earth and set all the stars in place, should come close to us and engage with us in the course of our everyday lives. We join with the words of the old hymn in saying, "When on others you are calling, do not pass me by!"[2] Meet with us, God of all our lives, and in our encounter transform and renew us, for we ask it in Jesus' holy name; Amen.

---

2 "Pass me not, O Gentle Savior", by Fanny Crosby (1868).

Key features from the four Gospels

Matthew

The faithful Israel and the new Moses
The teacher of righteousness
The holy mountain
The fulfilment of the Law
The Zoroastrians

Mark

The Son of God
The reinterpretation of leadership
Transfiguration – sight and insight
The unvarnished Jesus
The unnamed outsider

Luke

Finding the lost
Healing the sick
The Holy Spirit
A gospel for the whole world
Lifting up the lowly

John

The light of the world
The living Word
The body of Christ
The *ego eimi*
The way of love

Matthew

The faithful Israel and the new Moses

Bible passages

Matthew 1:1

This is the genealogy of Jesus the Messiah the son of David, the son of Abraham ...

Matthew 2:13–16

When they had gone, an angel of the Lord appeared to Joseph in a dream. "Get up," he said, "take the child and his mother and escape to Egypt. Stay there until I tell you, for Herod is going to search for the child to kill him."

So he got up, took the child and his mother during the night and left for Egypt, where he stayed until the death of Herod. And so was fulfilled what the Lord had said through the prophet: "Out of Egypt I called my son."

When Herod realised that he had been outwitted by the Magi, he was furious, and he gave orders to kill all the boys in Bethlehem and its vicinity who were two years old and under, in accordance with the time he had learned from the Magi.

Commentary

Matthew's Gospel is recognized as very Jewish in flavour, focusing on themes particularly apposite to Judaism. Yet its thrust is not towards finding favour with Jewish readers, but rather demonstrates how Jesus takes up the torch from Moses, brings to fruition by both his life and his insights the Law of Moses, and both heals and perfects the flawed and stumbling devotion of the people of God. Matthew presents Jesus as a new Moses and a faithful Israel.

The genealogy at the start of the Gospel traces the lineage of Jesus back to Abraham, the founding father of the Jewish religion (unlike Luke, who traces back to Adam, the founding father of the human race). Just as the baby Moses found refuge from massacre in Egypt, so does Jesus. Like Moses, he returns from Egypt to his people. As Moses ascends the mountain to receive the Law from God, so Jesus goes up the mountain to deliver his reinterpretation of that Law. As there are five books of Moses in the Jewish Scriptures (the Old Testament), so Jesus offers five distinct teaching discourses in Matthew's Gospel (chapters 5 –7, 10, 13, 18, and 22 – 25). As Moses fasted for forty days and forty nights in the wilderness, so does Jesus. As Moses mediated the covenant of blood between God and his people (Exodus 24:8), so Jesus describes the shedding of his blood as bringing about the new covenant (Matthew 26:28). Where Mark wrote of the "kingdom of God", Matthew adapts his words to "kingdom of heaven", as Jewish devotees would regard using the word "God" openly and directly as irreverent. Matthew stresses more than Luke and Mark the identity of Jesus as "Son of David".

It is thought that Matthew's church had significant numbers of Jewish members, and his Gospel expounds the relevance and importance of how Jesus develops and perfects what their tradition began and taught (see the study on "The fulfilment of the Law"). Matthew sees in Jesus a new Moses – someone who can restore the vitality of a corrupted faith tradition.

Questions

- Who in your lifetime has been a "new Moses" – someone who brought your faith to life when it had become dry and meaningless, inspiring you to a renewed faith and determination as a disciple of Jesus?

- Missionaries have said, "There is no gospel before culture," by which they mean that, wherever the gospel is preached, it is understood and interpreted according to the cultural traditions of those who receive it. So African Christianity will be different in flavour from Scandinavian or Italian or Chinese Christianity, even while sharing the essential truths of the gospel. Can you think of some differences in Christian cultures known to you?

- The story of Jesus is real history, but Matthew told it in a way that brings out different emphases from Luke's, Mark's, and John's versions. Some teachers see the Bible as a simple manual for daily life, and do not recognize that interpretation comes into the way we each relate to its wisdom. How do you personally read and relate to the Bible? Do you see some or all of it as literally true? Do you find it enriching and enlightening to study its interpretation? How do you experience its truth and authority in your own life?

Prayer

O God of all wisdom and truth, thank you for your word to us in the Bible, and for finding and accepting us just as we are, each so different, each needing the transformation of your Holy Spirit in our life. As we read, study, and discuss, may our faith be deepened and strengthened, and may we grow to know and understand Jesus better, so that we may better reflect the image of his glory in the day-to-day reality of our lives. For we ask it in his holy name; Amen.

The teacher of righteousness

Bible passages

Matthew 3:13–15

Then Jesus came from Galilee to the Jordan to be baptised by John. But John tried to deter him, saying, "I need to be baptised by you, and do you come to me?"

Jesus replied, "Let it be so now; it is proper for us to do this to fulfil all righteousness." Then John consented.

Matthew 5:6

Blessed are those who hunger and thirst for righteousness, for they will be filled.

Matthew 5:20

For I tell you that unless your righteousness surpasses that of the Pharisees and the teachers of the law, you will certainly not enter the kingdom of heaven.

Matthew 6:33

But seek first his kingdom and his righteousness, and all these things will be given to you as well.

Matthew 7:28–29

When Jesus had finished saying these things, the crowds were amazed at his teaching, because he taught as one who had authority, and not as their teachers of the law.

Matthew 25:46

"Then they will go away to eternal punishment, but the righteous to eternal life."

Commentary

Righteousness is a very strong theme in Matthew's Gospel. The word comes up many times more often than in the other three Gospels, in all translations.

At the beginning of each Gospel, the words Jesus first speaks encapsulate the emphasized theme of that evangelist. In Matthew's Gospel the first words Jesus speaks are: "Let it be so now; it is proper for us to do this to fulfil all righteousness."

In the teaching of Jesus, a strong distinction is made between the integrity of true righteousness and the hypocrisy of self-righteousness: "Be careful not to practise your 'righteousness' in front of others to be seen by them. If you do, you will have no reward from your Father in heaven" (Matthew 6:1; see also Matthew 23:28).

Jesus draws a contrast between religious correctness – adhering to all the rules – and purity of heart, which shows itself in compassion towards our fellow human beings and in implicit trust in God.

Questions

- How do you feel about the word "righteousness"? Does the idea of a "righteous person" attract you, or does it feel intimidating?
- Would you describe your own life as "righteous"? In what ways do you think it might be, and in what ways do you think it might be hypocritical or short of the mark?
- The scribes and Pharisees, devout religious folk, come in for a lot of stick from Jesus! Which of our own faith traditions do you think draw us closer to God – and are there any that might actually be getting in the way?

Prayer

"The prayer of a righteous man is powerful and effective."* O Lord God, we claim that Scripture for the cleansing and transformation of our own lives – for it is not we who are the righteous, but Jesus, who intercedes for us.

Where we have been self-righteous and hypocritical, in your mercy forgive us. Show us the way of true integrity, trust, and humility, so that we may live and walk as Jesus meant us to do, in the ways of kindness, justice, and peace. For we ask it in his holy name; Amen.

*(James 5:16)

The holy mountain

Bible passages

Matthew 4:8

Again, the devil took him to a very high mountain and showed him all the kingdoms of the world and their splendour. "All this I will give you," he said, "if you will bow down and worship me."

Matthew 5:1–2

Now when Jesus saw the crowds, he went up on a mountainside and sat down. His disciples came to him, and he began to teach them.

Matthew 14:23

After he had dismissed them, he went up on a mountainside by himself to pray.

Matthew 15:29–30

Jesus left there and went along the Sea of Galilee. Then he went up on a mountainside and sat down. Great crowds came to him, bringing the lame, the blind, the crippled, the mute and many others, and laid them at his feet; and he healed them.

Matthew 24:3

As Jesus was sitting on the Mount of Olives, the disciples came to him privately. "Tell us," they said, "when will this happen, and what will be the sign of your coming and of the end of the age?"

Matthew 28:16–17

Then the eleven disciples went to Galilee, to the mountain where Jesus had told them to go. When they saw him, they worshipped him; but some doubted.

Commentary

Mountains have immense imaginative power in Judaism (see for example Exodus 19). The Law was given to Moses on Mount Sinai (Exodus 24:12–18; Exodus 31:18), and God would call Moses to meet with him face to face on the mountain. Afterwards, his face shone so bright it had to be veiled.

The last blessing of Moses upon the tribes of his people speaks of the God who meets with them on the mountain (Deuteronomy 33:1–3). And after he has blessed them one last time the Lord calls him up the mountain, and from the mountain top shows him the Promised Land (Deuteronomy 34:1–4).

Both Jesus' prophetic ministry as the new Moses bringing the new Law, and his deity, are indicated by the numerous mentions of mountains in Matthew's Gospel. Jesus goes up to pray to God on the mountain; he teaches his disciples and the people on the mountain. The Sermon on the Mount is in Matthew's Gospel alone; Luke's equivalent takes place down on the plain. The mountains in Matthew's Gospel are telling us who Jesus is.

Notice the difference in order of the temptations in the desert between Matthew's and Luke's Gospels (Matthew 4:1–11; Luke 4:1–12). Do you notice that for Luke the climactic temptation is located on the Temple, whereas for Matthew it's on the mountain?

When Jesus comes down from the mount of transfiguration, he finds the disciples having trouble with a demon (Matthew 17:1–20). Contrast his comment about the mountain in verse 20 with Mark's version of the same story (Mark 9:2–29; see verses 28–29).

Questions

- Like Moses, Jesus would climb up into the mountains to pray and draw close to God. As well as climbing into the hills, he liked to walk by the lakeside. Where do you feel especially close to God? Do you have a favourite place to pray?

- As well as showing mountains as a place of spiritual exaltation, Matthew shows Jesus as having power over the "mountains" of our doubt, fear, and troubles. Can you think of a time in your own (or someone else's) life when faith in Jesus helped you "move a mountain"?

- The world's great religions all came from desert country and mountainous regions. Why do you think this might be?

Prayer

O mountain-moving God, you tower over the highest heights and can overcome our greatest difficulties. Before you, the psalmist says, the mountains – solid as they are – "skip like rams". How great is your power, but deeper and stronger and more wonderful still is your love. O God our rock, our strength, and our redeemer, surely we take refuge in you! In the name of Jesus; Amen.

The fulfilment of the Law

Bible passages

Matthew 5:17–20

"Do not think that I have come to abolish the Law or the Prophets; I have not come to abolish them but to fulfil them. For truly I tell you, until heaven and earth disappear, not the smallest letter, not the least stroke of a pen, will by any means disappear from the Law until everything is accomplished. Therefore anyone who sets aside one of the least of these commands and teaches others accordingly will be called least in the kingdom of heaven, but whoever practises and teaches these commands will be called great in the kingdom of heaven. For I tell you that unless your righteousness surpasses that of the Pharisees and the teachers of the law, you will certainly not enter the kingdom of heaven."

Matthew 5:43–45, 48

"You have heard that it was said, 'Love your neighbour and hate your enemy.' But I tell you, love your enemies and pray for those who persecute you, that you may be children of your Father in heaven. He causes his sun to rise on the evil and the good, and sends rain on the righteous and the unrighteous... Be perfect, therefore, as your heavenly Father is perfect."

Matthew 8:10–12

"Truly I tell you, I have not found anyone in Israel with such great faith. I say to you that many will come from the east and the west, and will take their places at the feast with Abraham, Isaac and Jacob in the kingdom of heaven. But the subjects of the kingdom will be thrown outside, into the darkness, where there will be weeping and gnashing of teeth."

Matthew 9:13 (Hosea 6:6, quoted again in Matthew 12:7)

"But go and learn what this means: 'I desire mercy, not sacrifice.' For I have not come to call the righteous, but sinners."

Matthew 12:6

"I tell you that something greater than the temple is here."

Matthew 13:17

"For truly I tell you, many prophets and righteous people longed to see what you see but did not see it, and to hear what you hear but did not hear it."

Commentary

Matthew's approach doesn't pull its punches. His Gospel speaks very directly into his own Jewish faith tradition (see Matthew 23). He criticizes severely the legalism and hypocrisy that have grown like invasive weeds in the vineyard of God's people. At the same time, the point is clearly made that Jesus did not come to trash or sweep away the faith history of Israel. He came to cleanse, renew, and fulfil it. The cleansing fire of the Spirit of Jesus is for purification to allow and foster healthy new growth in a plant left too long to ramble out of control, with parts dying and diseased.

Questions

- Imagine Jesus had been born into your own church tradition. In what ways might he have wanted to develop and perfect some of its ways and teaching? ("You have heard it said... but I say to you... ", Matthew 5:21–48.)
- Jesus shows us that the fulfilment of the Law is in unconditional love. Paul expresses this point very succinctly too (Galatians 5:22–25). In your own faith community, can you think of examples where rules or guidelines are needed to safeguard people from slipping into ways that are too liberal or permissive, and examples where legalism or ritual may be threatening the freedom of grace?
- Jesus made it clear that he valued and respected the Law – but the true underlying spirit of the Law, not a dry and heartless rendering of it. In what ways do you feel your own life and faith practice would benefit from firmer discipline, and where do you feel some inspiration and revitalization would be welcome?

Prayer

O God of Israel, how faithfully you have pruned and tended the vineyard that is your people. We open our lives also to your wisdom and care. Where you see unfruitfulness, sickness or withered branches, prune our lives that we may live again. Where you see our spirits hungry and dry and neglected, water us with your grace, feed us on your living Word, nurture us into new life. Train us, good Lord, and feed us, so that we may flourish and prove fruitful, and so bring glory to your name. We ask it for the sake of Jesus, your Son and our Lord; Amen.

The Zoroastrians

Bible passages

Matthew 2:1–2, 7–12

After Jesus was born in Bethlehem in Judea, during the time of King Herod, Magi from the east came to Jerusalem and asked, "Where is the one who has been born king of the Jews? We saw his star when it rose and have come to worship him"...

... Then Herod called the Magi secretly and found out from them the exact time the star had appeared. He sent them to Bethlehem and said, "Go and search carefully for the child. As soon as you find him, report to me, so that I too may go and worship him."

After they had heard the king, they went on their way, and the star they had seen when it rose went ahead of them until it stopped over the place where the child was. When they saw the star, they were overjoyed. On coming to the house, they saw the child with his mother Mary, and they bowed down and worshipped him. Then they opened their treasures and presented him with gifts of gold, frankincense and myrrh. And having been warned in a dream not to go back to Herod, they returned to their country by another route.

Matthew 7:13–14

"Enter through the narrow gate. For wide is the gate and broad is the road that leads to destruction, and many enter through it. But small is the gate and narrow the road that leads to life, and only a few find it."

Matthew 21:21

"Truly I tell you, if you have faith and do not doubt, not only can you do what was done to the fig-tree, but also you can say to this mountain, 'Go, throw yourself into the sea,' and it will be done."

Commentary

As well as Jewish worshippers, Matthew's congregation seems to have included Gentiles, and clues from his Gospel suggest a significant number of Zoroastrians. His church was probably Syrian, and Zoroastrianism began in Iran but was a huge and powerful world religion in Bible times – later decimated by Muslim persecution.

Matthew seems to have been writing to both affirm and challenge the different cultural elements within his congregation. The Magi were Zoroastrians, and their homage to Jesus, inspired by their own traditions, is welcomed and accepted. Some of their other teachings – such as the broad and flowery way of righteousness – are challenged. Other beliefs – such as that the world was once smooth, and turbulent spiritual struggle made its mountains and ravines, and once righteousness is attained it will be made smooth again – are seen as fulfilled in the person and power of Jesus.

Questions

- Is your congregation mainly one type of person, or does it hold in balance clearly defined sections of cultural types, or is it an eclectic mix of all kinds? Is the balance between all the people harmonious? How is this harmony maintained, or how could it be improved?

- If you had Matthew's job of writing the gospel of Jesus for your church congregation, what aspects of the life of Jesus would you like to emphasize and bring out, and why? The Zoroastrian Gentiles must have been really pleased to see their Magi given an important part in the opening chapters. To whom would you like to give a special part, to affirm people in your congregation? Matthew gives the scribes and the Pharisees a very hard time because of their hypocrisy. Are there any shortcomings in your own church culture that you would like to critique and highlight in your gospel?

- Matthew also puts himself and his own call to faith in his Gospel (Matthew 9:9–10). What story would you tell about your call to follow Jesus, in your gospel?

Prayer

O God and Father of all, in Jesus you draw together the people of every time and culture into one household of faith and love. Forgive us when we have been prejudiced or suspicious of our neighbours and fellow believers because of their cultural differences. Open our eyes to the value and beauty of their humanity and their faith. We give thanks for the great work of reconciliation wrought for us and all creation in Jesus' saving death on the cross. May we set the power of his cross at the heart of our lives and faith, and live every day in the light of his mercy, humility, and grace. We ask it for his love's sake; Amen.

Mark

The Son of God

Bible passages

Mark 1:1

The beginning of the good news about Jesus the Messiah, the Son of God...

Mark 1:9–11

At that time Jesus came from Nazareth in Galilee and was baptised by John in the Jordan. Just as Jesus was coming up out of the water, he saw heaven being torn open and the Spirit descending on him like a dove. And a voice came from heaven: "You are my Son, whom I love; with you I am well pleased."

Mark 9:2–7

After six days Jesus took Peter, James and John with him and led them up a high mountain, where they were all alone. There he was transfigured before them. His clothes became dazzling white, whiter than anyone in the world could bleach them. And there appeared before them Elijah and Moses, who were talking with Jesus.

Peter said to Jesus, "Rabbi, it is good for us to be here. Let us put up three shelters – one for you, one for Moses and one for Elijah." (He did not know what to say, they were so frightened.) Then a cloud appeared and covered them, and a voice came from the cloud: "This is my Son, whom I love. Listen to him!"

Mark 15:37–39

With a loud cry, Jesus breathed his last. The curtain of the temple was torn in two from top to bottom. And when the centurion, who stood there in front of Jesus, saw how he died, he said, "Surely this man was the Son of God!"

Commentary

Mark's Gospel is wonderfully crafted, with every aspect of it employed in conveying its message, even the way it is structured.

The first of our passages is the tiny prologue to Mark's Gospel, in which he "sets out his stall", declaring his purpose in writing the Gospel and announcing the spiritual identity of Jesus.

The next three passages form the framework around which Mark builds his Gospel. Three times a voice declares that Jesus is the Son of God: at his baptism at the beginning of the Gospel, at the transfiguration at the apex of the Gospel, and at the end when Jesus dies on the cross. The first two voices are the voice of God; the third is the voice of the Roman soldier, showing that the message has gone out to all the world.

Each of the three occasions is described as a glimpse into heaven – at Jesus' baptism we read of heaven being "torn open", at his transfiguration we see the light of heaven and the presence of great men of God from beyond the grave, and at his crucifixion the Temple veil, which hid the Holy of Holies from the ordinary people, was torn in two.

The structure of Mark's Gospel is like a sandwich – a piece of bread then the filling then the second piece of bread. The first slice is taken up with stories detailing the signs and wonders that demonstrate that Jesus is the Son of God – again and again Mark reports that people were amazed at his teaching and miraculous power over nature and demons. The other slice of bread is the story of his suffering and death. The filling is the teaching section that connects the two and helps us see how the sorrow and suffering belong together with the signs and wonders.

Questions

- Why did Jesus come to John to be baptized – surely he didn't need to? Perhaps this was a sign of: identifying himself with all people; his ministry commencing; leaving his parents and community of origin to claim God as his Father and the faith community as his people; his self-dedication to God; or that he is going before us through the waters of the Jordan, leading us to the freedom of new life. What do you think?

- It was seeing how Jesus died that made the centurion say, "Surely this man was the Son of God!" How about you? What made you put your faith in Jesus and choose him as your Lord?

- In what ways do you feel it changes things, to accept Jesus as your Lord? On a day-to-day basis, what difference does it make to your life?

Prayer

O God of our salvation, whose love and humility were made manifest to us in your Son, Jesus, may the revelation of his grace and power illuminate our hearts and minds, until by his Spirit we are transformed into his likeness. For we ask it in Jesus' holy name; Amen.

The reinterpretation of leadership

Bible passages

Mark 8:34

Then he called the crowd to him along with his disciples and said: "Whoever wants to be my disciple must deny themselves and take up their cross and follow me."

Mark 9:35

Sitting down, Jesus called the Twelve and said, "Anyone who wants to be first must be the very last, and the servant of all."

Mark 10:42–45

Jesus called them together and said, "You know that those who are regarded as rulers of the Gentiles lord it over them, and their high officials exercise authority over them. Not so with you. Instead, whoever wants to become great among you must be your servant, and whoever wants to be first must be slave of all. For even the Son of Man did not come to be served, but to serve, and to give his life as a ransom for many."

Commentary

The message of Mark's Gospel is twofold: first he sets out to teach and demonstrate that Jesus is the messiah, the Son of God; but second and just as importantly Mark wants to convey Jesus' radical reinterpretation of what it means to be the messiah.

Another King David is what the people expected: a wealthy, kingly, strong conqueror, an exalted leader to look up to. Jesus challenges this expectation with the news that "the Son of Man came not to be served but to serve, and to give his life as a ransom for many" (Mark 10:45).

Our three passages are all taken from the important central block of teaching about humility, integrity, and simplicity spanning chapters 8 to 10. Up to chapter 8 Mark shows us the many signs that Jesus is the Son of God – nature miracles, exorcisms, and healing. After chapter 10 begins the passion narrative, as we see enacted the way of suffering by which the Son reconciles the world to Father God. This middle block of teaching is the pivotal section in which Jesus explains that his type of power and leadership is demonstrated in humble, sacrificial love. This section thus links the power shown in the signs and wonders of the early chapters with the power of the cross in the passion narrative.

Three times in this central block of teaching Jesus predicts his death: once at the beginning of the section (Mark 8:31), once after the transfiguration, which is the apex of the Gospel and comes at the centre of this teaching block (Mark 9:30), and once at the closing of the section, before the passion narrative begins (Mark 10:32).

Our third passage (Mark 10:42–45) summarizes and concludes this important teaching section about what it means to be the messiah.

Questions

- Jesus redefined leadership as suffering servanthood. Thinking of positions of leadership familiar to you – such as a parent, a head teacher, a church pastor, the owner of a small business employing staff – in what ways do you think a Christian leader might go about balancing fulfilment of the authority the role requires with the humility we see in Jesus?

- As well as willingness to accept suffering, Jesus identifies simplicity as an essential characteristic of his followers (Mark 10:15, 21, 25). How might we modern-day disciples begin to put into practice the simplicity to which we are called?

- To humility and simplicity Jesus adds integrity as a hallmark of his followers (Mark 9:47–50; 10:9, 18–19). Jesus hated hypocrisy, and it is arguably the greatest stumbling block to evangelism and the credibility of the church. Where would you draw the line between actual hypocrisy and the ordinary human weakness we all share? Have there been times when you have had to make a stand for integrity in the face of the ways of the world, in your neighbourhood or workplace, or even in your home?

Prayer

Father of Jesus, creator of the world, how hard and high is our calling! Forgive us for the many times we have stumbled, the myriad ways we fall short every day, the choices we have made to build our own little empire instead of the peaceable kingdom. Have mercy upon us, and heal us. By your grace may we stay the course and stand firm in the faith. By your transforming love may we be made acceptable to you, and in the power of the cross prove victorious over the world, the flesh, and the devil. For we ask it in Jesus' holy name; Amen.

Transfiguration – sight and insight

Bible passages

Mark 8:22–25

They came to Bethsaida, and some people brought a blind man and begged Jesus to touch him. He took the blind man by the hand and led him outside the village. When he had spat on the man's eyes and put his hands on him, Jesus asked, "Do you see anything?"

He looked up and said, "I see people; they look like trees walking around."

Once more Jesus put his hands on the man's eyes. Then his eyes were opened, his sight was restored, and he saw everything clearly.

Mark 8:27–33

Jesus and his disciples went on to the villages around Caesarea Philippi. On the way he asked them, "Who do people say I am?"

They replied, "Some say John the Baptist; others say Elijah; and still others, one of the prophets."

"But what about you?" he asked. "Who do you say I am?"

Peter answered, "You are the Messiah."

Jesus warned them not to tell anyone about him.

He then began to teach them that the Son of Man must suffer many things and be rejected by the elders, the chief priests and the teachers of the law, and that he must be killed and after three days rise again. He spoke plainly about this, and Peter took him aside and began to rebuke him.

But when Jesus turned and looked at his disciples, he rebuked Peter. "Get behind me, Satan!" he said. "You do not have in mind the concerns of God, but merely human concerns."

Mark 10:51–52

"What do you want me to do for you?" Jesus asked [Bartimaeus].

The blind man said, "Rabbi, I want to see."

"Go," said Jesus, "your faith has healed you." Immediately he received his sight and followed Jesus along the road.

Commentary

Our three passages belong to the important central teaching section about what it means to be the messiah. In Mark's Gospel, "sight" works as a metaphor for "insight". So the section in which we will be taught to see what it means to be the messiah starts with the story of healing a blind man. Jesus has to persevere with the healing, because at first the man doesn't see properly. Then we move on to the story of Peter's declaration of faith. Jesus commends his insight, saying that it is God who has revealed to him that Jesus is the messiah. But in the next moment Jesus rebukes Peter for his inability to accept that the role of the messiah necessarily involves suffering and death. We realize that it is Peter who is the blind man – the one who begins to see but cannot yet see clearly.

The section reinterpreting the messiah's calling closes with the story of healing Blind Bartimaeus, whose response is to "follow Jesus in the Way". Our translation says "along the road", but that misses the deeper meaning, which is that once we see, we will follow, we will take the same road.

Questions

- Can you think of an occasion in your own life when you had an "Aha!" moment of suddenly seeing things differently?

- Mark's Gospel teaches that we have to see things differently to change what we do. Can you think of examples of people you know or people in the news – perhaps politicians of different parties – who see things very differently from each other, and who accordingly choose very different life paths? One person sees a terrorist where another sees a freedom fighter – how might we work towards reconciliation by helping to see one another's point of view?

- The Bible teaches that "without vision the people perish". Can you think of modern-day examples of people whose vision has inspired you or changed the way you see things?

Prayer

Your power alone can heal the blindness of our sight, O God. You alone can help us to see past our own fear and self-interest. Please open our eyes to your vision of humility, simplicity, and sacrificial love, for by ourselves we cannot see its wonder. Hold the light for us to see the path where you want us to go; take us by the hand and lead us, and once we have found the way, may we never leave the path for one moment, but walk with Jesus until we arrive safely home. For we ask it in his holy name; Amen.

The unvarnished Jesus

Bible passages

Mark 3:20–21, 31–34

Then Jesus entered a house, and again a crowd gathered, so that he and his disciples were not even able to eat. When his family heard about this, they went to take charge of him, for they said, "He is out of his mind"...

... Then Jesus' mother and brothers arrived. Standing outside, they sent someone in to call him. A crowd was sitting round him, and they told him, "Your mother and brothers are outside looking for you."

"Who are my mother and my brothers?" he asked.

Then he looked at those seated in a circle round him and said, "Here are my mother and my brothers! Whoever does God's will is my brother and sister and mother."

Mark 4:35–38

That day when evening came, he said to his disciples, "Let us go over to the other side." Leaving the crowd behind, they took him along, just as he was, in the boat. There were also other boats with him. A furious squall came up, and the waves broke over the boat, so that it was nearly swamped. Jesus was in the stern, sleeping on a cushion. The disciples woke him and said to him, "Teacher, don't you care if we drown?"

Mark 6:4–6

Jesus said to them, "A prophet is not without honour except in his own town, among his relatives and in his own home." He could not do any miracles there, except lay his hands on a few people who were ill and heal them. He was amazed at their lack of faith.

Commentary

Mark's Gospel, the first of the four written and a foundational resource for Matthew and Luke, is structured with extraordinary literary elegance and written with shrewd intelligence, yet the Greek is rough and the sense conveyed is one of immediacy, urgency, and unvarnished reality. One of Mark's favourite phrases is "at once" or "immediately" – you will notice how often this occurs if you read it straight through or listen to a recording of it.

Mark portrays Jesus as a real person, seeing no need to polish or tidy up the image of his Lord. This honesty of presentation becomes very clear when we compare Mark's version with the other Gospels. Luke also tells of Jesus' mother and brothers asking for him outside the house where he is teaching (Luke 8:19–21), but no mention is made of them thinking he is out of his mind, and Jesus' reception of them seems more polite.

Matthew (8:23–27) and Luke (8:22–25) also tell the story of the stilling of the storm, but change Mark's "they took him into the boat just as he was". Matthew has the disciples follow Jesus into the boat, and Luke has him get into the boat with his disciples and instruct them where to go – Matthew and Luke make it clear that Jesus is the leader. Only Mark has the vivid, personal detail of the cushion on which Jesus slept. And when in fear they rouse Jesus, Matthew's disciples say, "Save us, Lord; we are perishing", Luke's disciples say, "Master, Master, we are perishing!" Only Mark's say, "Teacher, don't you care if we drown?"

Matthew (13:53–58) also includes the story where Jesus comments that a prophet is without honour in his own town, but amends Mark's "He could not do any miracles there" to "… he did not do many miracles there".

Questions

- Mark says the disciples took Jesus into the boat with them "just as he was". Try to picture this. Was Jesus tired and harassed – even exhausted? Was he dishevelled, after being pulled about by desperate, needy people? Think about the boat of your life at the present time. Who is travelling with you? Do the seas feel dangerous or calm? Does it feel as if Jesus is on board with you? If so, is he awake or asleep? Is everything OK just now, or do you need to shake him awake?

- Mark says that in his own town Jesus could not do many miracles because of the people's lack of faith. Do you think that means faith in God and miracles, or faith in Jesus – "familiarity breeds contempt"? Is there any area in your own life where you long to see change and you wish you could trust Jesus more?

- What do you think it must have been like to have Jesus in your family? Can you imagine living with him from day to day?

Prayer

O God of truth, our companion in the everyday as well as our exalted Lord, help us to put our trust in you completely, so that your mighty power may be at work in our lives for everyone to see, bringing healing and wholeness, integrity, peace, and salvation: for we ask it in Jesus' holy name; Amen.

The unnamed outsider

Bible passages

Mark 15:37–39

> With a loud cry, Jesus breathed his last.
>
> The curtain of the temple was torn in two from top to bottom. And when the centurion, who stood there in front of Jesus, saw how he died, he said, "Surely this man was the Son of God!"

Mark 7:24–30

> Jesus left that place and went to the vicinity of Tyre. He entered a house and did not want anyone to know it; yet he could not keep his presence secret. In fact, as soon as she heard about him, a woman whose little daughter was possessed by an impure spirit came and fell at his feet. The woman was a Greek, born in Syrian Phoenicia. She begged Jesus to drive the demon out of her daughter.
>
> "First let the children eat all they want," he told her, "for it is not right to take the children's bread and toss it to the dogs."
>
> "Lord," she replied, "even the dogs under the table eat the children's crumbs."
>
> Then he told her, "For such a reply, you may go; the demon has left your daughter." She went home and found her child lying on the bed, and the demon gone.

Commentary

Mark wrote his Gospel to get across to us who Jesus is – the Son of God. One way he does this is by offering us pictures of people outside the accepted faith community recognizing and acknowledging the power and grace in Jesus. He is showing us that Jesus was more than a leader of a particular religious tradition – his ministry was universal; he came for everyone.

Mark gave his Gospel a particular structure conveying the message that Jesus is God's Son. Three times a voice is heard affirming this: at the beginning in the story of Jesus' baptism when the voice of God is heard; at the apex of the Gospel structure in the story of the transfiguration, a moment of shining revelation when the voice of God is heard again; and then at the end, when Jesus gives up his spirit to the Father, when the voice of the unnamed outsider, the Roman centurion, bookends the voice from the beginning of the Gospel, confirming that this is indeed the Son of God. Mark shows us by this means a gospel of universal relevance, of application far wider than religious cliques and élites.

In the story of the Syro-Phoenician woman, Mark brings home to us that Jesus was not there for just the inner circle of his own spiritual family, but for all people, even outsiders whose names we do not know.

It has been said that "all truth is God's truth", so people of quite different faith traditions from our own might be able to deepen and enrich our faith in God by the unexpected perspectives they offer us.

Questions

- Can you think of a time when you were surprised by truth spoken from an unexpected quarter? A child, maybe; or a homeless person; or someone of a different political or religious persuasion from your own?

- Jesus seems reluctant to help the Syro-Phoenician woman at first because he was sent as the messiah to the Jews, but he responds to her faith in him. Can you identify the faith groups you feel comfortable with, and the ones you feel more wary of or alien from? See if anyone in the study group can suggest some insights of truth that have come from the faith communities towards which you feel less warmth.

- Have you sometimes felt like an outsider or a nonentity or a lone voice in a church setting? How did you overcome this to feel more at home? Or, if you just gave up and left, can you think of ways to help make connections with those who might feel alone or ill at ease in the church you are part of now?

Prayer

You are a great, great God. You made every star and planet, every speck of dust, everything that ever was. You made us too, and you knew us, each one of us, from the days when we grew hidden from the world in our mother's womb. You know our hidden thoughts, the undisclosed yearning of our hearts, the quickening of joy, and the bitter roots of shame and sorrow deep in our souls. Help us, in our search for truth, to look always for the big picture, to look beyond the narrow horizons of our own tradition to the salvation in Jesus offered to all people of every culture we can possibly imagine. Keep us faithful, as you are faithful, but save us from the closed mind, the blinkered vision, and the stunting of possibilities. Give us the humility to remember who you are, and the imagination to spread our wings in the spacious sky of your unlimited love. In Jesus' holy name; Amen.

Luke

Finding the lost

Bible passage – Luke 15:1–10

Now the tax collectors and sinners were all gathering round to hear Jesus. But the Pharisees and the teachers of the law muttered, "This man welcomes sinners, and eats with them."

Then Jesus told them this parable: "Suppose one of you has a hundred sheep and loses one of them. Doesn't he leave the ninety-nine in the open country and go after the lost sheep until he finds it? And when he finds it, he joyfully puts it on his shoulders and goes home. Then he calls his friends and neighbours together and says, 'Rejoice with me; I have found my lost sheep.' I tell you that in the same way there will be more rejoicing in heaven over one sinner who repents than over ninety-nine righteous people who do not need to repent.

"Or suppose a woman has ten silver coins and loses one. Doesn't she light a lamp, sweep the house and search carefully until she finds it? And when she finds it, she calls her friends and neighbours together and says, 'Rejoice with me; I have found my lost coin.' In the same way, I tell you, there is rejoicing in the presence of the angels of God over one sinner who repents."

Commentary

Luke's Gospel is loved for its compassion and understanding, not least in its treatment of human sin. There is an essential kindness in Luke's portrayal of sinfulness as the state of being lost.

Only Luke tells the story of Zacchaeus, with Jesus' telling remark, "The Son of Man came to seek and to save the lost."

Luke devotes a whole chapter to the exploration of this concept. Chapter 15 is given over to the telling of three parables, The Lost Sheep, The Lost Coin, and The Lost Son, each of which helps us to see the faithful and tireless love of God. Luke shows us that, no matter how far we have strayed, God will never give up searching for us. Not only will he wait for us and run to meet us, like the father of the lost son, but he will search for us as the shepherd looked for his lost sheep. And Luke stresses in each of these parables that, when we are reunited with this loving God, we are not scolded or punished – the joy at our homecoming is exuberantly happy. God rejoices when his lost children come home.

We notice in the "chapter of the lost" a sense of God accepting responsibility for our wrongdoing. In the story of the coin, the woman has lost her treasure; you can hardly blame the coin. In the story of the sheep – well, sheep do wander; it is the responsibility of the shepherd to watch over them. This shows a wise compassion for human weakness, and suggests that God accepts us as we are. Even when we have sinned, he is still on our side; he does not blame us; he just does everything he can to put things right, and he wants us to do the same. This response of restitution also comes out very vividly in the story of Zacchaeus in chapter 19.

Questions

- Matthew also tells the story of the lost sheep, but with differences. Look at the story in Matthew 18:12–13. What differences do you notice between his telling of the story and Luke's version in our study passage? Do you see the "if" in Matthew and the "when" in Luke? What other differences can you find? Do you prefer one version to the other? What are your reasons, if you do?
- What do you think Luke wants to draw out about the nature of God, in his chapter of the lost? How does this match your own experience of God and what you have been taught about him in your childhood or in church?
- What experiences can you think of, in your own life or the life of someone you know, that reflect the kindness of God in finding you and bringing you home?

Prayer

O God our Father, how generous and forgiving is your love to us! We thank you from the bottom of our hearts for your gracious dealing with us, your patience, and your kindness. Plant in our souls the seeds of loving-kindness, so that we may look upon others with the same generosity with which you have regarded us. May your mercy and gentleness take root in our lives and flower in our hearts. May our relationships with one another bear the fruit of forgiveness and reconciliation that you long to see, and so witness to everyone who knows us that you are our true Father and we are indeed your children, bearing the family resemblance of compassion and grace. For we ask it in Jesus' holy name; Amen.

Healing the sick

Bible passages

Colossians 4:14, KJV

Luke, the beloved physician, and Demas, greet you.

Luke 13:11–13, KJV

And, behold, there was a woman which had a spirit of infirmity eighteen years, and was bowed together, and could in no wise lift up herself.

And when Jesus saw her, he called her to him, and said unto her, Woman, thou art loosed from thine infirmity.

And he laid his hands on her: and immediately she was made straight, and glorified God.

Luke 4:38–39 (compare Mark 1:30 and Matthew 8:14)

Jesus left the synagogue and went to the home of Simon. Now Simon's mother-in-law was suffering from a high fever, and they asked Jesus to help her. So he bent over her and rebuked the fever, and it left her. She got up at once and began to wait on them.

Luke 8:43–44, KJV (compare Mark 5:25–29 and Matthew 9:20–22)

And a woman having an issue of blood twelve years, which had spent all her living upon physicians, neither could be healed of any, came behind him, and touched the border of his garment: and immediately her issue of blood stanched.

Commentary

We know Luke was a doctor, because Paul says so in the greetings ending his letter to Colossae. This is the only direct mention of it, but evidence of Luke's medical knowledge and interest is sprinkled throughout his writing. Our study passages contain only some of numerous examples. I have used the KJV here where particular words used are helpful in making this clear.

In the story of the woman who was bent double, the Greek word rendered here as "infirmity" is *astheneias*, meaning "weakness" or "frailty". Luke goes on to a more specific description, using the word *sugkuptousa*, a medical term, meaning curvature of the spine. When Jesus heals her, saying, "Thou art loosed," this word "loosed" translates *apolelusai*, the ancient Greek medical term referring to relaxing tendons or tight skin, or removing bandages.

In the story about Peter's mother-in-law, Luke's account includes two medical terms we don't see in Mark or Matthew. He describes her as "taken with a great fever" (*sunechomene pureto megalo*), a phrase we find in the works of Hippocrates and Galen and in other contemporary medical books, but only in Luke in the New Testament. From Galen we know that Greek physicians differentiated fevers as "high" (*megas*) or "slight" (*mikros*). Where Mark and Matthew use the generalized term, Luke is medically specific.

In the story of the woman with an issue of blood, we note a difference in attitude to doctors between Mark and Luke! Mark notes that the woman had spent everything she had on medical care and instead of getting better had only got worse. Luke (characteristically kind and discreet – another doctor's habit) describes the situation more gently, saying she had spent her living on doctors' fees, but none of them had been able to heal her. He uses a precise medical term for the cessation of her bleeding, *este*, rightly given in the KJV as "stanched".

Luke probably never met Jesus personally, but relied on information from Mark's Gospel and his own sources (it is thought that Mary the mother of Jesus was one source) to write his Gospel. The medical detail in his accounts reveals his physician's discipline of careful questioning in taking a history.

Questions

- When you discover that Luke's medical background has influenced the Gospel text, are you excited and intrigued to have this extra insight or does the information seem to threaten your sense of the Bible being purely the word of God? How do you respond?

- How do you think Luke the doctor would have felt about Jesus the healer? How do you think, in our prayers and practice, we could balance the spiritual with the physical in our regular treatment of illness today?

- Where Mark is very direct in his expression, Luke is careful always to be courteous and kind. Can you think of examples from your own life when the direct approach has been necessary, and examples of times when it has been important to approach a difficult subject with tact and kindness?

Prayer

O God our healer and our strength, you see us and know us. You understand our weakness and frailty; our vulnerability is never hidden from the kindness of your love. Where we are lost, please find us; where we are infirm or diseased, please heal us. Thank you for the compassion of your gaze, and for the touch of your love, which makes us whole. In Jesus' holy name; Amen.

The Holy Spirit

Bible passages

Luke 3:15–16

The people were waiting expectantly and were all wondering in their hearts if John might possibly be the Messiah. John answered them all, "I baptise you with water. But one who is more powerful than I will come, the straps of whose sandals I am not worthy to untie. He will baptise you with the Holy Spirit and fire."

Luke 3:21–22 (compare Mark 1:10 and Matthew 3:16)

When all the people were being baptised, Jesus was baptised too. And as he was praying, heaven was opened and the Holy Spirit descended on him in bodily form like a dove.

Luke 4:1

Jesus, full of the Holy Spirit, left the Jordan and was led by the Spirit into the wilderness...

Luke 4:16–20

He went to Nazareth, where he had been brought up, and on the Sabbath day he went into the synagogue, as was his custom. He stood up to read, and the scroll of the prophet Isaiah was handed to him. Unrolling it, he found the place where it is written:

"The Spirit of the Lord is on me, because he has anointed me to proclaim good news to the poor. He has sent me to proclaim freedom for the prisoners and recovery of sight for the blind, to set the oppressed free, to proclaim the year of the Lord's favour."

Then he rolled up the scroll, gave it back to the attendant and sat down. The eyes of everyone in the synagogue were fastened on him. He began by saying to them, "Today this scripture is fulfilled in your hearing."

Luke 11:13

"If you then, though you are evil, know how to give good gifts to your children, how much more will your Father in heaven give the Holy Spirit to those who ask him!"

Luke 12:10–12

"And everyone who speaks a word against the Son of Man will be forgiven, but anyone who blasphemes against the Holy Spirit will not be forgiven.

"When you are brought before synagogues, rulers and authorities, do not worry about how you will defend yourselves or what you will say, for the Holy Spirit will teach you at that time what you should say."

Commentary

A particular characteristic of Luke's Gospel is his emphasis on the very real presence and power of the Holy Spirit. This ties in with his concern for the poor and the outcast (see our study entitled "Lifting up the lowly", and his emphasis on inclusion (see study on "A gospel for the whole world").

The opening chapters of Luke's Gospel take us through examples of the Holy Spirit residing in people often excluded from religious elites (Luke 1:15, 35, 41, 67; 2:25–26). Mary the unmarried girl is pregnant by the action of the Holy Spirit. John the Baptist, as yet unborn, leaps in his mother's womb in response to the presence of his Lord, and is described as being "strong in the Spirit" in childhood. His mother, Elizabeth, who had been barren, was also made fertile by the Holy Spirit's miracle. Old Anna and Simeon at the Temple are motivated and filled by the Holy Spirit. The old, the women, the little children (even unborn; and see also Luke 10:21), and those socially inferior (the unmarried mother, the barren woman) all are included in this blessing of the indwelling Holy Spirit.

Through his Gospel, Luke teaches that the Holy Spirit is for everyone, and that it is through his power that spiritual ministry is accomplished and the good news effectively passed on.

Questions

- What would you say is the role of the Holy Spirit in your life? Where do you see him at work?
- Can you think of examples of people you know whom you might describe as "full of the Holy Spirit"?
- What implications might the Gospel of Luke have for our understanding and treatment of the unborn child?

Prayer

Holy Spirit of God, without you we are nothing and can do nothing worthwhile. In your love and grace, please fill us; please stay with us and never depart from us. Transform us into the likeness of Jesus so that even the smallest details of our daily lives are illumined by the light of your presence. For we ask it in Jesus' holy name; Amen.

A gospel for the whole world

Bible passages

Luke 3:23a–38b

Now Jesus himself was about thirty years old when he began his ministry. He was the son, so it was thought, of Joseph... the son of Adam, the son of God.

Luke 17:11–20

Jesus travelled along the border between Samaria and Galilee. As he was going into a village, ten men who had leprosy met him. They stood at a distance and called out in a loud voice, "Jesus, Master, have pity on us!"

When he saw them, he said, "Go, show yourselves to the priests." And as they went, they were cleansed.

One of them, when he saw he was healed, came back, praising God in a loud voice. He threw himself at Jesus' feet and thanked him – and he was a Samaritan.

Jesus asked, "Were not all ten cleansed? Where are the other nine? Has no one returned to give praise to God except this foreigner?" Then he said to him, "Rise and go; your faith has made you well."

Once, on being asked by the Pharisees when the kingdom of God would come, Jesus replied, "The coming of the kingdom of God is not something that can be observed, nor will people say, "Here it is," or "There it is," because the kingdom of God is in your midst."

Luke 24:52–53

While he was blessing them, he left them and was taken up into heaven. Then they worshipped him and returned to Jerusalem with great joy. And they stayed continually at the temple, praising God.

Acts 1:4 (from the opening of the book of the Acts of the Apostles)

"Do not leave Jerusalem, but wait for the gift my Father promised, which you have heard me speak about."

Acts 28:28–31 (the ending of the book of Acts)

"Therefore I want you to know that God's salvation has been sent to the Gentiles, and they will listen!"

For two whole years Paul stayed there in his own rented house and welcomed all who came to see him. He proclaimed the kingdom of God and taught about the Lord Jesus Christ – with all boldness and without hindrance!

Commentary

Luke's Gospel portrays Jesus as a universal saviour for all humankind. Gentile soldiers come to John to be baptized (Luke 3:14), and Jesus is shown associating with Samaritans (Luke 9:51–52). In the first of our passages above, Luke traces the lineage of Jesus back to Adam, father of humanity (unlike Matthew, who traces the line back to Abraham, father of Judaism). In our second passage, we see a Gentile singled out from a group of people healed of leprosy, and commended for his faith. Following this story, Luke juxtaposes the teaching of Jesus in response to questioning by Jewish leaders, that the kingdom of God can never be monopolized or pinned down to a location – wherever and whoever we are, it can be found in the midst of us.

Luke wrote the book of Acts too, and they are best understood as one two-part work. It's instructive to trace the movement of the gospel, carried like a torch from Jerusalem, the heart of the Jewish religious world, to Rome, the heart of the secular Gentile Roman world, as Luke unfolds the story over the two books. In his Gospel, Jerusalem is central. He roots the opening chapters there; the first words we hear Jesus speak are in and of the Temple (Luke 2:49). In the wilderness temptation his order differs from Matthew's in climaxing at the Temple in Jerusalem, and the parting from Jesus' earthly ministry focuses on Jerusalem (Luke 24:52–53; Acts 1:3–14). We watch as Luke then shows us the gospel fanning out through and across the Gentile world to the triumphant conclusion (Acts 28:28): "God's salvation has been sent to the Gentiles, and they will listen!"

Questions

- What do you think it means to say the kingdom of God is in our midst? How do we find it? How do we realize it?
- Luke showed the gospel moving from the heart of Judaism to the heart of the Gentile world, but also from the heart of the religious world to the heart of the secular and political world. What challenge might this offer to our own faith practice? How might we make a similar journey as modern believers?
- If the modern-day church is the equivalent of the Pharisees and the Jewish people, who are the Gentiles and how might we reach them?

Prayer

O God of the whole world, of all people and all creation, words cannot express how glad and grateful we are that your plan had room for us too. Help us remember that your gospel is for all people. Help us to live generously and openly, sharing and offering what we know of the life and love of Jesus in every way we can think of to everyone we meet. For we ask it in his holy name; Amen.

Lifting up the lowly

Bible passages

Luke 1:51–53

He has performed mighty deeds with his arm;
  he has scattered those who are proud in their inmost thoughts.
He has brought down rulers from their thrones
  but has lifted up the humble.
He has filled the hungry with good things
  but has sent the rich away empty.

Luke 2:8–11

And there were shepherds living out in the fields near by, keeping watch over their flocks at night. An angel of the Lord appeared to them, and the glory of the Lord shone around them, and they were terrified. But the angel said to them, "Do not be afraid. I bring you good news that will cause great joy for all the people. Today in the town of David a Saviour has been born to you; he is the Messiah, the Lord."

Luke 15:1–2

Now the tax collectors and sinners were all gathering round to hear Jesus. But the Pharisees and the teachers of the law muttered, "This man welcomes sinners, and eats with them."

Luke 12:32–34

"Do not be afraid, little flock, for your Father has been pleased to give you the kingdom. Sell your possessions and give to the poor. Provide purses for yourselves that will not wear out, a treasure in heaven that will never fail, where no thief comes near and no moth destroys. For where your treasure is, there your heart will be also."

Luke 14:33

"In the same way, those of you who do not give up everything you have cannot be my disciples."

Luke 22:24–27

A dispute also arose among them as to which of them was considered to be greatest. Jesus said to them, "The kings of the Gentiles lord it over them; and those who exercise authority over them call themselves Benefactors. But you are not to be like that. Instead, the greatest among you should be like the youngest, and the one who rules like the one who serves. For who is greater, the one who is at the table or the one who serves? Is it not the one who is at the table? But I am among you as one who serves."

Commentary

Luke's Gospel places emphasis both on the non-negotiable essential discipline for a disciple of practising simplicity and humility, and also on the special place the poor and lowly and outcast have in the heart of God.

At the time and place of Christ's birth, shepherds were looked down upon – they were on the very bottom rung of the social ladder – yet it was to them the angel came.

The Song of Mary, which Luke sets out for us, rejoices in God's option for the poor, remembering and lifting up the lowly. Luke shows Jesus born in a stable because there was no room at the inn, the child of a couple who could afford only the poor man's sacrifice (Luke 2:24).

Teaching about money is prominent in Luke's Gospel, for example the parables of the Rich Fool (12:13–21) and Dives and Lazarus (16:19–26) – and Jesus warns that no one can serve God and money (16:10–13).

Questions

- Luke tells us that Jesus said "… those of you who do not give up everything you have cannot be my disciples". What do you suppose he meant by that?

- Mary in her song rejoiced that God had "filled the hungry with good things but has sent the rich away empty". What do you think about this? In what way has God "sent the rich away empty"? And how has he "filled the hungry with good things"?

- Jesus says, "Provide purses for yourselves that will not wear out, a treasure in heaven that will never fail… For where your treasure is, there your heart will be also." What are the purses he means? What is that "treasure in heaven"? Do you think you have it? How do we find it?

Prayer

O God of love, your heart burns with compassion for the poorest, the loneliest, and the lost. Your eye sees even the sparrow that falls. You feel the sorrow and despair of the poor, and your choice on earth was to share that with them. Help us, we pray. Forgive us where we are complacent, indifferent, and selfish. Find us where we ourselves are poor or lonely and forgotten. Strengthen us to serve, to share, and to love, and so bring us to the place where heaven's treasure is to be found in our midst here on earth. For we ask it in Jesus' holy name; Amen.

John
The light of the world

Bible passages

John 1:5–10, 14b

The light shines in the darkness, and the darkness has not overcome it. There was a man sent from God whose name was John. He came as a witness to testify concerning that light, so that through him all might believe. He himself was not the light; he came only as a witness to the light.

The true light that gives light to everyone was coming into the world. He was in the world, and though the world was made through him, the world did not recognize him...

We have seen his glory, the glory of the one and only Son, who came from the Father, full of grace and truth.

John 1:36–39 (my paraphrase)

Looking at Jesus treading the way, John said, "Perceive! – The Lamb of God!" Overhearing that, the two disciples followed Jesus. Jesus turned, turned his gaze upon them. He asked them, "What are you looking for?" They said, "Rabbi (which means "Teacher"), where are you staying?" "Come," he answered them, "and see for yourselves."

John 8:12 (see also 3:19–21; 12:35)

When Jesus spoke again to the people, he said, "I am the light of the world. Whoever follows me will never walk in darkness, but will have the light of life."

John 9:4–5

"As long as it is day, we must do the works of him who sent me. Night is coming, when no one can work. While I am in the world, I am the light of the world."

John 20:3–10

So Peter and the other disciple started for the tomb. Both were running, but the other disciple outran Peter and reached the tomb first. He bent over and **looked in at** the strips of linen lying there but did not go in. Then Simon Peter came along behind him and went straight into the tomb. He **saw** the strips of linen lying there, as well as the cloth that had been wrapped round Jesus' head. The cloth was still lying in its place, separate from the linen. Finally the other disciple, who had reached the tomb first, also went inside. He **saw** and believed... Then the disciples went back to where they were staying.

Commentary

Light and the corresponding themes of enabling sight and glory run like threads through John's Gospel. Jesus is characterized as the light of the world, unvanquished by opposing forces of darkness. John 1:5 encapsulates this concept wonderfully: "the darkness has not overcome it". That word "overcome" could be rendered as "comprehended", "grasped", "swallowed", "engulfed". The Greek is literally "down-got". In common parlance we say we have "got it down" when we have completely understood something; we also think of "bringing down" prey. John is saying the light both baffles and eludes the darkness, still shining clearly despite the brutalizing forces of blinding ignorance. The cross is described in terms of glory (see 17:1) – a moment of blazing light.

I have paraphrased the section where Jesus first speaks, to bring out John's emphasis in the Greek on seeing with understanding – "perceiving". The light of Jesus' presence enables in-sight. We see this again in the resurrection story (20:3–8), where three times John uses verbs for "to see" (I have emphasized the three words in the passage). In the Greek, the words have different meanings: glimpsed... examined... understood.

John is encouraging us to realize that the light we see in Jesus is a catching force, and can become indwelling light in our souls as we gaze upon Christ and his story, and as his gaze falls upon us. Notice the attachment, in both the resurrection story at the end and the meeting Jesus story at the beginning, of the concept of dwelling – where one is staying. This Gospel is about indwelling light, being at home with light, light coming home.

Questions

- John thinks of coming to faith as "seeing the light". How would you describe the process of finding faith, for you personally?
- John sees the presence of Christ as illuminating. Can you think of Christians whose faith seemed to "shine out" of them, or make them shine?
- "This little light of mine, I'm gonna let it shine!" What might this mean in practical, everyday terms? How are we going to actually do this?

Prayer

God of light and glory, may the radiance of your Holy Spirit so fill our hearts and lives that all we say and do reflects the beauty of Jesus, the light of the world. For we ask it in his holy name; Amen.

The living Word

Bible passages

John 1:1–3, 14

In the beginning was the Word, and the Word was with God, and the Word was God. He was with God in the beginning. Through him all things were made; without him nothing was made that has been made...

... The Word became flesh and made his dwelling among us.

John 5:23–24

"Whoever does not honour the Son does not honour the Father, who sent him. Very truly I tell you, whoever hears my word and believes him who sent me has eternal life and will not be judged but has crossed over from death to life."

John 6:62–63

"Then what if you see the Son of Man ascend to where he was before! The Spirit gives life; the flesh counts for nothing. The words I have spoken to you – they are full of the Spirit and life."

1 John 1:1–3

That which was from the beginning, which we have heard, which we have seen with our eyes, which we have looked at and our hands have touched – this we proclaim concerning the Word of life. The life appeared; we have seen it and testify to it, and we proclaim to you the eternal life, which was with the Father and has appeared to us. We proclaim to you what we have seen and heard, so that you also may have fellowship with us. And our fellowship is with the Father and with his Son, Jesus Christ.

1 John 1:10

If we claim we have not sinned, we make him out to be a liar and his word is not in us.

Commentary

John's portrayal of Jesus is sometimes called "the Cosmic Christ", because he shows Jesus as a transcendent, eternal figure, at work with the Father in the creation of the world. In the prologue (opening words) to his Gospel, John says that nothing was made except through the Word – Jesus.

"The Word" is a big term here. It has resonances in both Jewish and Greek religious culture. For the Jews, it recalls the words of creation: "Let there be light!"

The echoes of the opening of Genesis are clear and obvious in the prologue to John's Gospel. The breath of God, which confers and defines life (and is a term for the Holy Spirit), the Law, which structured the whole of their lives, and the word of God spoken through the prophets, are all key aspects of the Jewish faith. But in his prologue John, writing in Greek, uses the word *logos* (tr. "word"), which the Stoic philosophers of ancient Greece used to describe the life-giving divine principle. So John is showing us the mind-blowingly enormous wingspan of the Christ idea. In Jesus reside the full power and radiance of the creator himself. As the Christ, there is nothing limited or local about Jesus; he is for every time and culture, and his reach even extends beyond to before time began and after its ending.

Though Bible scholars inevitably question whether the authorship of the Gospel of John and the epistles of John are the same, they show many similarities in thought and composition, so I have included two excerpts from 1 John in our study passages, to fill out our knowledge and understanding of John's teaching that Jesus is the living Word of God.

Questions

- We often call the Bible the "Word of God", but the Bible calls Jesus the "Word of God". What difference might it make to our lives if we think the Word of God is the Bible, or if we think it's Jesus? Consider the difference between how we can know the Bible, and how we can know Jesus.
- It has been said that in the Bible the Word became flesh, and the main activity of the church has been to change it back to words again. Think about the balance of teaching and study with life and service in your church. Is it about right, or are there changes you would like to see?
- Jesus is called the "Word of life". He described his words as "giving life". Can you think of experiences of your own when someone's words have meant life to you?

Prayer

O God of love and life and power, we give you thanks for Jesus, the living Word, transforming and renewing our hearts and minds into his likeness of love. We beg you to breathe into us the vitalizing power of your Holy Spirit, enabling us to see and to grasp the way and teaching of Jesus. It may be true that we shall never be perfect followers, never understand completely all that he is and has done for us, but nevertheless we ask for grace to make a start, and to prove faithful in our daily walk with him. For we ask it in his holy name; Amen.

The body of Christ

Bible passages

John 17:20–26

"My prayer is not for them alone. I pray also for those who will believe in me through their message, that all of them may be one, Father, just as you are in me and I am in you. May they also be in us so that the world may believe that you have sent me. I have given them the glory that you gave me, that they may be one as we are one – I in them and you in me – so that they may be brought to complete unity. Then the world will know that you sent me and have loved them even as you have loved me.

"Father, I want those you have given me to be with me where I am, and to see my glory, the glory you have given me because you loved me before the creation of the world.

"Righteous Father, though the world does not know you, I know you, and they know that you have sent me. I have made you known to them, and will continue to make you known in order that the love you have for me may be in them and that I myself may be in them."

John 20:19–23, 26, 29

On the evening of that first day of the week, when the disciples were together, with the doors locked for fear of the Jewish leaders, Jesus came and stood among them and said, "Peace be with you!" After he said this, he showed them his hands and side. The disciples were overjoyed when they saw the Lord.

Again Jesus said, "Peace be with you! As the Father has sent me, I am sending you." And with that he breathed on them and said, "Receive the Holy Spirit. If you forgive anyone's sins, their sins are forgiven; if you do not forgive them, they are not forgiven."

... A week later his disciples were in the house again, and Thomas was with them...

... Then Jesus told him, "Because you have seen me, you have believed; blessed are those who have not seen and yet have believed."

John 15:5–6

"I am the vine; you are the branches. If you remain in me and I in you, you will bear much fruit; apart from me you can do nothing. If you do not remain in me, you are like a branch that is thrown away and withers; such branches are picked up, thrown into the fire and burned."

Commentary

John wrote his Gospel later than the others, when the church was being fiercely persecuted. We know from the epistles (for example 2 Thessalonians) that believers expected the second coming of Jesus to be at hand. Their faith centred on Jesus, and they saw the time they were in as a brief waiting period. John's Gospel is encouraging them to see things differently, answering their question, "Where is Jesus now? He rose from the dead – so where is he?"

Luke answers the question in one way, in telling us about the day of Pentecost, and the passing-on of the Holy Spirit. John answers in a different way, showing us that Christ is still present with us, but now to be found in the gathered people of God – the body of Christ. A clue to this theme is in the opening words Jesus speaks in John's Gospel. "Where are you staying?" the two disciples ask him, and he answers, "Come and see" (John 1:37–39).

Notice how, in the story of Doubting Thomas, John shows us the believers in a rhythm of weekly meetings (compare Acts 2:42–47). When Thomas didn't attend, he missed the risen Jesus. It was as he joined with the body of believers that he found the risen Christ.

Jesus' teaching about the vine in John 15, and his prayer in John 17, when put together with John's emphasis on Christ's divinity, give us a picture of organic wholeness – the body of believers united with each other, in Christ, in God. It is in this unity that Christ's presence is revealed.

Questions

- How do you personally experience the presence of Jesus in the gathering of the people of God? In the preaching? In the Eucharist? In the songs of worship? In direct ministry – of healing, for example?
- "Remain/abide in me," Jesus said. What do you think we have to do to remain in him?
- Do you think that ideally we should not have separate denominations but all belong to one group – or are they just different branches of one family?

Prayer

God of love, indivisibly one, Father of mercy, blessed saviour, Holy Spirit, we give you thanks that you have called us into union with you and communion with one another – all believers in every time and place. Keep us firm in the hope you have set before us, and bring us at the last into the fullness of your eternal presence. In Jesus' holy name we pray; Amen.

The *ego eimi*

Bible passages

Exodus 3:14

God said to Moses, "I am who I am. This is what you are to say to the Israelites: 'I am has sent me to you.'"

Isaiah 52:6, KJV

Therefore my people shall know my name: therefore they shall know in that day that I am he that doth speak: behold, it is I.

John 4:25–26

The woman said, "I know that Messiah" (called Christ) "is coming. When he comes, he will explain everything to us."

Then Jesus declared, "I, the one speaking to you – I am he."

John 8:58–59

"Very truly I tell you," Jesus answered, "before Abraham was born, I am!" At this, they picked up stones to stone him, but Jesus hid himself, slipping away from the temple grounds.

John 6:35

Then Jesus declared, "I am the bread of life. Whoever comes to me will never go hungry, and whoever believes in me will never be thirsty."

John 10:11

"I am the good shepherd. The good shepherd lays down his life for the sheep."

John 13:19

"I am telling you now before it happens, so that when it does happen you will believe that I am who I am."

John 18:4–6

Jesus, knowing all that was going to happen to him, went out and asked them, "Who is it you want?"

"Jesus of Nazareth," they replied.

"I am he," Jesus said. (And Judas the traitor was standing there with them.) When Jesus said, "I am he," they drew back and fell to the ground.

Commentary

The *ego eimi* is not entirely exclusive to John's Gospel, but is very prominently emphasized by John, occurring twenty-four times. Jesus says "*eimi*" (the usual form of "I am") forty-five times in this Gospel, but of these twenty-four are the *ego eimi*, giving the deliberate addition of the *ego* ("I"), unnecessary in Greek grammar, which alerts us to something special being said. Of these twenty-four times, seven (8:24; 8:28; 8:58; 13:19; 18:5; 18:6; and 18:8) are absolute emphatic statements of self-identification with the Father, the I Am that I Am. These are moments of epiphany, when the power of Jesus shines out dramatically. In one case those to whom he speaks fall to the ground as if stunned (John 18:6). In another case, faith in him is the result (John 4:26).

By using this form, Jesus is claiming to be God, for only God is the I Am that I Am. That's why he roused such anger in his hearers in 8:58–59. It is clear that, in his use of the phrase, Jesus is making an intentional link to its use in the Old Testament as the name of God. This "name" is no mere label, a random identifying moniker; it is like a compressed file in which is contained all the power and glory of the being of God himself, only waiting to be unzipped into our lives by personal encounter.

Questions

- "The name of the Lord is a fortress. When the righteous take refuge in it, they are kept safe" (Proverbs 18:10, my paraphrase). How do you respond to the idea of God's name as his actual self, a place of protection and security? Is that concept difficult for you, or does it resonate easily?
- How do you think we might actually in practical terms go about taking refuge in God's name?
- It seems clear from John's Gospel that it wasn't just other people who concluded that Jesus is God – he thought so himself. What are your thoughts and feelings about Jesus? Which divine aspect do you relate to most comfortably – the Father, the Son, or the Holy Spirit?

Prayer

Most glorious God, we praise and exalt your holy name, the quintessential expression of who you are – Ancient of Days, most mighty, the Mystery we can know and love as a fellow traveller in Jesus. Wrap the power and light of your name around us, we pray, so that, whatever happens to us in this world, our faith will hold firm in Jesus, in whose holy name we pray; Amen.

The way of love

Bible passages

John 3:16–17

For God so loved the world that he gave his one and only Son, that whoever believes in him shall not perish but have eternal life. For God did not send his Son into the world to condemn the world, but to save the world through him.

John 13:1

It was just before the Passover Festival. Jesus knew that the hour had come for him to leave this world and go to the Father. Having loved his own who were in the world, he loved them to the end.

John 13:34–35

"A new command I give you: love one another. As I have loved you, so you must love one another. By this everyone will know that you are my disciples, if you love one another."

John 14:21, 23–24

"Whoever has my commands and keeps them is the one who loves me. The one who loves me will be loved by my Father, and I too will love them and show myself to them...

"Anyone who loves me will obey my teaching. My Father will love them, and we will come to them and make our home with them. Anyone who does not love me will not obey my teaching. These words you hear are not my own; they belong to the Father who sent me."

John 15:9–17

"As the Father has loved me, so have I loved you. Now remain in my love. If you keep my commands, you will remain in my love, just as I have kept my Father's commands and remain in his love. I have told you this so that my joy may be in you and that your joy may be complete. My command is this: love each other as I have loved you. Greater love has no one than this: to lay down one's life for one's friends. You are my friends if you do what I command. I no longer call you servants, because a servant does not know his master's business. Instead, I have called you friends, for everything that I learned from my Father I have made known to you. You did not choose me, but I chose you and appointed you so that you might go and bear fruit – fruit that will last – and so that whatever you ask in my name the Father will give you. This is my command: love each other."

Commentary

To John's Gospel particularly we owe our concept of the hallmark of Christian faith and tradition: love. If we assume that the writer of the epistles of John is the same John as the Gospel writer, then we see the teaching on the centrality of love broadened and deepened.

Faithfulness, self-sacrifice, unconditional acceptance, and forgiveness – all these we see in Jesus' vision of the love that draws us into unity with each other and with the Father.

It is perhaps this emphasis above all that gives John's Gospel its mystical flavour. He shows us Jesus as a priestly, transcendent, cosmic figure – pre-existent and eternal, a being of light. But the heart of mysticism is not so much its transcendence as that it experiences the attraction of the soul towards God as a matter of the heart, not the intellect. The union with Mystery is at a level beyond words, reaching heights whose air only love can breathe.

In spite of this, the love John advocates is rooted in practical expression: "Simon, Son of John, do you love me? Feed my sheep" (John 21:15–18). As the epistle 1 John puts it (1 John 4:12): "No one has ever seen God; but if we love one another, God lives in us and his love is made complete in us."

Questions

- What does it mean to say we love God? Is it a feeling, a way of life, or both? How is our love of God experienced, and how is it expressed?
- Jesus said, "This is my command: love each other." How is it possible to command a person to love? Doesn't love have to grow naturally? How might we fulfil this command?
- Jesus charged us, "Now remain in my love." Do you feel loved by God – by Jesus? It may be easier to put into practice his command to love than to be loved! What do you think?

Prayer

O God your love brought us into being, gave everything to save us and set us free, and holds out to us the promise of abundant life, the joy of our salvation. Give us the grace to embrace with the eagerness and trust of children your love, which watches and waits for us; and give us grace to so dwell in your love that every day, without even thinking, we pass it on. For we ask it in Jesus' holy name; Amen.

Walking in the light

(15 studies)

Everyday essentials of the Christian life

Justice
Mercy
Bearing witness
Humility
Honesty and transparency
Kindness
Accountability
Simplicity
Discipline
Chastity
Joy
Compassion
Courage
Fidelity
Stewardship

Justice

Bible passages

1 Kings 3:7–13

"Now, Lord my God, you have made your servant king in place of my father David. But I am only a little child and do not know how to carry out my duties. Your servant is here among the people you have chosen, a great people, too numerous to count or number. So give your servant a discerning heart to govern your people and to distinguish between right and wrong. For who is able to govern this great people of yours?"

The Lord was pleased that Solomon had asked for this. So God said to him, "Since you have asked for this and not for long life or wealth for yourself, nor have asked for the death of your enemies but for discernment in administering justice, I will do what you have asked. I will give you a wise and discerning heart, so that there will never have been anyone like you, nor will there ever be. Moreover, I will give you what you have not asked for – both wealth and honour – so that in your lifetime you will have no equal among kings."

Amos 5:23–24

Away with the noise of your songs!
I will not listen to the music of your harps.
But let justice roll on like a river,
righteousness like a never-failing stream!

Hebrews 1:8–9

But about the Son he says,
"Your throne, O God, will last for ever and ever;
a sceptre of justice will be the sceptre of your kingdom.
You have loved righteousness and hated wickedness;
therefore God, your God, has set you above your companions
by anointing you with the oil of joy."

1 Peter 2:21–23

... Christ suffered for you, leaving you an example, that you should follow in his steps.

"He committed no sin, and no deceit was found in his mouth."

When they hurled their insults at him, he did not retaliate; when he suffered, he made no threats. Instead, he entrusted himself to him who judges justly.

Commentary

The teaching of Jesus and the apostles in the New Testament is built squarely on the Old Testament vision of the history of the people of God, the Law of Moses, the Prophets and the Wisdom literature. All these include justice as a non-negotiable essential feature of what pleases God and what he requires of his people.

What "justice" means in the Bible is giving a voice to the poor and marginalized (Proverbs 31:8–9), ensuring a place at the family table for the lowliest and least of God's people. The prophets speak up urgently for economic justice, and the Law makes provision for "sheltering the shorn lamb from the wind".

Since the ordering of society is the theme of the Law and the Prophets, it is hard to see how Christianity can ever realistically be expressed apolitically. Citizenship and social responsibility are integral to faithful discipleship, the big-picture outworking of Christ's command that we should love one another.

Questions

- It has been said that dependence on aid from overseas undermines the ability of the poor to get on their feet. In what way do you think we can best encourage, strengthen, and assist those trapped in poverty in our own country, and overseas? How would you advise people struggling with debt?
- Who would you identify as marginalized groups in our country? What strategies might we employ to help them?
- Apart from politics in the usual sense, in what ways might we seek to encourage social justice? Can consumer choices make a difference? Are the friendly links formed through sport helpful? What can we do to foster fairness, kindness, and responsibility in our society?

Prayer

O God of justice, Father of the poor, defender of the helpless and oppressed, show us how to live in faithfulness to your word in Scripture and in ways that bring honour to your name. Give us the humility to listen well and observe closely, the discernment to understand the implications of emerging social trends, the courage to stand up for what is right when necessary, and peaceful hearts that never seek a battle when gentleness will suffice to bring about change. This we ask in the name of Jesus, the Prince of Peace; Amen.

Mercy

Bible passages

Matthew 5:7

"Blessed are the merciful,
for they will be shown mercy."

Matthew 9:13

"But go and learn what this means: 'I desire mercy, not sacrifice.' For I have not come to call the righteous, but sinners."

Matthew 18:32–33

"Then the master called the servant in. 'You wicked servant,' he said, 'I cancelled all that debt of yours because you begged me to. Shouldn't you have had mercy on your fellow servant just as I had on you?'"

Luke 6:36–38

"Be merciful, just as your Father is merciful.
    "Do not judge, and you will not be judged. Do not condemn, and you will not be condemned. Forgive, and you will be forgiven. Give, and it will be given to you. A good measure, pressed down, shaken together and running over, will be poured into your lap. For with the measure you use, it will be measured to you."

Luke 10:36–38

"Which of these three do you think was a neighbour to the man who fell into the hands of robbers?"
    The expert in the law replied, "The one who had mercy on him."
    Jesus told him, "Go and do likewise."

Commentary

The mercy of God is a constant theme throughout the Bible, and the grace of God – his undeserved favour – is a central theme of the New Testament. A secondary theme that develops is our obligation to pass on to others the mercy we have ourselves received.

When we read these passages on mercy and forgiveness, it can look at first sight as though God's love is not, as we'd thought, unconditional. It looks as if his love and acceptance of us are made conditional upon our forgiving others and showing them mercy – when we read, for example, "Forgive, and you will be forgiven."

But when we look more closely, we see that the mercy and forgiveness we are asked to show others is a response to the mercy God has shown us – "Shouldn't you have had mercy on your fellow servant just as I had on you?"

This means that it is possible for our attitudes and impulses to flow from the wellspring of God's kindness; for gratitude, and the consciousness of how deeply we are loved, to shape and inform the people we become. But this is more than just a lovely feeling that might wash over us if we are lucky: it is an opportunity held out to us, and a responsibility we are expected to fulfil.

Questions

- Being quite honest, describe how you think God feels about you. Do you really feel he loves you, or is that just something you've heard people say?
- Can you remember an incident from your own life when you saw mercy in action? Can you think of instances when you wished somebody would show mercy and they didn't?
- Is there anything in your life right now where mercy is missing? Is there an area where you need mercy – from God or from a fellow human being? And, if you dig deep and are really honest, can you think of one relationship where you know you are not as merciful as God would want you to be? (But remember – it is possible to forgive and still keep appropriate boundaries.)

Prayer

Merciful God, your loving-kindness overflows into our lives without ceasing. You never give up on us; never withhold your love from us. Even when our hearts have been filled with hatred and resentment, in the instant we turn to you, your embrace is ready; we have the chance to start over, our sins all forgiven. So we ask you once again, God of infinite love: have mercy upon us and forgive us; cleanse us from all our sin. Renew a right spirit and a pure heart within us. O God, with whom all things are possible, fill us once again with your joy, with the full flowing of the abundant life that is your gift to us. And, by your grace, so soften our hearts that we may live every day from the power of your forgiveness, as generous with our mercy as you have been to us. For we ask it in Jesus' holy name; Amen.

Bearing witness

Bible passages

Luke 24:45–49

Then he opened their minds so they could understand the Scriptures. He told them, "This is what is written: the Messiah will suffer and rise from the dead on the third day, and repentance for the forgiveness of sins will be preached in his name to all nations, beginning at Jerusalem. You are witnesses of these things. I am going to send you what my Father has promised; but stay in the city until you have been clothed with power from on high."

John 1:6–8

There was a man sent from God whose name was John. He came as a witness to testify concerning that light, so that through him all might believe. He himself was not the light; he came only as a witness to the light.

Acts 1:8

"But you will receive power when the Holy Spirit comes on you; and you will be my witnesses in Jerusalem, and in all Judea and Samaria, and to the ends of the earth."

Acts 2:32 (see also Acts 3:15; 5:32; 13:31; 22:15)

"God has raised this Jesus to life, and we are all witnesses of it."

Acts 26:16

"Now get up and stand on your feet. I have appeared to you to appoint you as a servant and as a witness of what you have seen and will see of me."

1 Peter 3:15

Always be prepared to give an answer to everyone who asks you to give the reason for the hope that you have. But do this with gentleness and respect.

Commentary

Evangelism is sometimes mistaken for a form of product promotion, in which we have to wheedle, cajole, frighten, or trick people into sampling God. Our performance as reps is assessed on numbers as all performance is – how many did we sign up to giving our spiritual commodity a go?

Christian faith is more often than not seen as a personal attribute of the believer – "I wish I had your faith," people say, believing that faith arises from having a particular personality type, or being brought up in a home where spirituality was accepted and understood.

Our passages here would suggest otherwise. John the Baptist was not himself the light; he only bore witness to the light, John's Gospel says – faith is not an attribute of myself; it points beyond to a living Lord. "You are witnesses of these things," Jesus says – we are to report on what we have experienced first-hand for ourselves. And this is not to be pushed on people: always be ready to give an account of the hope that is in you, Peter says – but with gentleness and respect. And that's all. We don't need to knock on people's doors and harass them in their homes, or stop them in the street; what they see in us should be enough to make them be the ones to ask the questions.

Questions

- How did you learn about Jesus?
- "You are witnesses of these things," Jesus said to his disciples. We know what things they witnessed from reading the Gospels. How have you witnessed, in your own life, to the power and reality of God?
- Have you ever been encouraged to try styles of evangelism with which you feel uneasy? In what ways do you feel comfortable sharing your faith?

Prayer

Living Lord, we give you thanks for the hope and peace you have brought to our lives. Thank you for the times you have been our strength when trouble came to us. Thank you for the release and joy you have brought us in setting us free from sin. Here and now I invite you again: come into my heart, Lord Jesus; make your home with me. Cleanse and forgive anything I have done wrong. Heal the wounds that have been left by the hurly-burly of living. Make yourself real to me. Be the king of my life, of my heart. Stay with me, Lord Jesus, and never take your Holy Spirit from me. This prayer we ask in Jesus' holy name, for his glory; Amen.

Humility

Bible passages

Matthew 11:29

"Take my yoke upon you and learn from me, for I am gentle and humble in heart, and you will find rest for your souls."

Romans 12:3

For by the grace given me I say to every one of you: do not think of yourself more highly than you ought, but rather think of yourself with sober judgment, in accordance with the faith God has distributed to each of you.

Ephesians 4:2

Be completely humble and gentle; be patient, bearing with one another in love.

Philippians 2:1–4

Therefore if you have any encouragement from being united with Christ, if any comfort from his love, if any common sharing in the Spirit, if any tenderness and compassion, then make my joy complete by being like-minded, having the same love, being one in spirit and of one mind. Do nothing out of selfish ambition or vain conceit. Rather, in humility value others above yourselves, not looking to your own interests but each of you to the interests of the others.

Colossians 3:12

Therefore, as God's chosen people, holy and dearly loved, clothe yourselves with compassion, kindness, humility, gentleness and patience.

James 3:12–13

My brothers and sisters, can a fig-tree bear olives, or a grapevine bear figs? Neither can a salt spring produce fresh water.
    Who is wise and understanding among you? Let them show it by their good life, by deeds done in the humility that comes from wisdom.

Commentary

In his novel *David Copperfield*, Charles Dickens created the memorable character Uriah Heep – an obsequious, fawning, hand-wringing individual, who lives in his "'umble abode".

When the Bible recommends humility, it doesn't mean that kind of insincere abjection and self-abasement. God intended no human being to be a footstool or a doormat. Our passage from Romans sums up the biblical position nicely – that we are to do ourselves no special favours, but learn to look at ourselves with clear-sighted realism.

It's interesting to note that Jesus describes accepting his yoke of humility and gentleness as a service that will bring us rest. In humility is peace, because perpetual striving and pretending are exhausting.

Humility is not easy for us, because we are naturally eager to be the first and have the best. It feels embarrassing to admit our wrongdoing or ignorance or inadequacy. Yet it brings peace, and serenity.

Notice how the biblical writers so often pair humility with gentleness; it seems they go together, and both these quiet disciplines are beautiful to observe in others but are habits that are hard to learn and acquire.

Questions

- What images does the word "humble" conjure up for you? Are you attracted to people and things you could describe as "humble", or do you find them difficult?
- Run your mind through what would be an average day for you. If you were focusing on humility, how might that show up in your day? Would there need to be some changes, and what would they be?
- In our passage from Philippians 2, we read, "Rather, in humility value others above yourselves, not looking to your own interests but each of you to the interests of the others." Where is the balance between appropriate self-respect and humility?

Prayer

Humble God, who stooped down to earth to find and rescue us, who came to walk alongside us in Jesus, who washed our feet and accepted all the vulnerability of ordinary human life, please give us the grace to be ourselves humble and lowly in heart. May we be content with what you have apportioned us, finding happiness somewhere in all our circumstances; and may we learn gentleness along with humility, and so become like Jesus, in whose holy name we pray; Amen.

Honesty and transparency

Bible passages

Matthew 22:16

"Teacher," they said, "we know that you are a man of integrity and that you teach the way of God in accordance with the truth. You aren't swayed by others, because you pay no attention to who they are."

John 3:21

But whoever lives by the truth comes into the light, so that it may be seen plainly that what they have done has been done in the sight of God.

John 8:31–32

"If you hold to my teaching, you are really my disciples. Then you will know the truth, and the truth will set you free."

John 14:16–17

"And I will ask the Father, and he will give you another advocate to help you and be with you for ever – the Spirit of truth. The world cannot accept him, because it neither sees him nor knows him. But you know him, for he lives with you and will be in you."

Ephesians 4:22–25

You were taught, with regard to your former way of life, to put off your old self, which is being corrupted by its deceitful desires; to be made new in the attitude of your minds; and to put on the new self, created to be like God in true righteousness and holiness.

Therefore each of you must put off falsehood and speak truthfully to your neighbour, for we are all members of one body.

Ephesians 5:8–11

Live as children of light (for the fruit of the light consists in all goodness, righteousness and truth) and find out what pleases the Lord. Have nothing to do with the fruitless deeds of darkness, but rather expose them.

3 John 4

I have no greater joy than to hear that my children are walking in the truth.

Commentary

Jesus spoke out with passion against hypocrisy. He loved truth, and described the Holy Spirit as "the Spirit of truth". The Pharisees perceived him as a man who would never dress up the facts or put a spin on reality to make a good impression – a man of integrity who could be relied on to speak the truth.

Our passages from Ephesians bring in a further dimension – not only speaking but embodying truth. Our dealings should be transparent, and our lives characterized by holiness, as part of our commitment to truth. We are to be true as an arrow flies true, deflected by nothing, going straight to the target – "what pleases the Lord".

In our passage from Ephesians 4, we are encouraged to "put off your old self, which is being corrupted by its deceitful desires". A desire is not something we are used to thinking of in terms of dishonesty, and yet the things that catch our eye and take our fancy can often play us false, leading us into lifestyles or purchases that will do us no good and not lead to lasting happiness. Instead, we are urged "to be made new in the attitude of your minds", as the letter to the Romans (12:2) puts it: "Do not conform … to the pattern of this world, but be transformed by the renewing of your mind."

Questions

- A true statement is easy to define, but what is a true life, a true heart, or true righteousness?
- Is speaking the truth always advisable? Are there alternatives that we might choose without compromising our integrity?
- Jesus said that the truth will set us free. Can you think of examples showing how this is so, from everyday life?

Prayer

O God, you came to us in Jesus as the Way, the Truth, and the Life. Give us the grace to choose his living Way, and to become the friends and constant companions of Jesus the Truth, so that we catch the habit and learn the discipline of his absolute integrity, in the very detail of our lives; for we ask it in his holy name; Amen.

Kindness

Bible passages

1 Corinthians 4:12–13

We work hard with our own hands. When we are cursed, we bless; when we are persecuted, we endure it; when we are slandered, we answer kindly. We have become the scum of the earth, the garbage of the world – right up to this moment.

1 Corinthians 13:4

Love is patient, love is kind.

2 Corinthians 6:4, 6

Rather, as servants of God we commend ourselves in every way... in purity, understanding, patience and kindness...

Galatians 5:22–23

But the fruit of the Spirit is love, joy, peace, forbearance, kindness, goodness, faithfulness, gentleness and self-control.

Ephesians 4:32

Be kind and compassionate to one another, forgiving each other, just as in Christ God forgave you.

Colossians 3:12–17

Therefore, as God's chosen people, holy and dearly loved, clothe yourselves with compassion, kindness, humility, gentleness and patience. Bear with each other and forgive one another if any of you has a grievance against someone. Forgive as the Lord forgave you. And over all these virtues put on love, which binds them all together in perfect unity.

Let the peace of Christ rule in your hearts, since as members of one body you were called to peace. And be thankful. Let the message of Christ dwell among you richly as you teach and admonish one another with all wisdom through psalms, hymns, and songs from the Spirit, singing to God with gratitude in your hearts. And whatever you do, whether in word or deed, do it all in the name of the Lord Jesus, giving thanks to God the Father through him.

2 Timothy 2:24

And the Lord's servant must not be quarrelsome but must be kind to everyone, able to teach, not resentful.

Commentary

Keeping the discipline of kindness in all circumstances is one of the most exacting and demanding aspects of practising our faith. It means letting go of a witty putdown or a chance to vindicate ourselves. It means passing up the chance to humiliate people who have been mean to us.

Kindness makes us go out of our way when it's inconvenient, not letting it show when we are bored, sitting with the ones others have rejected as companions, listening to the interminable stories of the old, missing out on interesting conversations to get down on the floor and play with a child who feels ignored and left out.

Truth without kindness is deadly. Righteousness without kindness is chilling. A home or marriage without kindness cannot be happy.

How blessed are the children whose parents are kind, the congregations whose pastors are kind, the animals whose husbandmen are kind.

Without kindness, life is grim and lonely, hardly worth living.

A workaday, ordinary virtue, not designed to get anybody noticed, kindness is a jewel indeed, a fruit of the Spirit, a most precious manifestation of the presence of God.

Questions

- It has been said that it is better to be kind than to be right. What do you think?
- Can you think of instances when someone showed you great kindness? What difference did that make to you?
- Can you identify an area in your life where you would like to be kinder than you normally are?

Prayer

We thank you, God of love, for being so kind to us. When we were lost, you did not give up on us but brought us home. When we were afraid, you stayed with us and restored our peace. You came to us in Jesus and gave us a living hope and life in abundance. You have poured out blessing upon blessing to gladden our lives. Thank you, God of love, for your kindness. By your grace, may our hearts and minds be renewed in the likeness of Jesus, so that when others look upon our faces, they see his kindness in our eyes. For we ask it in his holy name; Amen.

Accountability

Bible passages

1 Corinthians 6:19–20

Do you not know that your bodies are temples of the Holy Spirit, who is in you, whom you have received from God? You are not your own; you were bought at a price. Therefore honour God with your bodies.

Matthew 8:7–9

Jesus said to him, "Shall I come and heal him?"

The centurion replied, "Lord, I do not deserve to have you come under my roof. But just say the word, and my servant will be healed. For I myself am a man under authority, with soldiers under me. I tell this one, 'Go,' and he goes; and that one, 'Come,' and he comes. I say to my servant, 'Do this,' and he does it."

Matthew 12:36–37

"But I tell you that everyone will have to give account on the day of judgment for every empty word they have spoken. For by your words you will be acquitted, and by your words you will be condemned."

Mark 10:42–45

Jesus called them together and said, "You know that those who are regarded as rulers of the Gentiles lord it over them, and their high officials exercise authority over them. Not so with you. Instead, whoever wants to become great among you must be your servant, and whoever wants to be first must be slave of all. For even the Son of Man did not come to be served, but to serve, and to give his life as a ransom for many."

Romans 14:7–13

For none of us lives for ourselves alone, and none of us dies for ourselves alone. If we live, we live for the Lord; and if we die, we die for the Lord. So, whether we live or die, we belong to the Lord. For this very reason, Christ died and returned to life so that he might be the Lord of both the dead and the living.

You, then, why do you judge your brother or sister? Or why do you treat them with contempt? For we will all stand before God's judgment seat. It is written:

"'As surely as I live,' says the Lord, 'Every knee will bow before me; every tongue will acknowledge God.'"

So then, each of us will give an account of ourselves to God.

Therefore let us stop passing judgment on one another. Instead, make up your mind not to put any stumbling block or obstacle in the way of a brother or sister.

Commentary

In the Bible, authority and accountability are always yoked together. Authority comes from taking one's place in a chain of command with God at the head. Even those things we assume to be ours – "my body… my life… my children…" are not our own but lent us on trust by God.

Far from being an irksome servitude, there is great freedom in this as well as wholesome discipline. For if it is to God that we are accountable, then we are free indeed – no man is our master, even if the world calls us slaves. And, however high our status may be in the eyes of the world, we bear continually in mind that for our every action, every word we have spoken, we must give account on the Day of Judgment. Those who know this are kept from pride and arrogance even when their status in human society sets them above the restraint of their fellow human beings. We also find peace more readily when faced with the wrongdoing of others – for we know that they too are accountable to God; one day there will be justice.

Questions

- How do you imagine the Day of Judgment? How do you think the judgment of God operates in day-to-day life now?
- What are some examples of injustices that we have to live with now, trusting that one day God will put them right?
- Can you think of examples from history or your own experience of individuals who held high-ranking authority yet always humbly bore in mind their accountability to God?

Prayer

O God of power and might, our Lord, our king, our judge, look with mercy upon our human frailty, we pray. We acknowledge our waywardness and wilfulness, the foolish empty things we have said – and the unkind, spiteful things too. We ask your forgiveness. Make us whole and strengthen us in your service, we beseech you, so that when the day comes that we stand before you as our judge, we shall know ourselves cleansed, justified, and free from sin, because we kept a short account with Jesus, in whose holy name we pray; Amen.

Simplicity

Bible passages

Deuteronomy 2:27–29

"Let us pass through your country. We will stay on the main road; we will not turn aside to the right or to the left. Sell us food to eat and water to drink for their price in silver. Only let us pass through on foot – as the descendants of Esau, who live in Seir, and the Moabites, who live in Ar, did for us – until we cross the Jordan into the land the Lord our God is giving us."

Ecclesiastes 7:29, Good News Bible

This is all that I have learned: God made us plain and simple, but we have made ourselves very complicated.

Matthew 6:19–21, 24–26

"Do not store up for yourselves treasures on earth, where moths and vermin destroy, and where thieves break in and steal. But store up for yourselves treasures in heaven, where moths and vermin do not destroy, and where thieves do not break in and steal. For where your treasure is, there your heart will be also.

"No one can serve two masters. Either you will hate the one and love the other, or you will be devoted to the one and despise the other. You cannot serve both God and Money.

"Therefore I tell you, do not worry about your life, what you will eat or drink; or about your body, what you will wear. Is not life more than food, and the body more than clothes? Look at the birds of the air; they do not sow or reap or store away in barns, and yet your heavenly Father feeds them."

Matthew 18:3

And he said: "Truly I tell you, unless you change and become like little children, you will never enter the kingdom of heaven."

2 Corinthians 6:10, New English Bible

In our sorrows, we always have reason to rejoice: poor ourselves, we bring wealth to many: penniless, we own the world.

1 John 2:15

Do not love the world or anything in the world. If anyone loves the world, the love for the Father is not in them.

Commentary

Nobody progresses far on any spiritual path without keeping a discipline of simplicity. The more stuff we have to defend, maintain, and organize, and the more harassed we are by complex finances and cluttered schedules, the less room we have for reality. Either our prayer life and passion for the gospel gradually push out our involvement with cruising the internet, hanging out in the mall, or obsessing over the housework, or vice versa. This is what Jesus meant when he said, "You cannot serve God and Mammon" (Matthew 6:24). Mammon is not just money and the love of money; it's the creeping worldliness that gets its claws into our whole lives until it takes us over completely.

The practice of simplicity is a matter of watching our boundaries to see that our lives are protected for God (Leviticus 20:26) – we are not to let the Temple turn into a high street.

In a high-tech world of mass production and growth economics, where multi-tasking is admired and everyone you know has a diagnosis of stress or depression, maintaining a discipline of simplicity is foreign territory, but without it no one can follow Jesus.

Questions

- How does your time budget work out? Is there enough allocation for fun, for learning and growing, for home and family, for prayer and study, for broadening your horizons, for rest and peace and thinking, and to spend time in nature? How is the balance? Does one aspect of commitment crowd out the others?
- How are your finances? Are you driven by debts or enmeshed in complex investments? Do you worry about money? Do you spend more than you should? If all is going well, how did you find, and how do you keep, that balance?
- Are you a hoarder or a chucker-out? What are your systems of organizing what you have? How easy would you find it to walk away from your possessions as the first disciples did? What would you miss most if the house burned down?

Prayer

O God of life and hope and freedom, give us the wisdom, courage, and vision to hold fast to a discipline of simplicity, so that we may make and keep space for the abundant life you promised would be ours in Jesus, in whose holy name we pray; Amen.

Discipline

Bible passages

Proverbs 25:28

Like a city whose walls are broken through is a person who lacks self-control.

1 Corinthians 9:23–27, Good News Bible

All this I do for the gospel's sake, in order to share in its blessings. Surely you know that many runners take part in a race, but only one of them wins the prize. Run, then, in such a way as to win the prize. Every athlete in training submits to strict discipline, in order to be crowned with a wreath that will not last; but we do it for one that will last forever. That is why I run straight for the finish line; that is why I am like a boxer who does not waste his punches. I harden my body with blows and bring it under complete control, to keep myself from being disqualified after having called others to the contest.

2 Timothy 1:7

For the Spirit God gave us does not make us timid, but gives us power, love and self-discipline.

Titus 1:6a, 8

An elder must be... hospitable, one who loves what is good, who is self-controlled, upright, holy and disciplined.

Titus 2:11–14

For the grace of God has appeared that offers salvation to all people. It teaches us to say "No" to ungodliness and worldly passions, and to live self-controlled, upright and godly lives in this present age, while we wait for the blessed hope – the appearing of the glory of our great God and Saviour, Jesus Christ, who gave himself for us to redeem us from all wickedness and to purify for himself a people that are his very own, eager to do what is good.

Hebrews 12:11

No discipline seems pleasant at the time, but painful. Later on, however, it produces a harvest of righteousness and peace for those who have been trained by it.

Galatians 5:24–25

Those who belong to Christ Jesus have crucified the flesh with its passions and desires. Since we live by the Spirit, let us keep in step with the Spirit.

Commentary

Since we are called to be "in the world but not of the world" (John 17:13–16), to an extent the people of God will always be swimming against the stream of the social current. "Follow your bliss" is not our mantra.

So self-discipline is required of us in making daily choices as we move through whichever milieu is native to us, "discerning the spirits" (1 Corinthians 12:10) of what sometimes feels like every darn thing – every TV programme, investment, and purchase; the clothes we wear, the company we keep, the language we use, the nature and quality of our friendships and sexual relationships, the business practices in which we engage. All of it is to be brought under scrutiny to determine not whether we can get away with it and still go to church, but whether it is wholesome, pure, edifying, and holy, building the peaceable kingdom that will be good news in a fallen world.

Evangelism – the extension of the reign of Christ in our society – is an every-believer ministry, not the job of missionaries working somewhere else and supported by donations from the rest of us.

This daily, week-in, week-out attention to integrity and virtue in godly living requires more self-discipline than any of us actually has. And when we fall down on the job we go to God and humbly ask forgiveness; then we start again.

Questions

- What are the areas of Christian discipline that you find hardest?
- How do you think we should teach our children discipline?
- Which areas of Christian discipline are emphasized in your church congregation? Are there any you think could be given a higher profile?

Prayer

O God, our rock, our strength, and our redeemer, we rest in you, we trust in you. Unless you build the house, we who labour work in vain. Make us wise to see what is worth our priority and focus, give us courage to choose and hold on to what is good, and give us tenacity and perseverance to run the race set before us with our eyes fixed upon the prize of eternal life. In Jesus' holy name we pray; Amen.

Chastity

Bible passages

1 Thessalonians 4:3–7

It is God's will that you should be sanctified: that you should avoid sexual immorality; that each of you should learn to control your own body in a way that is holy and honourable, not in passionate lust like the pagans, who do not know God; and that in this matter no one should wrong or take advantage of a brother or sister. The Lord will punish all those who commit such sins, as we told you and warned you before. For God did not call us to be impure, but to live a holy life. Therefore, anyone who rejects this instruction does not reject a human being but God, the very God who gives you his Holy Spirit.

Colossians 3:5

Put to death, therefore, whatever belongs to your earthly nature: sexual immorality, impurity, lust, evil desires and greed, which is idolatry.

1 Corinthians 6:12–20

"I have the right to do anything," you say – but not everything is beneficial. "I have the right to do anything"– but I will not be mastered by anything. You say, "Food for the stomach and the stomach for food, and God will destroy them both." The body, however, is not meant for sexual immorality but for the Lord, and the Lord for the body. By his power God raised the Lord from the dead, and he will raise us also. Do you not know that your bodies are members of Christ himself? Shall I then take the members of Christ and unite them with a prostitute? Never! Do you not know that he who unites himself with a prostitute is one with her in body? For it is said, "The two will become one flesh." But whoever is united with the Lord is one with him in spirit.

Flee from sexual immorality. All other sins a person commits are outside the body, but whoever sins sexually, sins against their own body. Do you not know that your bodies are temples of the Holy Spirit, who is in you, whom you have received from God? You are not your own; you were bought at a price. Therefore honour God with your bodies.

Hebrews 13:4

Marriage should be honoured by all, and the marriage bed kept pure, for God will judge the adulterer and all the sexually immoral.

Commentary

Jesus famously said that whoever looks lustfully upon a woman has already committed adultery with her in his heart, putting his finger on the reality that chastity begins with our imagination. Purity is more an attitude of mind or a disposition of the soul than how we dress or what we read. Getting this attitude of mind right is infinitely more effective than trying to limit behaviour by prohibition.

On the issue of chastity, the standards and traditions held by people of faith vary. Some frown on dating at all while others think that sexual intercourse between a couple intending to get married is acceptable. Some feel there should be no sex education in schools at all and the "facts of life" should be discovered within, or in preparation for, marriage. Some see teenagers reading pornographic magazines as harmless and inevitable; others view it as a corrupting evil.

Perhaps a first base is to bear in mind that children learn by imitation. To call pornographic films "adult" is to make them a magnet for every growing child. The way to protect the innocence of children is for their parents, and the other adults around them, to cultivate and safeguard their own innocence of mind.

Questions

- Do you think attitudes to chastity might be changed by parenthood? Might someone change the standards they held as a teenager and young adult once they become responsible for a growing child? Why might this be?
- Where would you like to see the boundaries set for sexual expression in intimate personal relationships? At what point is a relationship no longer chaste, in a couple preparing for marriage? How might we define chastity within marriage?
- They say our biggest sex organ is the brain! Without sexual urges and sexual fantasy, the human race could not have generated. How might we channel and manage our sexuality so that it is alive and well, but chaste rather than simply concealed?

Prayer

O God of life and love, who made us male and female, pronouncing all things good, we thank you for our sexuality. So fill us with your spirit of love and compassion that our humanity is always directed to behaviour and attitudes of gentleness, affirmation, and respect, giving us grace to turn away from all exploitation of others. For we ask it in Jesus' holy name; Amen.

Joy

Bible passages

Psalm 16:11, KJV

Thou wilt shew me the path of life: in thy presence is fulness of joy; at thy right hand there are pleasures for evermore.

Psalm 118:24, KJV

This is the day which the Lord hath made; we will rejoice and be glad in it.

Isaiah 55:12

You will go out in joy
and be led forth in peace;
the mountains and hills
will burst into song before you,
and all the trees of the field
will clap their hands.

Romans 14:17

For the kingdom of God is not a matter of eating and drinking, but of righteousness, peace and joy in the Holy Spirit.

Romans 15:13

May the God of hope fill you with all joy and peace as you trust in him, so that you may overflow with hope by the power of the Holy Spirit.

Galatians 4:15, NIV

What has happened to all your joy?

Philippians 4:4

Rejoice in the Lord always. I will say it again: rejoice!

1 Thessalonians 2:20

Indeed, you are our glory and joy.

James 1:2–3

Consider it pure joy, my brothers and sisters, whenever you face trials of many kinds, because you know that the testing of your faith produces perseverance.

Commentary

In times of economic recession, in a world where so many people feel squeezed and stressed, where depression and competition are rife – how urgently needed are people who know how to keep a discipline of joy!

Christian joy is not a passing feeling; it is an attitude and a habit, but it is a fire that does have to be fed – it won't run on nothing.

Joy is fed by keeping company with Jesus, for his Spirit is joyous and free, and if we spend time with him we become more like him. Deep and rich fellowship with people who know the Lord also feeds our joy; it is exhilarating and inspiring, and helps us persevere. Nature is also a source of joy, and spending time every day in the woods, hills or parkland, or by the sea, a lake or a stream, will feed our joy. For many people, spending time with animals and children also creates joy. Art and music inspire joy. Joy is also found in service. Everyone I know who has helped out in a hospice or prison, with disabled people needing support, or visiting old, frail or housebound folk, has testified that they went to give but came away humbled by how much they had received. Joy is fostered by eating nutritious food, and taking enough rest and exercise. Tired, malnourished, toxic bodies defy anyone's power to hold to a discipline of joy!

Joy needs space. We greatly diminish our chances of staying in joy if we allow the pressures of life to accumulate.

Questions

- How might you differentiate between happiness, fun, contentment, inspiration, and joy? Do we need all those things, or is there one or more you feel you could do without?
- Can you think of a person or occasion you could describe as joyous – where joy really radiated?
- What have been the times of joy in your life? Does joy characterize your life right now? If so, can you describe the source of your joy? If not, what happened to it, and how do you feel about that?

Prayer

Joy streams from you like light, O God our Father, and joy is the energy and radiance of Jesus. Help us so to walk in your will, in your perfect plan for us, that our lives overflow with joy, healing and lifting every life that touches ours. For we ask it in Jesus' precious name; Amen.

Compassion

Bible passages

Isaiah 49:15

Can a mother forget the baby at her breast
and have no compassion on the child she has borne?
Though she may forget,
I will not forget you!

Mark 6:34

When Jesus landed and saw a large crowd, he had compassion on them, because they were like sheep without a shepherd. So he began teaching them many things.

2 Corinthians 1:3–4

Praise be to the God and Father of our Lord Jesus Christ, the Father of compassion and the God of all comfort, who comforts us in all our troubles, so that we can comfort those in any trouble with the comfort we ourselves receive from God.

Galatians 6:1–2

Brothers and sisters, if someone is caught in a sin, you who live by the Spirit should restore that person gently. But watch yourselves, or you also may be tempted. Carry each other's burdens, and in this way you will fulfil the law of Christ.

Luke 10:30–37, New Living Translation

Jesus replied with a story: "A Jewish man was traveling from Jerusalem down to Jericho, and he was attacked by bandits. They stripped him of his clothes, beat him up, and left him half dead beside the road.

By chance a priest came along. But when he saw the man lying there, he crossed to the other side of the road and passed him by. A Temple assistant walked over and looked at him lying there, but he also passed by on the other side.

Then a despised Samaritan came along, and when he saw the man, he felt compassion for him. Going over to him, the Samaritan soothed his wounds with olive oil and wine and bandaged them. Then he put the man on his own donkey and took him to an inn, where he took care of him. The next day he handed the innkeeper two silver coins, telling him, 'Take care of this man. If his bill runs higher than this, I'll pay you the next time I'm here.'

Now which of these three would you say was a neighbour to the man who was attacked by bandits?" Jesus asked.

The man replied, "The one who showed him mercy."

Then Jesus said, "Yes, now go and do the same."

Commentary

Compassion literally means "suffer with" (from its Latin origin). It implies empathy, the ability to share in the feelings of someone else as if they were one's own. This is the art of standing in someone else's shoes, imaginatively experiencing their point of view.

It has been suggested that a brilliant way to achieve reconciliation in resolving conflict is to have each opposing party argue for the other's point of view as passionately as if it were his/her own. What a wonderful way that might be of encouraging compassion!

Compassion can also be called sympathy, and technically means the same – yet sympathy has overtones of mere feeling – crying on each other's shoulders – whereas compassion implies either taking action to help or exercising restraint in a situation where one has power over another.

Questions

- In this section of the book, we also have a study on "mercy". Notice the word is used interchangeably with "compassion" in the parable of the Good Samaritan. How would you differentiate compassion from mercy – or are they really the same?
- Who have you met or read about, whose life exemplifies Christian compassion?
- What is the place for compassion in your life at the moment? Where does your heart cry out for it? Where are you needing to exercise it?

Prayer

O God of righteousness, justice, and power, we thank you humbly for the compassion you have shown to us. You have stayed your hand when we chose greed and violence; you waited for us to learn better when we chose destruction and indifference. When we were lost in sin, you came to us yourself in Jesus, to teach us, heal us, and show us the way to heaven. Compassionate God, may we be transformed by the renewing of our minds into the likeness of your compassion, until we come to reflect the beauty of Jesus in the time and place in which we live. For we ask it in his holy name; Amen.

Courage

Bible passages

Deuteronomy 31:6

Be strong and courageous. Do not be afraid or terrified because of them, for the Lord your God goes with you; he will never leave you nor forsake you.

1 Samuel 17:45

David said to the Philistine, "You come against me with sword and spear and javelin, but I come against you in the name of the Lord Almighty, the God of the armies of Israel, whom you have defied."

Psalm 27:14

Wait for the Lord;
be strong and take heart
and wait for the Lord.

Daniel 3:16–18

Shadrach, Meshach and Abednego replied to him, "King Nebuchadnezzar, we do not need to defend ourselves before you in this matter. If we are thrown into the blazing furnace, the God we serve is able to deliver us from it, and he will deliver us from Your Majesty's hand. But even if he does not, we want you to know, Your Majesty, that we will not serve your gods or worship the image of gold you have set up."

Matthew 14:29

Then Peter got down out of the boat, walked on the water and came towards Jesus.

John 16:33

"I have told you these things, so that in me you may have peace. In this world you will have trouble. But take heart! I have overcome the world."

Acts 5:29

Peter and the other apostles replied: "We must obey God rather than human beings!"

Ephesians 6:10, 12–13

Finally, be strong in the Lord and in his mighty power... For our struggle is not

against flesh and blood, but against the rulers, against the authorities, against
the powers of this dark world and against the spiritual forces of evil in the
heavenly realms. Therefore put on the full armour of God, so that when the day
of evil comes, you may be able to stand your ground, and after you have done
everything, to stand.

Commentary

Our passages look at different facets of Christian courage. The verse from Psalm 27
recommends cool courage that remembers not to panic – to wait… wait… and do
everything in the Lord's timing, listening and watching for his "Go!"

The Ephesians' passage reminds us to have the courage not to get paranoid
about our fellow human beings, however they appal us. God is on the side of
humanity; our neighbour isn't the enemy; we must look deeper than that.

The verse from Matthew challenges us to have the courage to take risks.

The wonderful passage from Daniel holds up the example of men with the
courage to trust in God whatever life throws at them, whether they see a happy
ending or whether they don't. This is the courage we need when we watch a good
life end with a grim cancer, or a faithful family sitting at the bedside of a dying
child: "… the God we serve is able to deliver us from it… But even if he does not",
we stand firm in trusting him. This is courage.

Questions

- Can you think of two examples from your own life when it took courage to
  stand firm in faith?
- Taking risks (Matthew 14:29) is one kind of courage, endurance (Ephesians
  6:13) is another, staying calm in a tight spot (John 16:33) is another, standing
  up to authority (Acts 5:29), what Quakers call "speaking Truth to Power", yet
  another. Which come more easily to you and which do you find harder?
- What is the bravest thing you have ever seen a person do for their faith?

Prayer

O God, our rock, we know that you are always there for us and will never abandon
us. It's easy to say that in times of calm and peace, but we pray here today that when
the storm hits our own little boat and it looks as if we will go under, you will give us
grace then to go on trusting, and never let go of our faith in Jesus. Keep us strong,
keep us loving, keep us faithful. May we never forget we asked this, and may we see
it fulfilled in our lives: for we ask it in Jesus' holy name; Amen.

Fidelity

Bible passages

Psalm 91:4

> He will cover you with his feathers,
> and under his wings you will find refuge;
> his faithfulness will be your shield and rampart.

Matthew 4:10

> Jesus said to him, "Away from me, Satan! For it is written: 'Worship the Lord your God, and serve him only.'"

John 6:66–68

> From this time many of his disciples turned back and no longer followed him.
> "You do not want to leave too, do you?" Jesus asked the Twelve.
> Simon Peter answered him, "Lord, to whom shall we go? You have the words of eternal life. We have come to believe and to know that you are the Holy One of God."

John 14:15

> "If you love me, keep my commands."

Romans 12:2

> Do not conform to the pattern of this world, but be transformed by the renewing of your mind. Then you will be able to test and approve what God's will is – his good, pleasing and perfect will.

Revelation 2:10, KJV

> Be thou faithful unto death, and I will give thee a crown of life.

Commentary

Faithfulness is much to be prized in the Christian character, because it is an attribute that the Scriptures continually praise in God himself.

As we read the New Testament, most of which was written to church communities enduring relentless and fierce persecution, not surprisingly we find significant emphasis on enduring to the end and remaining faithful, standing firm in the face of adversity. Still today there are places in the world where to embrace the gospel of Christ is to sign your own death warrant, and standing firm in the faith is a matter of great courage. But even in countries with religious tolerance or a

Christian majority, there are many areas of life in which it is hard to remain faithful to our Christian convictions.

Faithfulness in marriage is increasingly under fire in a society in which divorce is rife and entirely acceptable. Faithfulness as an employee or employer is less easy to fulfil in a highly mobile society and an economic recession.

Sometimes we have to choose between conflicting calls on our fidelity: should a woman whose husband is a violent drinker, taking her family down into poverty and abusing their children, be faithful to her marriage vows or faithful to ensuring stability and safety for her children? Should an employee who witnesses his boss do something seriously illegal be faithful as an employee or as a citizen? Should a Christian who finds his church unfulfilling be faithful to that faith community or look for somewhere more inspiring to attend? Faithfulness is important, but not always easy!

Questions

- Can you think of some instances in your life when it has been hard to be faithful, or hard to work out what faithfulness meant in a particular context? What happened?
- Who are the people you can identify in your own life, to whom you are grateful for being faithful to you? And who can you think of whose faithfulness to God has inspired you personally?
- Can you see examples of God's faithfulness to you in the outworking of your life? Have there been clear moments when you can say, "Yes, God kept his promise to me there"?

Prayer

Faithful God, you call us to walk with you in your ways of fidelity. By your grace, may we mature into responsible and trustworthy souls, the kind of people that others know they could trust with their lives. May our love be like your love – wise, tough, enduring, and reliable to the very end. When we have run our race, may Christ say to us the words we long to hear: "Well done, thou good and faithful servant." For we ask it in Jesus' holy name; Amen.

Stewardship

Bible passages

Genesis 1:28

God blessed them and said to them, "Be fruitful and increase in number; fill the earth and subdue it. Rule over the fish in the sea and the birds in the sky and over every living creature that moves on the ground."

Matthew 25:23 (see also Luke 12:42–44)

"His master replied, 'Well done, good and faithful servant! You have been faithful with a few things; I will put you in charge of many things. Come and share your master's happiness!'"

Luke 16:8–12

"The master commended the dishonest manager because he had acted shrewdly. For the people of this world are more shrewd in dealing with their own kind than are the people of the light. I tell you, use worldly wealth to gain friends for yourselves, so that when it is gone, you will be welcomed into eternal dwellings.

"One who is faithful in a very little is also faithful in much, and one who is dishonest in a very little is also dishonest in much. If then you have not been faithful in the unrighteous wealth, who will entrust to you the true riches? And if you have not been faithful in that which is another's, who will give you that which is your own?"

1 Corinthians 4:2

Now it is required that those who have been given a trust must prove faithful.

Commentary

Personal property looms large in our lives. From admonitions by teachers and parents to respect the property of others, to signs such as "Keep off the grass" and "Trespassers will be prosecuted", and razor wire coiled round the top of high fences as a security measure, we learn a lesson of ownership that is entirely misleading. It is augmented by phrases such as "me-time" and "personal income". Actually, nothing belongs to us at all. As the first epistle to Timothy (6:7) says, "we brought nothing into the world, and we can take nothing out of it". Furthermore, during the time we are in the world nothing belongs to us, either: "The earth is the Lord's, and everything in it, the world, and all who live in it" (Psalm 24:1).

We are not the owners but the stewards of our time, our money, our homes, our land, and our possessions. All of it belongs to God and so do we ourselves: "Know that the Lord is God. It is he who made us, and we are his; we are his people, the sheep of his pasture" (Psalm 100:3).

In our Bible passages we are commanded to be aware of the trust placed in us, and to prove faithful in our management of so great a responsibility, always remembering that we are not the owners but only the estate managers, and must learn and apply the principles of our Master in the disposition of what passes through our hands.

The two paragraphs from Luke 16 come at the tail end of Jesus' story of the unjust steward – you might like to look it up and read the whole story. In our two paragraphs, two quite separate points are being made: the first belongs to the story and encourages us to remember that goodwill is as important a benefit to have on account as hard cash. The second is related in that it is on the subject of stewardship, and is Jesus' teaching (see also Matthew 25:23) that, as we prove trustworthy in little things, both God and our fellow human beings will see that they can depend on us and trust us with greater things.

Questions

- Can you think of some responsibilities with which God has entrusted you personally in this life? Where do you feel you could do better in fulfilling these responsibilities? What has helped you to do well?

- Can you think of some responsibilities where the challenge is to work together rather than as individuals? Perhaps as husband and wife, as church members, as a neighbourhood, or as citizens of a nation. Where do you think we are fulfilling these well, and where are we falling down?

- Can you think of examples from life where it has been prudent to forgo the acquisition of money in the bank for the preservation of goodwill?

Prayer

Wise and faithful God, we marvel that you have made us the stewards of the works of your hands! We look at the trust you have placed in us, in the relationships and good things with which you have blessed us, and the wonderful natural ecosystem of which we are a part, and it is amazing to consider that you have made us the stewards of all this. Unless you help us, we are not equal to the task, so we ask that day by day you will guide and direct us in your ways of wisdom, reconciliation, and peace, so that the works of our hands tend always towards integrity, wholeness, and well-being. For we ask in Jesus' holy name; Amen.

Tracing the circle of the church's year

(15 Studies)

Three Advent studies (there are four weeks in Advent – three studies leave space for a Christmas party)

Five Lent studies (there are six weeks in Lent – five studies leave space for an Easter party)

A study for Ascension

A study for Pentecost

A study for the Holy Trinity

Two studies for Ordinary Time

A study for Harvest Thanksgiving

A study for All Saints

Three Advent studies

Church-year themes for the four weeks of Advent are: The Patriarchs, The Prophets (see our section of studies on "Insights from the Law and the Prophets", beginning p. 224), John the Baptist (study on p. 58) and Mary the mother of Jesus (study on p. 56). We have only three studies here as, by the fourth week of Advent, home groups usually either have adjourned for Christmas or want to have a festive party.

Advent week one – Stars

Bible passages

Genesis 15:5

He took him outside and said, "Look up at the sky and count the stars – if indeed you can count them." Then he said to him, "So shall your offspring be."

Job 38:4, 6–7

"Where were you when I laid the earth's foundation? On what were its footings set, or who laid its cornerstone – while the morning stars sang together and all the angels shouted for joy?"

Psalm 8:3–4, KJV

When I consider thy heavens, the work of thy fingers, the moon and the stars, which thou hast ordained; what is man, that thou art mindful of him? and the son of man, that thou visitest him?

Psalm 147:4

He determines the number of the stars and calls them each by name.

Psalm 148:3

Praise him, sun and moon; praise him, all you shining stars.

Matthew 2:1–2, 7–10 (see also study on The Zoroastrians, p. 84)

After Jesus was born in Bethlehem in Judea, during the time of King Herod, Magi from the east came to Jerusalem and asked, "Where is the one who has been born king of the Jews? We saw his star when it rose and have come to worship him."

    ... Then Herod called the Magi secretly and found out from them the exact time the star had appeared. He sent them to Bethlehem and said, "Go and search carefully for the child. As soon as you find him, report to me, so that I too may go and worship him."

    After they had heard the king, they went on their way, and the star they had seen when it rose went ahead of them until it stopped over the place where the child was. When they saw the star, they were overjoyed. On coming to the house, they saw the child with his mother Mary, and they bowed down and worshipped him.

Revelation 22:16–17

"I, Jesus, have sent my angel to give you this testimony for the churches. I am the Root and the Offspring of David, and the bright Morning Star."

Commentary

Stars have a beautiful place in the Scriptures. The book of Job speaks of the singing of the stars on the day of creation, and the book of Psalms offers a picture of intimate relationship between the stars and their creator, who ordains the movements of their dance and knows them all by name.

In the book of Genesis comes that magical moment when God takes Abram outside into the desert and bids him look up at the stars. What he saw was not quite the same as we see in our light-polluted cities. If you can get away from the streetlights, car headlights, and house security lights, the night sky is ablaze with myriad stars beyond counting. "So shall your offspring be," God said.

As the years went by, the time came for Jesus to be born – one of those stars of Abram's descent. In the Bible he is sometimes called the Morning Star (i.e. the sun), and John the Baptist's father Zechariah prophesies, regarding the birth of Jesus, of "the tender mercy of our God, by which the rising sun will come to us from heaven to shine on those living in darkness and in the shadow of death, to guide our feet into the path of peace" (Luke 1:78–79).

Questions

• Can you remember times when you have been out in the country, where you could see the stars with less light pollution? What was it like?

• Can you think of a friend who has been to you like a star in a dark night?

• They call celebrities "stars". Who are the "stars" of your life, the ones you look up to?

Prayer

We thank you, O God, for frosty nights and starry heavens. Thank you for the beauty and majesty of the wide sky above us, lifting our hearts, moving our souls, speaking to us of wonder and glory. Thank you for the clear shining of the Evening Star as night comes down, and the Morning Star, the sun that rises in such splendour, reminding us of Jesus. The stars are too many for us to count, dear Lord, but you know every one of them by name. How great is our God, how great is our God! In all times of our darkness, whenever our life passes through a night-time, remind us, God of our journeys, to look up at the stars. For we ask it in Jesus' name; Amen.

Advent week two – Light

Bible passages (see also our study on John, "The light of the world", p. 106)

Isaiah 9:2

The people walking in darkness have seen a great light; on those living in the land of deep darkness a light has dawned.

Luke 2:29–32

"Sovereign Lord, as you have promised, you may now dismiss your servant in peace. For my eyes have seen your salvation, which you have prepared in the sight of all nations: a light for revelation to the Gentiles, and the glory of your people Israel."

John 3:19–21

This is the verdict: light has come into the world, but people loved darkness instead of light because their deeds were evil. Everyone who does evil hates the light, and will not come into the light for fear that their deeds will be exposed. But whoever lives by the truth comes into the light, so that it may be seen plainly that what they have done has been done in the sight of God.

Matthew 6:22–23

"The eye is the lamp of the body. If your eyes are healthy, your whole body will be full of light. But if your eyes are unhealthy, your whole body will be full of darkness. If then the light within you is darkness, how great is that darkness!"

Matthew 5:14–16

"You are the light of the world. A town built on a hill cannot be hidden. Neither do people light a lamp and put it under a bowl. Instead they put it on its stand, and it gives light to everyone in the house. In the same way, let your light shine before others, that they may see your good deeds and glorify your Father in heaven."

1 Corinthians 3:10–13

But each one should build with care. For no one can lay any foundation other than the one already laid, which is Jesus Christ. If anyone builds on this foundation using gold, silver, costly stones, wood, hay or straw, their work will be shown for what it is, because the Day will bring it to light. It will be revealed with fire, and the fire will test the quality of each person's work.

Commentary

When Christianity was embraced by the Taoist Chinese in the seventh century, they called it "the light religion". Everywhere in the New Testament the metaphor of light is used to clarify aspects of our faith.

Jesus is identified as the light of the world. Even in our two short passages from Isaiah and Luke 2, three different facets of what that can mean are included. Isaiah foretells the coming of Jesus (see this taken up in Matthew 4:16) as a light to people condemned to live in a dark place. This is light as salvation, comfort, rescue, and hope. In the Song of Simeon (sometimes called the *Nunc Dimittis*) in Luke 2, the light of Jesus is seen both as revelation – opening the eyes of the Gentiles to new truth – and as glory, the radiance or *shekinah* of God in the midst of his people.

Our text from John 3 identifies the necessity of light for discernment, for the exposure of truth and reality. Our text from Matthew 6 considers how what we focus on illuminates our thinking and experience – if we focus on goodness, our whole selves and lives are enlightened. If we focus on evil, in place of illumination we have only shadows and confusion.

The passage from Matthew 5 looks at light as radiance – goodness which both lights up the world and shines a spotlight on the beauty of God. And our Corinthians passage reminds us to be mindful of how we live, remembering that the day will come when the light of God will reveal everything we chose and did for what it really is. Light is about integrity.

Questions

- Can you think of examples of light that you have found especially beautiful?
- Can you think of lives or actions you have known whose faith and goodness made them seem to shine?
- At Christmas time, the pure white light of God comes to earth in the multicoloured lights of humanity. What colour light would you be, and why?

Prayer

Jesus, light of the world, shine into our hearts and expose what is really there. Where there is sadness and gloom, may your light shine joyfully. Where there are shadows of pretence and hypocrisy, may the radiance of your truth chase them away. May your light so illumine our hearts and minds that our lives may shine forth like lanterns of hope, and beacons of the gospel of truth. This we ask in your holy name; Amen.

Advent week three – Emmanuel

(See also the study on his birth at Bethlehem in the section on the life of Jesus; p. 182)

Bible passages

Matthew 1:18–25, KJV

Now the birth of Jesus Christ was on this wise: When as his mother Mary was espoused to Joseph, before they came together, she was found with child of the Holy Ghost.

Then Joseph her husband, being a just man, and not willing to make her a public example, was minded to put her away privily.

But while he thought on these things, behold, the angel of the Lord appeared unto him in a dream, saying, Joseph, thou son of David, fear not to take unto thee Mary thy wife: for that which is conceived in her is of the Holy Ghost.

And she shall bring forth a son, and thou shalt call his name Jesus: for he shall save his people from their sins.

Now all this was done, that it might be fulfilled which was spoken of the Lord by the prophet, saying,

Behold, a virgin shall be with child, and shall bring forth a son, and they shall call his name Emmanuel, which being interpreted is, God with us.

Then Joseph being raised from sleep did as the angel of the Lord had bidden him, and took unto him his wife: and knew her not till she had brought forth her firstborn son: and he called his name Jesus.

Philippians 2:5–8

In your relationships with one another, have the same mindset as Christ Jesus: who, being in very nature God, did not consider equality with God something to be used to his own advantage; rather, he made himself nothing by taking the very nature of a servant, being made in human likeness. And being found in appearance as a man, he humbled himself by becoming obedient to death – even death on a cross!

Luke 15:4

"Suppose one of you has a hundred sheep and loses one of them. Doesn't he leave the ninety-nine in the open country and go after the lost sheep until he finds it?"

Commentary

"Emmanuel" means "God with us". In Jesus, God comes to find us. Our walk with him offers us as many challenges as we can take, and asks of us probably more than we are willing to give: "In your relationships with one another, have the same mindset as Christ Jesus", says our passage from Philippians – there's a steep hill to climb! But the challenges of discipleship are not a means by which we earn our salvation – that is already freely given. The coming to us of God in Jesus is free grace and unconditional love, with no strings attached. He is "with us". He is on our side.

In the Christmas story we marvel again at how God in Jesus chose vulnerability; he put himself at our mercy just as we in turn depend on his mercy – he levelled the playing field in his Son.

Humanity does not come out of the story of the life of Jesus very creditably. Right from his infancy there was always somebody trying to kill him – not because he did anything wrong but because power, violence, and corruption do not like healing, truth, and simplicity. The innate authority that was in Jesus posed a threat to what Paul calls "the powers of this dark world and … the spiritual forces of evil in the heavenly realms" (Ephesians 6:12). But then that was the very reason Jesus came; because we needed to be redeemed. He saw us with the eyes of a shepherd; because we were lost, he would come to find us, and never give up searching until he could lift us up onto his shoulders and bring us home.

Questions

- "Emmanuel" is one of the names of Jesus: "God with us". In what ways do you feel that he is with us – and with you personally – today?
- In our personal relationships, how do we create a balance between loving unconditionally and encouraging responsible behaviour?
- What do you like best – and least! – about Christmas?

Prayer

Thank you, Father, for sending Jesus. Thank you for his courage, his vulnerability, his tenderness, and his strength. Thank you for the full and free salvation he won for us. As the time draws near for us to remember again his birth at Bethlehem, we pray for all who are homeless, for refugees, and for those who are persecuted or afraid. And we pray for peace in the Middle East, peace for all humanity. May your kingdom come, and your will be done here on earth. We ask it for his love's sake; Amen.

Five Lent studies

(There are six weeks in Lent – five studies leave space for an Easter party)

Lent 1 – The wilderness

Bible passages

Deuteronomy 2:7

The Lord your God has blessed you in all the work of your hands. He has watched over your journey through this vast wilderness. These forty years the Lord your God has been with you, and you have not lacked anything.

Deuteronomy 8:2

Remember how the Lord your God led you all the way in the wilderness these forty years, to humble and test you in order to know what was in your heart, whether or not you would keep his commands.

Psalm 63:1

You, God, are my God, earnestly I seek you; I thirst for you, my whole being longs for you, in a dry and parched land where there is no water.

Ezekiel 20:10

I led them out of Egypt and brought them into the wilderness.

Mark 1:12–14

The Spirit sent him out into the wilderness, and he was in the wilderness for forty days, being tempted by Satan. He was with the wild animals, and angels attended him.

Luke 4:1

Jesus, full of the Holy Spirit, left the Jordan and was led by the Spirit into the wilderness.

Leviticus 16:21–22

He is to lay both hands on the head of the live goat and confess over it all the wickedness and rebellion of the Israelites – all their sins – and put them on the goat's head. He shall send the goat away into the wilderness in the care of someone appointed for the task. The goat will carry on itself all their sins to a remote place; and the man shall release it in the wilderness.

Commentary

There are three ways for us to look at the wilderness.

It can be seen as a beautiful and absolutely necessary part of the earth's life. Unless a huge proportion of the earth's surface is left as wilderness, a high percentage of species will be driven into extinction, and the climate will no longer sustain life. We cannot live without wilderness. If we see wilderness as a metaphor, this is still true. We all need breathing space, time to just be, peace and quiet, and the opportunity to retreat, regroup, and get a better perspective on life.

Wilderness can be seen as a situation of austerity – a desert place offering no luxury. Intimidating, disheartening, and downright dangerous, time in the wilderness is daunting and not something to look forward to. It's a place where survival skills are called for. Metaphorically, it is about loneliness or depression, about adversity – maybe bereavement; tough times.

Wilderness can also be a place of formation. Luke (1:80) says of John the Baptist: "And the child grew and became strong in spirit; and he lived in the wilderness." It has been pointed out that the world's great religions emerged from desert cultures, and suggested that perhaps in the desert there is time and space to think and pray, whereas in wetter climates the mind naturally focuses on organizing stout houses, umbrellas, and gumboots.

Questions

- Can you describe a time in your life that you would identify as "wilderness"?
- Why do you think the Spirit led Jesus out into the wilderness to be tempted?
- Our first passage speaks of how God "watched over your journey through this vast wilderness". Can you recall times of struggle or aridity where you experienced moments of encouragement or felt close to God?

Prayer

Whatever happens to us in life, dear Lord, even when the road is rocky and leads us through wild or frightening passes, help us to hold on tight to you and to drink from the springs of grace along the way. Thank you for the endurance and courage of Jesus, and his steadfastness in temptation. May we learn from him, may our faith in him never fail, and may we grow more like him as we follow – slowly, stumblingly – after him. We ask our prayer in his name and for his glory; Amen.

Lent 2 – Fasting

Bible passages

Luke 4:2

For forty days he was tempted by the devil. He ate nothing during those days, and at the end of them he was hungry.

Matthew 6:16–18

"When you fast, do not look sombre as the hypocrites do, for they disfigure their faces to show others they are fasting. Truly I tell you, they have received their reward in full. But when you fast, put oil on your head and wash your face, so that it will not be obvious to others that you are fasting, but only to your Father, who is unseen; and your Father, who sees what is done in secret, will reward you."

Mark 2:18–20

Now John's disciples and the Pharisees were fasting. Some people came and asked Jesus, "How is it that John's disciples and the disciples of the Pharisees are fasting, but yours are not?"

Jesus answered, "How can the guests of the bridegroom fast while he is with them? They cannot, so long as they have him with them. But the time will come when the bridegroom will be taken from them, and on that day they will fast."

Acts 13:2 (see also Acts 14:23)

While they were worshipping the Lord and fasting, the Holy Spirit said, "Set apart for me Barnabas and Saul for the work to which I have called them." So after they had fasted and prayed, they placed their hands on them and sent them off.

Luke 2:36

There was also a prophet, Anna, the daughter of Penuel, of the tribe of Asher. She was very old; she had lived with her husband seven years after her marriage, and then was a widow until she was eighty-four. She never left the temple but worshipped night and day, fasting and praying. Coming up to them at that very moment, she gave thanks to God and spoke about the child to all who were looking forward to the redemption of Jerusalem.

Commentary

Fasting has been a discipline of the church from its earliest days, and is common in other religions too.

It can mean abstaining from some luxury foods on a temporary or permanent basis – as for example many monastic communities abstain from eating meat permanently, and all Roman Catholics traditionally abstained from meat on Fridays as a form of fasting. Or it can mean complete abstinence from food and all drinks other than water (or sometimes herbal tea) for a length of time. Jesus' forty-day fast is the longest a person practised in fasting might undertake; beyond that it is inadvisable for health reasons.

Abstinence from food is not the only kind of fast. Fasting from watching TV is a popular alternative – or maybe fasting from shopping. During Lent many Christians choose to give something up as a form of fasting – this may be a kind of food, for example giving up chocolate or sugar in tea, or it can be some kind of comfort – perhaps sitting on a hard chair instead of in an armchair.

In every case it is done as a reminder, a help in focusing the mind – either to free oneself for complete availability to God, or as a small discomfort serving to recall attention again and again to focus on prayer. In our passages above we see Anna fasting and praying as part of her dedication to God, the church fasting and praying in preparation for anointing leaders, and Jesus' reference to fasting in response to sorrow and bereavement. Jesus points out that the one really bad reason for fasting is to show off!

Questions

- Have you ever fasted as a spiritual discipline? What was your experience like? In what ways did you find it helpful?
- Can you think of some things that you believe every Christian should always fast from, as part of their commitment to personal holiness?
- If you feel led to try fasting as part of your prayer, what kind of fast do you think might be appropriate for you? How would you time it to fit in with the obligations of your regular commitments?

Prayer

O Holy Spirit of God, as you led Jesus into the wilderness to fast and pray by himself for forty long days and nights, so you call us to practise a discipline of self-denial to help us draw closer to him. Speak quietly in our hearts, Spirit of God, so that we may know what you are asking us to undertake and what to relinquish. Give us, we pray, the wisdom to discern your voice in our hearts, and the grace to follow your leading. This we ask in Jesus' holy name; Amen.

Lent 3 – Solitude

Bible passage – 1 Kings 19:1–14 (see also Matthew 4; Luke 4; Mark 1)

Now Ahab told Jezebel everything Elijah had done and how he had killed all the prophets with the sword. So Jezebel sent a messenger to Elijah to say, "May the gods deal with me, be it ever so severely, if by this time tomorrow I do not make your life like that of one of them."

Elijah was afraid and ran for his life. When he came to Beersheba in Judah, he left his servant there, while he himself went a day's journey into the wilderness. He came to a broom bush, sat down under it and prayed that he might die. "I have had enough, Lord," he said. "Take my life; I am no better than my ancestors." Then he lay down under the bush and fell asleep.

All at once an angel touched him and said, "Get up and eat." He looked around, and there by his head was some bread baked over hot coals, and a jar of water. He ate and drank and then lay down again.

The angel of the Lord came back a second time and touched him and said, "Get up and eat, for the journey is too much for you." So he got up and ate and drank. Strengthened by that food, he travelled for forty days and forty nights until he reached Horeb, the mountain of God. There he went into a cave and spent the night. And the word of the Lord came to him: "What are you doing here, Elijah?"

He replied, "I have been very zealous for the Lord God Almighty. The Israelites have rejected your covenant, torn down your altars, and put your prophets to death with the sword. I am the only one left, and now they are trying to kill me too."

The Lord said, "Go out and stand on the mountain in the presence of the Lord, for the Lord is about to pass by."

Then a great and powerful wind tore the mountains apart and shattered the rocks before the Lord, but the Lord was not in the wind. After the wind there was an earthquake, but the Lord was not in the earthquake. After the earthquake came a fire, but the Lord was not in the fire. And after the fire came a gentle whisper. When Elijah heard it, he pulled his cloak over his face and went out and stood at the mouth of the cave. Then a voice said to him, "What are you doing here, Elijah?"

He replied, "I have been very zealous for the Lord God Almighty. The Israelites have rejected your covenant, torn down your altars, and put your prophets to death with the sword. I am the only one left, and now they are trying to kill me too."

Commentary

When we read (in Matthew 4, Luke 4, and Mark 1) about Jesus in the wilderness, we see the resonances of the faith story in which the gospel is rooted. The first

(Jewish) Christians hearing of Jesus' forty days' and nights' solitary fasting in the wilderness would remember Israel wandering for forty years in the wilderness, Moses spending forty days and nights in solitude on Mount Sinai receiving the Law, Elijah encountering God in the wilderness after forty days' and nights' travel to Mount Horeb ("the Mount of God", where Moses met with God in the burning bush), and the striking similarities between Elijah's commission on Horeb with the sending-forth from Horeb of the people of God in Exodus 33. The connections are clear; the Gospels are written in such a way as will enable us to see and grasp them, helping us understand who Jesus is – the holy one of God.

The story of Elijah on Mount Horeb is especially helpful for us in imagining the sense of solitude permeating Jesus' experience. "I am the only one... " Elijah says, and "they are trying to kill me... " When he reached Beersheba in his flight, bread miraculously appeared amid the stones of the wilderness to sustain him. On Mount Horeb the still small voice of the Lord spoke to him.

Do you see the connections with Jesus (Matthew 4:1–11)? The scriptural precedents give his temptation power. He too is alone, facing the magnitude of his ministry – and he really *is* "the only one". From infancy "they" have been trying to kill him. Like Elijah, he goes deep into the wilderness, and he too hears a little voice, suggesting that he too might find bread, and leading him too up a mountain to demonstrate divinity. Thank God for the shrewd, inspired, down-to-earth humility and integrity of Jesus, who even in the loneliness of the desert, facing the enormity of the task before him, sees through the tempter's ruse and discerns that voice from the Father's voice, knows who he himself is, does not need the ego-boost of being like Moses or Elijah, and has the integrity to stand firm.

Questions

- Can you remember specific times in your life when you felt very alone?
- Have you a clear sense of your ministry? What were you sent here to do?
- What helps you discern the guidance of God in your life when you are unsure which way to take?

Prayer

When we are alone, when we are afraid, may we always reach out for you, O Lord; for you are always with us, mighty to save. May we hold fast to you our whole life long – this we ask in the holy name of Jesus, your faithful Son, our faithful Lord; Amen.

Lent 4 – Temptation

Bible passages

Matthew 4:1–4

Then Jesus was led by the Spirit into the wilderness to be tempted by the devil. After fasting for forty days and forty nights, he was hungry. The tempter came to him and said, "If you are the Son of God, tell these stones to become bread."

Jesus answered, "It is written: 'Man shall not live on bread alone, but on every word that comes from the mouth of God.'" (See Deuteronomy 8:3.)

Matthew 4:5–7

Then the devil took him to the holy city and set him on the highest point of the temple. "If you are the Son of God," he said, "throw yourself down. For it is written: 'He will command his angels concerning you, and they will lift you up in their hands, so that you will not strike your foot against a stone.'"

Jesus answered him, "It is also written: 'Do not put the Lord your God to the test.'" (See Deuteronomy 6:16.)

Matthew 4:8–10

Again, the devil took him to a very high mountain and showed him all the kingdoms of the world and their splendour. "All this I will give you," he said, "if you will bow down and worship me."

Jesus said to him, "Away from me, Satan! For it is written: 'Worship the Lord your God, and serve him only.'" (See Deuteronomy 6:13.)

Mark 14:38

"Watch and pray so that you will not fall into temptation. The spirit is willing, but the flesh is weak."

Galatians 6:1

Brothers and sisters, if someone is caught in a sin, you who live by the Spirit should restore that person gently. But watch yourselves, or you also may be tempted.

James 1:13–14

When tempted, no one should say, "God is tempting me." For God cannot be tempted by evil, nor does he tempt anyone; but each person is tempted when they are dragged away by their own evil desire and enticed.

Commentary

Temptation is not sin, but it encourages you to peep over the fence!

The Pharisees created a practice called the "hedge around the Law"; they added a plethora of secondary laws to ensure that the Mosaic Law was not infringed. Similarly, the Society of Friends developed what is known as the "Quaker Hedge", the plain customs of speech, dress, and life that created a quarantine or buffer zone between the holy and the worldly, to ensure they did not fall into sin. Modest dress, "custody of the eyes" (basically minding one's own business!), and avoiding some centres of leisure where there will be a lot of alcohol consumed and raucous, bawdy behaviour are normal; they are all measures we might put in place to guard against temptation. For we know too well that we are but frail and human, and can so easily make mistakes we later regret.

In our study passages, we see some of the weapons against temptation identified: Jesus' intimate knowledge of the Scriptures safeguards him from the wiliness of temptation; Jesus urges his friends to keep watch in prayer as a defence against temptation; Paul reminds us that a humble attitude will be a shield against the temptation to self-righteousness when we have to sort out situations arising from someone else's sin; and James says what should be obvious but so often is not – the mess we get ourselves into is not God's fault!

Questions

- Jesus was tempted to break his discipline to satisfy his senses: can you think of examples of this in our modern society?
- Jesus was tempted to show off his spiritual status for his own glory: have you sometimes been tempted to name-drop or show off for your personal advantage?
- Jesus was offered power in exchange for forming a corrupt alliance and creating an unholy allegiance. In modern politics, do you think it is possible to avoid this and retain personal integrity?

Prayer

We take refuge with you, O God our redeemer and our rock. You who made us and understand us know so well that we are weak-willed and a lot less clever than we think. Help us and protect us, we pray; strengthen us and hold on to our hands, that we may not lose our footing as we walk the straight and narrow way of eternal life. For we ask it in Jesus' holy name; Amen.

Lent 5 – Preparation

Bible passages

Exodus 24:18; 31:18

Then Moses entered the cloud as he went on up the mountain. And he stayed on the mountain forty days and forty nights.

When the Lord finished speaking to Moses on Mount Sinai, he gave him the two tablets of the covenant law, the tablets of stone inscribed by the finger of God.

Mark 1:9–15

At that time Jesus came from Nazareth in Galilee and was baptised by John in the Jordan. Just as Jesus was coming up out of the water, he saw heaven being torn open and the Spirit descending on him like a dove. And a voice came from heaven: "You are my Son, whom I love; with you I am well pleased."

At once the Spirit sent him out into the wilderness, and he was in the wilderness for forty days, being tempted by Satan. He was with the wild animals, and angels attended him.

After John was put in prison, Jesus went into Galilee, proclaiming the good news of God. "The time has come," he said. "The kingdom of God has come near. Repent and believe the good news!"

Matthew 3:1–6, 11–12 (optional: read to the end of the chapter)

In those days John the Baptist came, preaching in the wilderness of Judea and saying, "Repent, for the kingdom of heaven has come near." This is he who was spoken of through the prophet Isaiah:

"A voice of one calling in the wilderness, 'Prepare the way for the Lord, make straight paths for him.'"

John's clothes were made of camel's hair, and he had a leather belt round his waist. His food was locusts and wild honey. People went out to him from Jerusalem and all Judea and the whole region of the Jordan. Confessing their sins, they were baptised by him in the River Jordan...

... "I baptise you with water for repentance. But after me comes one who is more powerful than I, whose sandals I am not worthy to carry. He will baptise you with the Holy Spirit and fire. His winnowing fork is in his hand, and he will clear his threshing floor, gathering his wheat into the barn and burning up the chaff with unquenchable fire."

Commentary

Withdrawal into the wilderness is part of the scriptural story of preparation for ministry. Moses would draw apart from his people to meet with God on the mountain and find the way forward for God's people, Jesus often withdrew into the hills to commune with the Father, Abram was led out into the desert to find a new identity, and Jacob wrestled with God in the desert and found a new name (Israel – see our study on Jacob on p. 72). Solitude, austere simplicity, and nature are the context in which the giants of our spiritual heritage sought the face of God.

Here, after thirty years spent growing up in Nazareth and working as a carpenter, Jesus goes into the wilderness to prepare. The time has come. Joseph, in whose house he grew up, has died (he is present when Jesus is lost as a boy [Luke 2:48], but by the time Jesus has embarked on his teaching ministry it is Jesus who is head of the household [Matthew 12:46]); John the Baptist, his childhood friend, his cousin, and his herald, has been put to death; it is time – his early support networks have been withdrawn. Just as John the Baptist prepared for this in the wilderness, so Jesus now withdraws to the wilderness to make himself ready. The striking difference is that whereas Abraham, Jacob, Moses, and Elijah encounter God in the desert, Jesus meets the devil. This of itself is a huge clue to who Jesus is, and a preparation for the cosmic confrontation that is to come. In Luke's Gospel we read (Luke 4:13): "When the devil had finished all this tempting, he left him until an opportune time." That "opportune time" comes at the Last Supper (Luke 22:3): "Then Satan entered Judas, called Iscariot, one of the Twelve." The adversary who met him at his preparation in the wilderness is back, and the battle lines are drawn. This is what Jesus came here to do.

Questions

- Have you experienced, or do you feel drawn to, making a retreat?
- In your church, how are people prepared to undertake new ministry?
- Where do you go when you want to think something through, or prepare for ministry?

Prayer

O God of all our journeys, you call us on. Help us to hear your call, to grasp what you are asking of us, and to have the courage to undertake it. Help us to find the right friends to advise us and the right circumstances to prepare privately with you, so that we are ready for what you want of us. In Jesus' holy name we make our prayer; Amen.

Ascension

Bible passages

John 20:17

Jesus said, "Do not hold on to me, for I have not yet ascended to the Father. Go instead to my brothers and tell them, 'I am ascending to my Father and your Father, to my God and your God.'"

Luke 24:50–51 (please also read the full account in Acts 1:3–11)

When he had led them out to the vicinity of Bethany, he lifted up his hands and blessed them. While he was blessing them, he left them and was taken up into heaven.

Ephesians 4:7–13

But to each one of us grace has been given as Christ apportioned it. This is why it [Psalm 68:18] says: "When he ascended on high, he took many captives and gave gifts to his people."

(What does "he ascended" mean except that he also descended to the lower, earthly regions? He who descended is the very one who ascended higher than all the heavens, in order to fill the whole universe.) So Christ himself gave the apostles, the prophets, the evangelists, the pastors and teachers, to equip his people for works of service, so that the body of Christ may be built up until we all reach unity in the faith and in the knowledge of the Son of God and become mature, attaining to the whole measure of the fullness of Christ.

Hebrews 4:14–16

Therefore, since we have a great high priest who has ascended into heaven, Jesus the Son of God, let us hold firmly to the faith we profess. For we do not have a high priest who is unable to empathize with our weaknesses, but we have one who has been tempted in every way, just as we are – yet he did not sin. Let us then approach God's throne of grace with confidence, so that we may receive mercy and find grace to help us in our time of need.

Commentary

The work of salvation Jesus did for us had stages. First, we read that the Christ/ Logos/Word was there in our making at the beginning of the universe; nothing was made without him, so he intimately understands us. Second, it was in Jesus Christ that God came to be with us when we were lost in sin and incapable of finding our way back to him. Third, he taught and showed us how to live so that once he had redeemed us we would know how to sustain a life of holiness, without which we would be fragmented into isolationism and chaos. Fourth, with unbelievable courage he entered into the heart of suffering, sin, and death, carrying his light into the heart of darkness to redeem creation, restore the pattern of life from the tangle and wreckage human sin had made, and set at the heart of creation the living reconciliation of the cross, which holds all things together in unity for eternity. Fifth, God raised him from the dead, thus opening a path of victorious life through the Omega gate of death. The bridge thus created formed a living way of connection between the state of being separated off and that of being able to reach God. We need no longer fear death. Immediately after his resurrection, Jesus was physically present with his followers, yet warned Mary not to cling to him – his resurrection body was not the form by which he would relate to us now; only the ascension would make him once more fully accessible. Sixth, Jesus was taken up to the Father, and in so doing took with him "captives", everything he held together through his redeeming death, drawn up with him to the throne of grace. Seventh, because his humanity was now subsumed into heaven, by this living connection his Spirit was able to be poured out on all flesh, available to all who turn to him and dwell in him. The ascension is the fulcrum, the pivotal event completing the work of salvation that only Jesus could do, and inaugurating the body of Christ present throughout the church in the power of the Holy Spirit.

Questions

- Where and when have you felt closest to Jesus?
- How did you first learn about Jesus?
- Thinking of your everyday life, can you identify areas of struggle where you would especially like Jesus' help just now?

Prayer

Jesus, Lord of life, living Word, God with us, fount of our salvation, we look to you. Ascended Master, enable us through the power of your Holy Spirit, poured out into our hearts, to follow you faithfully, to please you in our choices and ways of living, and to be fruitful in your service from now until the end of our lives. This we ask in your holy name; Amen.

Pentecost

Bible passages

John 20:19–22

On the evening of that first day of the week, when the disciples were together, with the doors locked. for fear of the Jewish leaders, Jesus came and stood among them and said, "Peace be with you!" After he said this, he showed them his hands and side. The disciples were overjoyed when they saw the Lord.

Again Jesus said, "Peace be with you! As the Father has sent me, I am sending you." And with that he breathed on them and said, "Receive the Holy Spirit."

Acts 2:1–4

When the day of Pentecost came, they were all together in one place. Suddenly a sound like the blowing of a violent wind came from heaven and filled the whole house where they were sitting. They saw what seemed to be tongues of fire that separated and came to rest on each of them. All of them were filled with the Holy Spirit and began to speak in other tongues as the Spirit enabled them.

Acts 2:38–39

Peter replied, "Repent and be baptised, every one of you, in the name of Jesus Christ for the forgiveness of your sins. And you will receive the gift of the Holy Spirit. The promise is for you and your children and for all who are far off – for all whom the Lord our God will call."

1 Corinthians 12:7–11

Now to each one the manifestation of the Spirit is given for the common good. To one there is given through the Spirit a message of wisdom, to another a message of knowledge by means of the same Spirit, to another faith by the same Spirit, to another gifts of healing by that one Spirit, to another miraculous powers, to another prophecy, to another distinguishing between spirits, to another speaking in different kinds of tongues, and to still another the interpretation of tongues. All these are the work of one and the same Spirit, and he distributes them to each one, just as he determines.

Galatians 5:22–23, 25

But the fruit of the Spirit is love, joy, peace, forbearance, kindness, goodness, faithfulness, gentleness and self-control... Since we live by the Spirit, let us keep in step with the Spirit.

Commentary

In the Old Testament, God communicated with his people through specially chosen individuals – the patriarchs and prophets: Abraham, Isaac, Jacob, Moses, Elijah, Isaiah, etc. He did not communicate with the people directly, but only through these individuals who were called into his presence to receive his word for them.

In the Gospels, God came to us in Jesus, who is described as like the light of God moving through a dark world; the radiance of the Godhead was concentrated in him.

At the moment of his death on the cross when he cried "It is finished!" the Temple veil keeping the people out of the Holy of Holies was torn from top to bottom; Jesus took humanity into the throne room of God. So it was that, when he had ascended to the Father, this living connection he had made between heaven and humanity allowed for the Holy Spirit to be poured out on all believers.

This happened on the day of Pentecost. Ever since that time it has been the privilege and responsibility of every believer to open their life to complete saturation in the Holy Spirit of God. No longer does God's heart have to be mediated to us through specially called individuals; now all of us can enter personal and direct communion with God, because Jesus has made that possible. The priestly and prophetic ministries of the Old Testament are now conferred upon the whole people of God. Biblical Christianity does not have any kind of caste system. The Holy Spirit is for us all.

Questions

- Can you think of three different ways you have seen the Holy Spirit at work in the world?
- In what ways is your church best at expressing the work of the Holy Spirit?
- Do you experience the presence of the Holy Spirit most intensely in gatherings or in solitude?

Prayer

Come to us now, Holy Spirit, and fill us anew. Transform us; renew our minds so that we are no longer conformed to the ways of the world but are set free to follow Jesus. Make us bold, fill us with hope, infuse us with your peace and light. Shine through us so that everyone we know may be blessed by the touch of your love: for we ask it in Jesus' holy name; Amen.

The Holy Trinity

Bible passages

John 1:18

No one has ever seen God, but the one and only Son, who is himself God and is in the closest relationship with the Father, has made him known.

John 6:45–46

"Everyone who has heard the Father and learned from him comes to me. No one has seen the Father except the one who is from God; only he has seen the Father."

John 10:30

"I and the Father are one."

Colossians 2:9, KJV

For in him dwelleth all the fulness of the Godhead bodily.

John 16:7–15

"But very truly I tell you, it is for your good that I am going away. Unless I go away, the Advocate will not come to you; but if I go, I will send him to you. When he comes, he will prove the world to be in the wrong about sin and righteousness and judgment: about sin, because people do not believe in me; about righteousness, because I am going to the Father, where you can see me no longer; and about judgment, because the prince of this world now stands condemned.

"I have much more to say to you, more than you can now bear. But when he, the Spirit of truth, comes, he will guide you into all the truth. He will not speak on his own; he will speak only what he hears, and he will tell you what is yet to come. He will glorify me because it is from me that he will receive what he will make known to you. All that belongs to the Father is mine. That is why I said the Spirit will receive from me what he will make known to you."

John 16:28

"I came from the Father and entered the world; now I am leaving the world and going back to the Father."

Acts 16:7

When they came to the border of Mysia, they tried to enter Bithynia, but the Spirit of Jesus would not allow them to.

Commentary

The mystery of the Holy Trinity became part of the Christian understanding of God during the first three hundred years after the resurrection of Jesus. By the time of the Council of Nicea in 325, the church was ready to agree on a doctrine, a definite article of faith, which would define orthodox Christian belief. This doctrine is drawn from the Scriptures and Christian experience, but is not specifically outlined or defined in Scripture.

The substance of this understanding is that we experience God in three distinct ways. We encounter him as God the Father who is transcendent and all-powerful, over and above us, our creator who watches over us but who is infinitely greater than our intellectual or spiritual capacity can possibly encompass. It is this aspect of God of which Isaiah's prophecy (55:9) says, "As the heavens are higher than the earth, so are my ways higher than your ways and my thoughts than your thoughts."

We also experience him as God the Son in Jesus, both in the story of his teaching and ministry and in personal direct encounter with him in the here and now. It is possible to meet Jesus.

And we experience God as the Holy Spirit dwelling in our hearts, "transformed by the renewing of your mind", as Romans 12:2 puts it.

The Holy Trinity is God above us, God alongside us, and God within us; Father, Son, and Holy Spirit – not three gods but three ways of experiencing or encountering one God. This is hard to understand intellectually because it is a mystery; it can be understood only spiritually and experientially.

Questions

- Is there one of these three aspects of God that you find it easier to relate to?
- Does your church emphasize one of the three aspects more than the others?
- Which aspect of God do you think is easiest for children to start with?

Prayer

Holy God, Ancient of Days, Lord of Hosts, we thank you that you are our Father, loving us and watching over us. Thank you that you are Emmanuel, God with us in Jesus, our saviour, our brother, and our friend. Thank you for coming to us as Holy Spirit, breath of God that illumines and enlivens us, transforming and renewing our minds. Enable us by your grace to enter the power of this mystery, so that we may know for ourselves the wonder of relationship with you. This we ask you, Father, in the name of Jesus and in the power of the Holy Spirit; Amen.

Two studies for Ordinary Time

Ordinary Time 1 – Daily life

Bible passages

1 Thessalonians 4:11–12

... make it your ambition to lead a quiet life: you should mind your own business and work with your hands, just as we told you, so that your daily life may win the respect of outsiders and so that you will not be dependent on anybody.

Philippians 4:4–9

Rejoice in the Lord always. I will say it again: rejoice! Let your gentleness be evident to all. The Lord is near. Do not be anxious about anything, but in every situation, by prayer and petition, with thanksgiving, present your requests to God. And the peace of God, which transcends all understanding, will guard your hearts and your minds in Christ Jesus.

Finally, brothers and sisters, whatever is true, whatever is noble, whatever is right, whatever is pure, whatever is lovely, whatever is admirable – if anything is excellent or praiseworthy – think about such things. Whatever you have learned or received or heard from me, or seen in me – put it into practice. And the God of peace will be with you.

Hebrews 13:1–5

Keep on loving one another as brothers and sisters. Do not forget to show hospitality to strangers, for by so doing some people have shown hospitality to angels without knowing it. Continue to remember those in prison as if you were together with them in prison, and those who are mistreated as if you yourselves were suffering.

Marriage should be honoured by all, and the marriage bed kept pure, for God will judge the adulterer and all the sexually immoral. Keep your lives free from the love of money and be content with what you have, because God has said, "Never will I leave you; never will I forsake you."

1 Peter 4:9–11

Offer hospitality to one another without grumbling. Each of you should use whatever gift you have received to serve others, as faithful stewards of God's grace in its various forms. If anyone speaks, they should do so as one who speaks the very words of God. If anyone serves, they should do so with the strength God provides, so that in all things God may be praised through Jesus Christ.

Commentary

The word "ordinary" means both unexceptional and ordained. In the church year, some parts that are not special festivals are designated "ordinary time". This reminds us that it's in the regular everyday relationships, work, and leisure activities that our main service to God is carried out. This is the arena of our faithfulness, the field in which we sow the seeds of heaven.

The letters of the New Testament are full of encouragement and wisdom to help us in this; they recommend cheerfulness, kindness, honesty, and quietness in our daily living, and caution us against discontentment, grudges, criticism, and quarrelling.

Christian chastity is also identified in the New Testament as an important aspect of faithful conduct. In an age where divorce is everywhere we look, we have much to learn from the New Testament about conducting our lives with love and faithfulness, building households with habits of peace and understanding, and learning the arts of communication and reconciliation.

The New Testament also challenges us to consider how we spend our money and share our resources, reminding us to be unselfish, hospitable, and compassionate in our choices (see for example 2 Corinthians 9:6–11).

Questions

- Which aspects of the Christian life come naturally to you, and which do you find the biggest challenge?
- Describe somebody you know whose life you feel is a wonderful example of how a Christian should live.
- Can you think of some advice or experiences that have helped you overcome your weaknesses and walk more faithfully in the way of grace?

Prayer

Wise and loving God, how generous you have been to us, how faithfully you have provided for us! At times when we have been tempted to despair, you have been there for us with your miracles of provision, lifting us up to new beginnings. Sow in our hearts the seed of your grace; make us cheerful souls, quick to smile, to comfort, and to encourage. Sweeten our homes with the fragrance of your Spirit, dispelling the stale and sour odours of resentment, grudges, and criticism. Set us free from heaviness and introspection, so that with light hearts and minds renewed we may follow in the way of Jesus, for we love him, Lord. Amen.

Ordinary Time 2 – A certain hope

Bible passages

Hebrews 13:11–14

The high priest carries the blood of animals into the Most Holy Place as a sin offering, but the bodies are burned outside the camp. And so Jesus also suffered outside the city gate to make the people holy through his own blood. Let us, then, go to him outside the camp, bearing the disgrace he bore. For here we do not have an enduring city, but we are looking for the city that is to come.

Romans 8:24–25

For in this hope we were saved. But hope that is seen is no hope at all. Who hopes for what they already have? But if we hope for what we do not yet have, we wait for it patiently.

Colossians 1:3–6

We always thank God, the Father of our Lord Jesus Christ, when we pray for you, because we have heard of your faith in Christ Jesus and of the love you have for all God's people – the faith and love that spring from the hope stored up for you in heaven and about which you have already heard in the true message of the gospel that has come to you.

Colossians 1:21–23

Once you were alienated from God and were enemies in your minds because of your evil behaviour. But now he has reconciled you by Christ's physical body through death to present you holy in his sight, without blemish and free from accusation – if you continue in your faith, established and firm, and do not move from the hope held out in the gospel. This is the gospel that you heard and that has been proclaimed to every creature under heaven, and of which I, Paul, have become a servant.

1 Timothy 4:10

That is why we labour and strive, because we have put our hope in the living God, who is the Saviour of all people, and especially of those who believe.

1 Timothy 6:17

Command those who are rich in this present world not to be arrogant nor to put their hope in wealth, which is so uncertain, but to put their hope in God, who richly provides us with everything for our enjoyment.

Commentary

Paul introduces his first letter to Timothy with the words: "Paul, an apostle of Christ Jesus by the command of God our Saviour and of Christ Jesus our hope… "

Christian hope is like a home to live in – the sturdy, stone-walled crofter's cottage of the heart, fit to withstand the onslaught of any and every weather. We dwell in hope.

So our hope is not an uncertain thing – "Are you saved?" "I'm not sure, but I hope so" – we have what we describe as a "certain hope", and our hope is Jesus Christ himself.

The reason we call this confident security in Jesus a "hope" is that it is not yet fulfilled or finally revealed. As our passage from Hebrews says, "here we do not have an enduring city, but we are looking for the city that is to come". Jesus taught us to pray, "Thy kingdom come on earth as it is in heaven," and this teaches us that our hope in him certainly begins to be realized and revealed here on earth in day-to-day life and prayer, but that heaven is our home and our destination, and the kingdom will be fulfilled beyond this passing earthly realm, in eternity.

So the hope in which we live is like the embassy of heaven; a place where, even in a twisted and cynical world, the rules of the kingdom apply.

Questions

- Christians are only human, sometimes downcast and even despairing. When that happens to you, what do you do to restore an attitude of good hope?
- Paul advises the wealthy to put their hope in God, not in money. How should Christians make decisions about medical/life/property insurance?
- Paul says that as an apostle he labours and strives because of his hope in Jesus. Can you think of times when hope has kept you going through adversity?

Prayer

Covenant God, we put our trust and hope in you. You came to us in Jesus, setting us free from sin, showing us how to live, and giving us a glimpse of heaven. May we all our lives remain faithful to this living hope, and walk life's path with our eyes fixed on Jesus, remembering that heaven is our home. For we ask it in his holy name; Amen.

Harvest Thanksgiving

Bible passages

Genesis 8:21–22

[The Lord said to Noah] "Never again will I curse the ground because of humans, even though every inclination of the human heart is evil from childhood. And never again will I destroy all living creatures, as I have done.

"As long as the earth endures, seedtime and harvest, cold and heat, summer and winter, day and night will never cease."

Exodus 23:10–11

"For six years you are to sow your fields and harvest the crops, but during the seventh year let the land lie unploughed and unused. Then the poor among your people may get food from it, and the wild animals may eat what is left. Do the same with your vineyard and your olive grove."

Exodus 23:16

"Celebrate the Festival of Harvest with the firstfruits of the crops you sow in your field. Celebrate the Festival of Ingathering at the end of the year, when you gather in your crops from the field."

Leviticus 23:22 (see also Leviticus 19:9–10)

"When you reap the harvest of your land, do not reap to the very edges of your field or gather the gleanings of your harvest. Leave them for the poor and for the foreigner residing among you. I am the Lord your God."

Galatians 6:7–10

Do not be deceived: God cannot be mocked. A man reaps what he sows. Whoever sows to please their flesh, from the flesh will reap destruction; whoever sows to please the Spirit, from the Spirit will reap eternal life. Let us not become weary in doing good, for at the proper time we will reap a harvest if we do not give up. Therefore, as we have opportunity, let us do good to all people, especially to those who belong to the family of believers.

Matthew 9:36–38

When he saw the crowds, he had compassion on them, because they were harassed and helpless, like sheep without a shepherd. Then he said to his disciples, "The harvest is plentiful but the workers are few. Ask the Lord of the harvest, therefore, to send out workers into his harvest field."

Commentary

In our passage from Genesis, God reassures us that the basic, stable rhythms of the earth, seedtime and harvest, will continue *as long as the earth endures*. This is reassuring, because we are part of the earth and it's comforting to know that God is watching over it and that its beauty and plenty will continue, blessed by him. It is also a reminder that the earth is an organism just as a person is – it will not last for ever; it is subject to disease and decay, and it can be destroyed by abuse. If we are wise we will tend it well so that it endures for as long as possible – for we are not separate from the earth but part of it. Yet we remember that our real home is with God, and that is where our lasting treasure, the love of our hearts, must be invested.

In our first passage from Exodus 23, we look at the strong themes of justice and the well-being of creation in the Law. The land, the animals, and the people are all to enjoy a rhythm of Sabbath rest. What is important is not the rigid religious observance of particular days (see Matthew 12:1–12), but the principle of compassion for both animal and human workers who need rest, and allowing the land to rest and recover. We ignore the Sabbath principle at our peril. The second passage from Exodus reminds us of the importance of giving thanks to God, and the passage from Leviticus reminds us to share, and to make space for the poor and needy to better themselves.

In our New Testament passages we remember that harvest is about how we live our whole lives, not just food, and the true harvest of God is a faithful soul.

Questions

- What do you consider your life's main crop?
- What have you gleaned from other people's lives and work?
- How is the principle of Sabbath rest expressed in your life?

Prayer

Lord of the harvest, we bring you thanks for the abundant blessing of our lives. Thank you for all that has nourished us – good food, wise words, simple kindness, and love. We acknowledge that all we have comes from you. Help us so to live that we ourselves become part of your harvest of love, remembering compassion, justice, and kindness in our daily lives, and observing the principle of Sabbath rest in setting appropriate boundaries so that the rhythm of our lives is attuned to peace. Our prayer we ask in Jesus' holy name; Amen.

All Saints

Bible passages

1 Thessalonians 3:12–13, KJV

The Lord make you to increase and abound in love one toward another, and toward all men, even as we do toward you: to the end he may stablish your hearts unblameable in holiness before God, even our Father, at the coming of our Lord Jesus Christ with all his saints.

Ephesians 1:18–19, KJV

The eyes of your understanding being enlightened; that ye may know what is the hope of his calling, and what the riches of the glory of his inheritance in the saints, and what is the exceeding greatness of his power to us-ward who believe, according to the working of his mighty power.

Ephesians 2:19–20, KJV

Now therefore ye are no more strangers and foreigners, but fellow citizens with the saints, and of the household of God; and are built upon the foundation of the apostles and prophets, Jesus Christ himself being the chief corner stone.

Romans 8:26–28, KJV

Likewise the Spirit also helpeth our infirmities: for we know not what we should pray for as we ought: but the Spirit itself maketh intercession for us with groanings which cannot be uttered. And he that searcheth the hearts knoweth what is the mind of the Spirit, because he maketh intercession for the saints according to the will of God. And we know that all things work together for good to them that love God, to them who are the called according to his purpose.

Revelation 8:3–4, KJV

And another angel came and stood at the altar, having a golden censer; and there was given unto him much incense, that he should offer it with the prayers of all saints upon the golden altar which was before the throne. And the smoke of the incense, which came with the prayers of the saints, ascended up before God out of the angel's hand.

Revelation 14:12, KJV

Here is the patience of the saints: here are they that keep the commandments of God, and the faith of Jesus.

Commentary

All our passages for this study are taken from the King James Version, because the New International Version does not use the term "saints". The terms it uses instead are "God's people" (Romans 8:27; Ephesians 2:19; Revelation 8:3), "the people of God" (Revelation 14:12), "his holy ones" (1 Thessalonians 3:13), "his holy people" (Ephesians 1:19). These modern terms are illuminating, bringing out the twin aspects of meaning in the word "saints". A saint is someone who is holy, set apart, consecrated unto God – and a saint is a common-or-garden, every-believer member of the household of faith. You don't have to be perfect to be a saint, you just have to believe in Jesus; it is living by this faith in him that will slowly sanctify you as you practise your salvation. It is a wonderful privilege to be part of the communion of saints; as our passage from Revelation 8 reminds us, our prayers arise like incense into the presence of God. Amazing.

The feast of All Saints is when we call to mind that we are part of the whole procession of witness to the lordship of Jesus, part of his family everywhere on earth and also in heaven. The communion of saints is present with us in every prayer, every act of worship, and in our faithful lives – for we are one with the whole company of believers.

Questions

- Do you think of yourself as a saint? Because…?
- When you think of the word "saint", who comes to mind out of people you have known?
- To live up to being a saint, what aspect of your faith practice do you think you should be working on most?

Prayer

Strengthen your saints, Lord Jesus, in every place on earth, especially where they are ostracized or persecuted for their faith, and where they struggle on as a lonely minority. Help them to hold in mind the great company that worships alongside them. Thank you for including us in your great family. Help us to live in a way that is worthy of the communion of the saints, remembering that we stand shoulder to shoulder with St Francis of Assisi, with your mother, Mary, and with Mother Teresa and St Peter and Dietrich Bonhoeffer and Martin Luther King as we bring you this prayer, which we offer in your holy name; Amen.

Learning from the life of Jesus

(20 Studies)

His birth at Bethlehem

His home at Nazareth

His fasting in the wilderness

His healing work

His teaching work

His prophetic spirit

His servant spirit

His attitude to authority

His attitude to women

His emphasis on forgiveness

His emphasis on personal faith and choice

His emphasis on thanksgiving

His proclamation of the kingdom

His teaching about freedom

His relationship with creation

His path of simplicity

His faithfulness in prayer

His passion and death

His work of reconciliation

His resurrection and glorious ascension

His birth at Bethlehem

Bible passage – Luke 2:1–20

In those days Caesar Augustus issued a decree that a census should be taken of the entire Roman world. (This was the first census that took place while Quirinius was governor of Syria.) And everyone went to their own town to register.

So Joseph also went up from the town of Nazareth in Galilee to Judea, to Bethlehem the town of David, because he belonged to the house and line of David. He went there to register with Mary, who was pledged to be married to him and was expecting a child. While they were there, the time came for the baby to be born, and she gave birth to her firstborn, a son. She wrapped him in cloths and placed him in a manger, because there was no guest room available for them.

And there were shepherds living out in the fields nearby, keeping watch over their flocks at night. An angel of the Lord appeared to them, and the glory of the Lord shone around them, and they were terrified. But the angel said to them, "Do not be afraid. I bring you good news that will cause great joy for all the people. Today in the town of David a Saviour has been born to you; he is the Messiah, the Lord. This will be a sign to you: you will find a baby wrapped in cloths and lying in a manger."

Suddenly a great company of the heavenly host appeared with the angel, praising God and saying,

"Glory to God in the highest heaven, and on earth peace to those on whom his favour rests."

When the angels had left them and gone into heaven, the shepherds said to one another, "Let's go to Bethlehem and see this thing that has happened, which the Lord has told us about."

So they hurried off and found Mary and Joseph, and the baby, who was lying in the manger. When they had seen him, they spread the word concerning what had been told them about this child, and all who heard it were amazed at what the shepherds said to them. But Mary treasured up all these things and pondered them in her heart. The shepherds returned, glorifying and praising God for all the things they had heard and seen, which were just as they had been told.

Commentary

Back in the 1980s I took part in a national Methodist investigation into all aspects of poverty. My role was to explore with individuals and families living in poverty what were their experiences, hopes, and aspirations. I learned that, though money was short in every case, it was not money that mattered most to the people with whom I talked. What they really wanted was someone to stand by them – a friend to go with them, a companion on the journey. With that, they could tackle their problems one by one without handouts. As I listened, I realized that this was exactly what Jesus did: he came to be with us, one of us, in our poverty. He found us where we were and came to make the journey with us.

In his birth at Bethlehem, Jesus came to be the child of poor parents (we know this because they gave the offering of the poor when they took him as a baby to the Temple). Not only that, but he was born at a time when they had to be on the road, going from place to place, turned away at every door. And not only that, but he shortly afterwards became a refugee, in flight from Herod's persecution. On the occasion of his birth at Bethlehem, angels announced his arrival – but to shepherds, not to dignitaries. Herding sheep was a lowly occupation; the guests invited by angels to adore the infant messiah were rough and humble people.

The birth of Jesus at Bethlehem introduces us to what will be a radical reinterpretation of what it means to be the messiah. The words "humble", "simple", and "unnoticed" all apply. And "accessible". And "miracle".

Questions

- What areas of your life would you identify as poor? And in what areas are you rich?
- Can you think of any occasions when you have witnessed (or heard of) a great or famous person humbling him-/herself for the sake of someone else?
- If you had seen an angel that holy night, and been privileged to worship the baby in the manger, what would you have taken as a gift?

Prayer

God of love, we can never thank you enough for coming to be with us in Jesus. As we think of his birth at Bethlehem, the difficult start of a life that was to ask everything of him, we acknowledge that without him we are nothing, that our lives depend upon his love, his grace, his humility. And in his holy name we give you thanks for so great a salvation. Amen.

His home at Nazareth

Bible passage – Luke 2:39–52

When Joseph and Mary had done everything required by the Law of the Lord, they returned to Galilee to their own town of Nazareth. And the child grew and became strong; he was filled with wisdom, and the grace of God was on him.

Every year Jesus' parents went to Jerusalem for the Festival of the Passover. When he was twelve years old, they went up to the festival, according to the custom. After the festival was over, while his parents were returning home, the boy Jesus stayed behind in Jerusalem, but they were unaware of it. Thinking he was in their company, they travelled on for a day. Then they began looking for him among their relatives and friends. When they did not find him, they went back to Jerusalem to look for him. After three days they found him in the temple courts, sitting among the teachers, listening to them and asking them questions. Everyone who heard him was amazed at his understanding and his answers. When his parents saw him, they were astonished. His mother said to him, "Son, why have you treated us like this? Your father and I have been anxiously searching for you."

"Why were you searching for me?" he asked. "Didn't you know I had to be in my Father's house?" But they did not understand what he was saying to them.

Then he went down to Nazareth with them and was obedient to them. But his mother treasured all these things in her heart. And Jesus grew in wisdom and stature, and in favour with God and man.

Commentary

Though we have so little information about this period of Jesus' life, the inspiration we can glean from what we do know is very precious.

Jesus grew up in the home of Joseph, who is remarkable not least because he plays so vital a role yet we do not know of a single word he said (see the study on Joseph on p. 70). Perhaps Joseph shows us that the living Word is nurtured and protected by silence, and grows to maturity in the company of silence. This leads us to consider the role of silence in our own lives, and how time spent in silence might help the presence of Christ to grow from infancy to maturity in our hearts.

The childhood of Jesus was spent in a carpenter's household, with a family who lived in simplicity on modest means. This speaks to us of the humility of God's grace, but suggests also that simplicity, making do for ourselves, honest work, and the labour of our hands are all part of a spiritual environment.

Joseph and Mary lost Jesus on their pilgrimage to the Temple because they assumed someone else was looking after him. That speaks volumes about the society in which they lived – where anyone's child was everyone's child, and all children were welcomed and loved. Jesus grew up knowing the meaning of community.

When they found their lost child, they expected an explanation, but treated him with gentleness. He had caused great inconvenience and anxiety and they told him so – but there were no angry scenes. Nobody hit him. Jesus grew up with gentleness, and this helped him to mature into what he was meant to be.

Questions

- What was your childhood home like? Whose life introduced you to Jesus, and showed you the path of grace?
- Think honestly, now. If Jesus had been your child, and you had lost him in the crowd and taken three days to find him, what would have happened?
- Joseph was a quiet man and we read of Mary "treasuring" or "pondering" things that happen, in her heart. In your own life and home, what priority is given to quiet reflection? Is there space to think things through, or is life very busy and active? Would you describe the emphasis in your home as "being" or "doing"?

Prayer

Patient and gentle God, you watch in wisdom and love over our homes and families. So direct our feet in the way of grace that we are fit travelling companions for Jesus. May his light so shine among us that gradually we are changed to become like him. Help us, good Lord, not only to sing about him and talk about him, but really to live with him. May Jesus abide among us as a member of our family, and may the family likeness grow more evident day by day. For we ask it in his holy name; Amen.

His fasting in the wilderness

Bible passage – Luke 4:1–13

Jesus, full of the Holy Spirit, left the Jordan and was led by the Spirit into the wilderness, where for forty days he was tempted by the devil. He ate nothing during those days, and at the end of them he was hungry.

The devil said to him, "If you are the Son of God, tell this stone to become bread."

Jesus answered, "It is written: 'Man shall not live on bread alone.'"

The devil led him up to a high place and showed him in an instant all the kingdoms of the world. And he said to him, "I will give you all their authority and splendour; it has been given to me, and I can give it to anyone I want to. If you worship me, it will all be yours."

Jesus answered, "It is written: 'Worship the Lord your God and serve him only.'"

The devil led him to Jerusalem and had him stand on the highest point of the temple. "If you are the Son of God," he said, "throw yourself down from here. For it is written:

"'He will command his angels concerning you
to guard you carefully;
they will lift you up in their hands,
so that you will not strike your foot against a stone.'"

Jesus answered, "It is said: 'Do not put the Lord your God to the test.'"

When the devil had finished all this tempting, he left him until an opportune time.

Commentary

The Bible is full of truth, and we can depend on it to lead us into the way of truth. But there are difficulties when we say that every word of the Bible is to be taken literally. This passage, taken from Luke's Gospel, is a good example. It tells of Jesus fasting in the wilderness in preparation for his ministry, experiencing temptation as hunger and solitude intensify. The three temptations Luke describes climax in Jerusalem on the pinnacle of the Temple. But if you read the same story in Matthew's Gospel (also chapter 4), the final temptation is not the one at the Temple in Jerusalem, but the one in which Jesus is shown all the kingdoms of the world, and tempted to choose worldly power instead of spiritual authority.

For people who look for a literalistic interpretation, this poses a problem – they can't both be accurate records because the order differs. This should alert us to the reality that each evangelist is describing these events in such a way as to bring out the particular emphasis of his Gospel. Matthew, portraying Jesus as the teacher of righteousness, the true Israel, shows him here choosing integrity over power and thus earning real authority. Luke is showing the centrality of the Temple at Jerusalem, the heart of the Judeo-Christian religious tradition, here at the start of a story that will spread out until it reaches Rome, the secular centre of the Gentile world – a gospel for all people.

Questions

- Jesus said, "Man shall not live by bread alone." What are the things in your life that are as necessary to you as food and drink – the things that nourish your soul?

- Jesus was led by the Spirit into the wilderness. Many people feel led to spend time quietly, alone, in nature, to get their minds clear and to pray. What environments help you to really think, and to feel close to God?

- The devil showed Jesus all the kingdoms of the world and said to him, "I will give you all their authority and splendour; it has been given to me, and I can give it to anyone I want to. If you worship me, it will all be yours." Yet Romans 13:1 says, "Let everyone be subject to the governing authorities, for there is no authority except that which God has established. The authorities that exist have been established by God." What do you think about this? In our daily lives, how can we exercise faithful Christian citizenship, discerning and differentiating between the reign of Mammon and authority established by God?

Prayer

God of power and might, our lives are in your hands, and we trust you for our salvation. So fill us with your Holy Spirit that we may grow in discernment and grace, choosing well in a complicated world. We pray for our national leaders, for those set in authority over us in local government, and for those who hold the reins of power in big international companies that can even determine the fate of nation states and ecosystems. May the peace and justice of your kingdom reign supreme over the kingdoms of the earth, and may our little lives reflect faithfully the priorities of the Lord Jesus, for we ask it in his holy name; Amen.

His healing work

Bible passage – Mark 1:32–42, KJV

And at even, when the sun did set, they brought unto him all that were diseased, and them that were possessed with devils.

And all the city was gathered together at the door.

And he healed many that were sick of diverse diseases, and cast out many devils; and suffered not the devils to speak, because they knew him.

And in the morning, rising up a great while before day, he went out, and departed into a solitary place, and there prayed.

And Simon and they that were with him followed after him.

And when they had found him, they said unto him, All men seek for thee.

And he said unto them, Let us go into the next towns, that I may preach there also: for therefore came I forth.

And he preached in their synagogues throughout all Galilee, and cast out devils.

And there came a leper to him, beseeching him, and kneeling down to him, and saying unto him, If thou wilt, thou canst make me clean.

And Jesus, moved with compassion, put forth his hand, and touched him, and saith unto him, I will; be thou clean.

And as soon as he had spoken, immediately the leprosy departed from him, and he was cleansed.

Commentary

Our Bible passage comes right after the story of Jesus healing Simon Peter's mother-in-law. Word spread, and soon everyone in the neighbourhood was beating a path to Jesus' door to have their ailments fixed. In a day when medicine had not yet advanced to include antibiotics, analgesics, sophisticated surgical techniques, and many of the medical remedies we take for granted today, how urgently his help must have been sought!

The passage has been quoted from the KJV rather than the NIV because of the part near the end which says that Jesus, looking at the man with leprosy, was "moved with compassion". The NIV says, "Jesus was indignant", which communicates less fully the response to our troubles that we see in Jesus.

It is interesting to see in this passage how Jesus divides his time between solitary prayer in the peace of the hills, confronting by exorcism evil that has a grip on people, healing the sick, and preaching the good news. And we know that he also made time to teach his disciples, guiding them and discussing spiritual truths with them.

In establishing our own priorities, we might like to make a study of this passage. Perhaps we could establish four areas of priority: quiet times to nurture and strengthen our spirit, time for sharing truth and insight with others, working to bring peace and well-being in our own community, and standing up against evil where we are confronted with it.

Questions

- Where and how have you experienced the healing of Jesus in your own life?
- In what way do you feel led to share in the healing work of Jesus?
- Jesus would often say to people in healing them, "Your faith has made you whole." What is the difference between being cured and being made whole? Is it possible to be made whole without being cured? How do you think we could work towards holistic health in our regular practice of medicine in hospitals and doctors' surgeries?

Prayer

You made us, God of love; you understand us, and you make us whole. Today we offer you our lives and hearts, asking you to look deeply into us, and heal us. Where you find anything poisonous or dangerous, please cut it out and burn it, so it can do no more damage. Where we are weak and fragile, please strengthen us by the presence of your Spirit. Where we are bruised and broken, please salve us with your kindness and splint us with your steady strength. And please nourish by your word and your Spirit whatever is good in our hearts and lives; for we ask this in Jesus' holy name; Amen.

His teaching work

Bible passages

Matthew 5:1–14

Now when Jesus saw the crowds, he went up on a mountainside and sat down. His disciples came to him, and he began to teach them.

The Beatitudes

He said:
"Blessed are the poor in spirit, for theirs is the kingdom of heaven.
Blessed are those who mourn, for they will be comforted.
Blessed are the meek, for they will inherit the earth.
Blessed are those who hunger and thirst for righteousness, for they will be filled.
Blessed are the merciful, for they will be shown mercy.
Blessed are the pure in heart, for they will see God.
Blessed are the peacemakers, for they will be called children of God.
Blessed are those who are persecuted because of righteousness, for theirs is the kingdom of heaven.
"Blessed are you when people insult you, persecute you and falsely say all kinds of evil against you because of me. Rejoice and be glad, because great is your reward in heaven, for in the same way they persecuted the prophets who were before you.
"You are the salt of the earth. But if the salt loses its saltiness, how can it be made salty again? It is no longer good for anything, except to be thrown out and trampled underfoot.
"You are the light of the world. A town built on a hill cannot be hidden. Neither do people light a lamp and put it under a bowl. Instead they put it on its stand, and it gives light to everyone in the house. In the same way, let your light shine before others, that they may see your good deeds and glorify your Father in heaven..."

Matthew 7:28–29

... When Jesus had finished saying these things, the crowds were amazed at his teaching, because he taught as one who had authority, and not as their teachers of the law.

Commentary

Our Bible passage shows the beginning and end of the Sermon on the Mount. Reading through this whole passage of teaching (Matthew 5:1 – 7:29) quietly at home in preparation for the group may be helpful in thinking about Jesus' teaching ministry.

In Matthew's Gospel, where Jesus is seen as a teacher of righteousness, the five blocks of teaching (see the study on p. 76 on Matthew's Gospel, "The faithful Israel and the new Moses") remind us of the books of the Law that taught the people of God how to live. The Sermon on the Mount forms part of these blocks of teaching, instructing us on the lifestyle of a Christian.

But Jesus also taught in parables; indeed, Matthew says elsewhere (13:34) that he always and only taught the crowds in parables. His parables (Matthew 13 gives a good selection) are often described as "parables of the kingdom", and they expound the nature of God and the kingdom of heaven. The parables help us to grasp imaginatively what Jesus elsewhere teaches in his discourses (for example Matthew 23:12 and Luke 18:9–14).

The teachings of Jesus emphasize faith that is genuine and stands firm, prayer that never gives up, forgiveness and mercy, God's constancy and love, the trustworthy generosity of God in providing for us, love as the hallmark of the disciple, willingness to embrace the sacrificial way, and the importance of simplicity.

Questions

- What do you find most encouraging and uplifting in what you know of the teaching of Jesus?
- Is there anything in Jesus' teaching that you find hard to understand or too hard to put into practice?
- When he taught, Jesus told stories (and sometimes just left his hearers to figure out what he was getting at), sometimes preached, and sometimes discussed or asked searching questions. He also sent his disciples out on missions, or involved them in miracles, where they learned by doing. What is your preferred way of learning?

Prayer

O God of wisdom, you know how dim our understanding can be, how slow we are to grasp what you are showing us. Thank you for your patience with us. As we walk the disciple's way, help us to keep our eyes fixed on Jesus, for we learn best of all by watching him. In his holy name we pray; Amen.

His prophetic spirit

Bible passages

Deuteronomy 18:18–19

I will raise up for them a prophet like you [Moses] from among their fellow Israelites, and I will put my words in his mouth. He will tell them everything I command him. I myself will call to account anyone who does not listen to my words that the prophet speaks in my name.

Luke 12:49–59

"I have come to bring fire on the earth, and how I wish it were already kindled! But I have a baptism to undergo, and what constraint I am under until it is completed! Do you think I came to bring peace on earth? No, I tell you, but division. From now on there will be five in one family divided against each other, three against two and two against three. They will be divided, father against son and son against father, mother against daughter and daughter against mother, mother-in-law against daughter-in-law and daughter-in-law against mother-in-law."

He said to the crowd: "When you see a cloud rising in the west, immediately you say, 'It's going to rain,' and it does. And when the south wind blows, you say, 'It's going to be hot,' and it is. Hypocrites! You know how to interpret the appearance of the earth and the sky. How is it that you don't know how to interpret this present time?"

Mark 6:1–6

Jesus left there and went to his home town, accompanied by his disciples. When the Sabbath came, he began to teach in the synagogue, and many who heard him were amazed.

"Where did this man get these things?" they asked. "What's this wisdom that has been given him? What are these remarkable miracles he is performing? Isn't this the carpenter? Isn't this Mary's son and the brother of James, Joseph, Judas and Simon? Aren't his sisters here with us?" And they took offence at him.

Jesus said to them, "A prophet is not without honour except in his own town, among his relatives and in his own home."

Luke 24:19–23 (from the story of the road to Emmaus)

"About Jesus of Nazareth," they replied. "He was a prophet, powerful in word and deed before God and all the people... "

Commentary

At the end of the book of Deuteronomy is a section about the death of Moses. It states : "Since then, no prophet has risen in Israel like Moses, whom the Lord knew face to face, who did all those signs and wonders the Lord sent him to do in Egypt – to Pharaoh and to all his officials and to his whole land. For no one has ever shown the mighty power or performed the awesome deeds that Moses did in the sight of all Israel" (Deuteronomy 34:10–12). But earlier in the book (18:18; see our Bible passages above) God speaks to Moses of another prophet like him who will be raised from among the Jewish people – a new Moses.

Speculation continued as time went by and no one fitting this description appeared, until Jesus came. Then the speculation centred on him (see Matthew 16:13–16) and people began to identify him as a prophet, possibly the prophet spoken of to Moses. At the time of his death (see our passage from Luke 24 above), he was understood to have been a great prophet. At that point the acceptance that he was the messiah, the saviour of the world, had not yet taken root.

Jesus' prophetic ministry is not emphasized as much as his teaching and healing nowadays, but it was revered during his earthly life. It is seen both in his fore-telling of events to come, and in his forth-telling – interpreting and understanding the spiritual significance of the events of his day, and seeing into the hearts of his fellow men, discerning truth and announcing the will of God.

Questions

- At Pentecost the Spirit of Jesus was poured out upon the church. Where can you see signs in the church today of the prophetic ministry of Jesus?
- When you hear the words "a prophet", what comes to mind? What does it mean to you, to be a prophet? What is the nature of prophetic ministry?
- Can you think of an example in modern life of someone you could describe as a prophet?

Prayer

O God of all truth, things hidden away in secret are exposed by the daylight of your presence. May we, by your mighty power and your Spirit at work within us, learn to see and discern what is wise and good for our nation, our time. Then give us the strength and the courage to work for our vision to come into being. In Jesus' holy name we pray; Amen.

His servant spirit

Bible passages

Mark 8:34 (also Luke 9:23; Matthew 16:24 – check variations)

Then he called the crowd to him along with his disciples and said: "Whoever wants to be my disciple must deny themselves and take up their cross and follow me."

Mark 10:42–45

Jesus called them together and said, "You know that those who are regarded as rulers of the Gentiles lord it over them, and their high officials exercise authority over them. Not so with you. Instead, whoever wants to become great among you must be your servant, and whoever wants to be first must be slave of all. For even the Son of Man did not come to be served, but to serve, and to give his life as a ransom for many."

Luke 17:7–10

"Suppose one of you has a servant ploughing or looking after the sheep. Will he say to the servant when he comes in from the field, 'Come along now and sit down to eat'? Won't he rather say, 'Prepare my supper, get yourself ready and wait on me while I eat and drink; after that you may eat and drink'? Will he thank the servant because he did what he was told to do? So you also, when you have done everything you were told to do, should say, 'We are unworthy servants; we have only done our duty.'"

John 13:12–17

When he had finished washing their feet, he put on his clothes and returned to his place. "Do you understand what I have done for you?" he asked them. "You call me 'Teacher' and 'Lord', and rightly so, for that is what I am. Now that I, your Lord and Teacher, have washed your feet, you also should wash one another's feet. I have set you an example that you should do as I have done for you. Very truly I tell you, no servant is greater than his master, nor is a messenger greater than the one who sent him. Now that you know these things, you will be blessed if you do them."

Commentary

There is hardly a page of the Gospels you can open without coming across either direct teaching from Jesus, or an example from his life, about the servant spirit that is to be at the core of our discipleship.

This was massively important to Jesus, and without it we cannot be his followers at all. On one occasion we read of his disciples arguing about which of them was the greatest: "Sitting down, Jesus called the Twelve and said, 'Anyone who wants to be first must be the very last, and the servant of all'" (Mark 9:35). The "sitting down" indicates this to be a teaching, a serious instruction.

In his parables of the kingdom, Jesus speaks often of God as a master and of human beings as his servants. In teaching about the servant spirit, he tells us that we are to be humble and obedient servants of God, asking no reward but to do the Father's will, which was how Jesus himself lived. But he asks us to go further than that, and extend the attitude of the servant spirit towards each other, humbly accepting the lowest place and the most menial tasks.

Not only will doing this make our homes and communities loving and harmonious, it will also protect our faith. So often people bitterly denounce God and turn away from him because of adversity, disappointment, or tragedy in their lives. They see God as a resource or commodity, there to ensure their personal happiness: the centre of their lives is themselves, not God. On one occasion, reporting at Sunday-morning church on a tent mission, one of the team said, "God was really working for us last night!" He saw no incongruity in his words. It is important for us to get things the right way round – only with God as master, and ourselves as humble servants, can we ever find contentment and peace.

Questions

- How do you think we can fulfil Christ's command to be the servants of one another without becoming exhausted and resentful? Where would you draw the line to set appropriate and healthy boundaries while at the same time maintaining a cheerful and humble servant spirit?
- What do you think it really means, to take up our cross every day and follow Jesus?
- If someone is a leader – the principal of a college, the chief executive of a company, the teacher of a class, or the parent of a family – in what way is it appropriate to express the servant spirit in that context?

Prayer

O God our Father, how can we thank you enough for Jesus our Master and Lord, who came among us as a humble servant to set us free from sin and show us how to live in peace with one another? By your grace at work in our hearts, may we find the strength of spirit to humble ourselves as he did, and live as your faithful servants, kindly and cheerfully serving each other. For we ask it in Jesus' holy name; Amen.

His attitude to authority

Bible passages

Matthew 12:22–30

Then they brought him a demon-possessed man who was blind and mute, and Jesus healed him, so that he could both talk and see. All the people were astonished and said, "Could this be the Son of David?"

But when the Pharisees heard this, they said, "It is only by Beelzebul, the prince of demons, that this fellow drives out demons."

Jesus knew their thoughts and said to them, "Every kingdom divided against itself will be ruined, and every city or household divided against itself will not stand. If Satan drives out Satan, he is divided against himself. How then can his kingdom stand? And if I drive out demons by Beelzebul, by whom do your people drive them out? So then, they will be your judges. But if it is by the Spirit of God that I drive out demons, then the kingdom of God has come upon you.

"Or again, how can anyone enter a strong man's house and carry off his possessions unless he first ties up the strong man? Then he can plunder his house.

"Whoever is not with me is against me, and whoever does not gather with me scatters."

John 5:16–23

So, because Jesus was doing these things on the Sabbath, the Jewish leaders began to persecute him. In his defence Jesus said to them, "My Father is always at his work to this very day, and I too am working." For this reason they tried all the more to kill him; not only was he breaking the Sabbath, but he was even calling God his own Father, making himself equal with God.

Jesus gave them this answer: "Very truly I tell you, the Son can do nothing by himself; he can do only what he sees his Father doing, because whatever the Father does the Son also does. For the Father loves the Son and shows him all he does. Yes, and he will show him even greater works than these, so that you will be amazed. For just as the Father raises the dead and gives them life, even so the Son gives life to whom he is pleased to give it. Moreover, the Father judges no one, but has entrusted all judgment to the Son, that all may honour the Son just as they honour the Father. Whoever does not honour the Son does not honour the Father, who sent him."

Commentary

Jesus' attitude to authority possibly looked quite different to him from the way it looked to those in authority. He enraged the Pharisees by such incidents as this:

"'Very truly I tell you,' Jesus answered, 'before Abraham was born, I am!' At this, they picked up stones to stone him, but Jesus hid himself, slipping away from the temple grounds" (see John 8:59). From the point of view of the Pharisees, it looked as though Jesus were arrogantly and delusionally blasphemous; from the point of view of Jesus, it was a matter of stating simple truth.

He respected both cultural and religious frameworks (see Matthew 5:17, 39–41), yet in such a way as to promote freedom and self-respect. For example, his instruction that if a Roman soldier compels you to carry his pack for a mile you should carry it for two miles is not as simple as it first appears. Yes, it is humble, but it would also get the soldier into trouble with his superiors, because a mile was the statutory distance he could make you carry his bag. Jesus insisted he had come to fulfil the Law not abolish it – yet how scathing he was of religious leaders who observed the letter of the Law in minute detail while losing the spirit of it from their hearts (Matthew 23:23–24).

Jesus looked with complete focus to the Father for his directions, saying that he did nothing except what he saw the Father do (see our passage above from John 5). He aligned himself completely with the will of God, living in trusting obedience under God's authority, nourishing his connection with deep knowledge of the Scriptures and constant prayer.

Questions

- The Pharisees were always trying to catch Jesus out and discredit him (see our passage about exorcisms above). Why do you think this was? Why did he get under their skin so badly?
- Jesus severely criticizes religious leaders (Matthew 23) for the hypocrisy that so often infects people in positions of power. Can you think of examples of leaders who have managed to maintain their integrity (as far as you know!)?
- Have you ever had to choose between the authority of God and the authority of an institution? What did you do?

Prayer

Lord God of hosts, Ancient of Days, our eyes are fixed upon you. Write in our hearts the Law of your love, and give us the grace to trust and obey you in every step of the road ahead, for we ask it in Jesus' holy name; Amen.

His attitude to women

Bible passages

Matthew 19:3–9

Some Pharisees came to him to test him. They asked, "Is it lawful for a man to divorce his wife for any and every reason?"

"Haven't you read," he replied, "that at the beginning the Creator 'made them male and female,' and said, 'For this reason a man will leave his father and mother and be united to his wife, and the two will become one flesh'? So they are no longer two, but one flesh. Therefore what God has joined together, let no one separate."

"Why then," they asked, "did Moses command that a man give his wife a certificate of divorce and send her away?"

Jesus replied, "Moses permitted you to divorce your wives because your hearts were hard. But it was not this way from the beginning. I tell you that anyone who divorces his wife, except for sexual immorality, and marries another woman commits adultery."

Luke 10:38–42

As Jesus and his disciples were on their way, he came to a village where a woman named Martha opened her home to him. She had a sister called Mary, who sat at the Lord's feet listening to what he said. But Martha was distracted by all the preparations that had to be made. She came to him and asked, "Lord, don't you care that my sister has left me to do the work by myself? Tell her to help me!"

"Martha, Martha," the Lord answered, "you are worried and upset about many things, but few things are needed – or indeed only one. Mary has chosen what is better, and it will not be taken away from her."

Matthew 12:46–50

While Jesus was still talking to the crowd, his mother and brothers stood outside, wanting to speak to him. Someone told him, "Your mother and brothers are standing outside, wanting to speak to you."

He replied to him, "Who is my mother, and who are my brothers?" Pointing to his disciples, he said, "Here are my mother and my brothers. For whoever does the will of my Father in heaven is my brother and sister and mother."

Commentary

In traditional societies everywhere you find women who can be called "the power behind the throne". Denied status of their own, they must rely on manipulating their men. It seems Jesus had very little time for this (John 2:1–5; Matthew 20:20–22), but he did stand up for the women themselves (John 8:2–11), defending them against the discrimination of tradition.

In our passage from Matthew 19, the Pharisees ask Jesus' opinion on "divorce for any cause", which allowed a man to divorce his wife for a burnt dinner or any reason whatever. Jesus' insistence on the seriousness of the marriage vow protected women against destitution in a society where their only security lay in their menfolk.

In the passage from Luke 10 (see our study on Martha on p. 50), Jesus defends Mary's bold choice to sit in the place of and enjoy the privileges reserved for male disciples, refusing to accept her inevitable female role as household servant.

In our passage from Matthew 12 we see Jesus extend the privilege of access traditionally held by family to create a radically inclusive society. All those who honoured the fatherhood of God were henceforth protected and upheld by belonging as surely as if they had been born of the same bloodline. What a lifeline for the widows in his company!

Questions

- Even though feminism has revolutionized society, a widow in the 1990s remarked that without a husband she no longer had anyone to stand up for her. What are your perceptions of the advantages and disadvantages of modern Western society for women? And for men?

- Jesus did not try to overturn social traditions but worked within them so that they served the purposes of justice and love. Do you think the parameters of traditional societies offer enough protection for women?

- In what ways do you think men and women are created equal?

Prayer

O God of justice and mercy, you created men and women to live in harmony, bound together by ties of family love and tenderness. Amid the pressures and confusion of modern life, may we by your grace find who we truly are in Jesus. Give us the wisdom to discern how to live together in ways that honour one another, understanding our gender differences and needs. And, knowing that in Christ there is neither male nor female, but we all are one in him, lead us into the freedom of his Holy Spirit, for we ask it in his name; Amen.

His emphasis on forgiveness

Bible passages

Matthew 18:21–35

Then Peter came to Jesus and asked, "Lord, how many times shall I forgive my brother or sister who sins against me? Up to seven times?"

Jesus answered, "I tell you, not seven times, but seventy-seven times.

"Therefore, the kingdom of heaven is like a king who wanted to settle accounts with his servants. As he began the settlement, a man who owed him ten thousand bags of gold was brought to him. Since he was not able to pay, the master ordered that he and his wife and his children and all that he had be sold to repay the debt.

"At this the servant fell on his knees before him. 'Be patient with me,' he begged, 'and I will pay back everything.' The servant's master took pity on him, cancelled the debt and let him go.

"But when that servant went out, he found one of his fellow servants who owed him a hundred silver coins. He grabbed him and began to choke him. 'Pay back what you owe me!' he demanded.

"His fellow servant fell to his knees and begged him, 'Be patient with me, and I will pay it back.'

"But he refused. Instead, he went off and had the man thrown into prison until he could pay the debt. When the other servants saw what had happened, they were outraged and went and told their master everything that had happened.

"Then the master called the servant in. 'You wicked servant,' he said, 'I cancelled all that debt of yours because you begged me to. Shouldn't you have had mercy on your fellow servant just as I had on you?' In anger his master handed him over to the jailers to be tortured, until he should pay back all he owed.

"This is how my heavenly Father will treat each of you unless you forgive your brother or sister from your heart."

Luke 23:33–34

When they came to the place called the Skull, they crucified him there, along with the criminals – one on his right, the other on his left. Jesus said, "Father, forgive them, for they do not know what they are doing."

Commentary

Jesus taught that the process of forgiveness is initiated by God (see our passage from Matthew 18). Our responsibility to forgive proceeds only from having been forgiven ourselves; it is part of our gratitude for what God has done in our lives. We do not have to earn forgiveness – but we are expected to pass it on, and to treat others as God has treated us.

So it comes about that our broken relationships and sustained grudges create a barrier between us and God (Matthew 5:23–24); we cannot bring our gift to the altar, cannot offer our worship to God, until we do all that is in our power to reach out and establish peace.

But Jesus offers practical, pragmatic teaching about this (Matthew 18:15–17). He expects our relationships to be realistic and fair; he is not talking about "peace at any price". Even when he taught his disciples to "turn the other cheek" (Matthew 5:39), what he is recommending sustains our self-respect. To hit someone on the left cheek would require the backhanded slap with which a man punished a servant. To offer the right cheek invited the open-handed slap of aggression between equals. Jesus taught humility and forgiveness but not self-annihilation.

Even in the extremity of his torture and death (see the passage from Luke 23 above), he remained compassionately practical, recognizing that brutality is an inevitable characteristic of spiritual blindness and failure to understand.

Questions

- Forgiveness is never easy. In difficult circumstances, what has helped you to forgive?
- Do you feel as though God has forgiven you, or do you find that hard to believe?
- Are there any situations of unforgivingness in your life for which you would like the group to pray right now?

Prayer

How blessed are we, God of love, that in your loving-kindness you have chosen to forgive all our sins. In the cross of Jesus, everything we have done wrong has been taken and turned to good account – death transformed to life by the power of his sacrificial death. It is hard for us to take in all that he has done for us, and impossible for us to fully understand the mystery of this act of saving grace. But we know its power to heal and to redeem. May the transformational power of the cross be at work in our lives, informing our own attitudes and choices by the generosity of grace; in the name of Jesus, who died that we might be forgiven; Amen.

His emphasis on personal faith and choice

Bible passages

Matthew 16:24–26

Then Jesus said to his disciples, "Whoever wants to be my disciple must deny themselves and take up their cross and follow me. For whoever wants to save their life will lose it, but whoever loses their life for me will find it. What good will it be for someone to gain the whole world, yet forfeit their soul? Or what can anyone give in exchange for their soul? For the Son of Man is going to come in his Father's glory with his angels, and then he will reward each person according to what they have done."

Matthew 19:16–22

Just then a man came up to Jesus and asked, "Teacher, what good thing must I do to get eternal life?"

"Why do you ask me about what is good?" Jesus replied. "There is only One who is good. If you want to enter life, keep the commandments."

"Which ones?" he enquired.

Jesus replied, "'You shall not murder, you shall not commit adultery, you shall not steal, you shall not give false testimony, honour your father and mother,' and 'love your neighbour as yourself.'"

"All these I have kept," the young man said. "What do I still lack?"

Jesus answered, "If you want to be perfect, go, sell your possessions and give to the poor, and you will have treasure in heaven. Then come, follow me."

When the young man heard this, he went away sad, because he had great wealth.

Revelation 3:20

"Here I am! I stand at the door and knock. If anyone hears my voice and opens the door, I will come in and eat with that person, and they with me."

Commentary

You can be a member of some religions simply by being born into a family who follow that religion, and some religions (such as Hinduism) do not have a strong sense of a perimeter boundary defining who does and does not belong.

But Christianity has always been decision-based. "Come – follow me" was the challenge Jesus offered seekers who found their way to him. The writers of the

New Testament speak in terms of opening a door (Revelation 3:20; Matthew 7:7), sight being gained by the blind (Matthew 13:13–16; Mark 8:17–18), and joining a group (Acts 2:41). Baptism was (and still is) undergone as an initiation rite, a sign of new birth (John 3:3–6).

In his healing ministry (see the study on p. 188), Jesus often asked those he healed to participate by expressing a conscious decision (see Mark 10:51; Matthew 8:7), and said to some he healed, "Your faith has made you whole."

Jesus spoke of taking up the cross and following him – a choice to accept sacrifice and suffering for the sake of the kingdom. Our passage above from Matthew 19 shows the struggle of decision – a man at a crossroads having to make up his mind which way to go.

Because the Christian faith is essentially about relationship – a personal relationship with Jesus – it is necessary to meet Jesus in order to fully embrace it. This is made possible by the resurrection (see the study on p. 220). Opening the door of our heart to Jesus is a free choice, and is the simple, basic, essential step we undertake to become a Christian (see Acts 9:1–19).

Questions

- Can you think of a decision you have taken that changed the course of your whole life?
- Have there been moments in your life so profoundly transformative that they felt like being born again?
- How would you describe your experience of faith?

Prayer – copy and circulate first. Participation in this should be optional

Dear Lord Jesus, light of the world, I ask you to come into my heart as my Lord and Master. I am not a strong person and I am afraid of suffering, and I am not sure where this road will lead. I doubt my strength to follow. Even so, I give my life to you. Come into my heart, Lord Jesus. Forgive me for all I have done wrong; heal me of all that hinders and harms me. I know that where your presence is, light has come and darkness vanishes, goodness grows and evil is driven out. I trust that you will dwell in my heart for ever, and bring to completion your good work in me, so that I will belong to you for all eternity. Make your presence known to me. Fill me with your Spirit. May I walk the way of life with you through every single day. Lord Jesus, I open my heart to you, I give my life to you, I belong to you now. Amen.

His emphasis on thanksgiving

Bible passages

Mark 14:22–23

While they were eating, Jesus took bread, and when he had given thanks, he broke it and gave it to his disciples, saying, "Take it; this is my body."

Then he took a cup, and when he had given thanks, he gave it to them, and they all drank from it.

Luke 17:11–19

Now on his way to Jerusalem, Jesus travelled along the border between Samaria and Galilee. As he was going into a village, ten men who had leprosy met him. They stood at a distance and called out in a loud voice, "Jesus, Master, have pity on us!"

When he saw them, he said, "Go, show yourselves to the priests." And as they went, they were cleansed.

One of them, when he saw he was healed, came back, praising God in a loud voice. He threw himself at Jesus' feet and thanked him – and he was a Samaritan.

Jesus asked, "Were not all ten cleansed? Where are the other nine? Has no one returned to give praise to God except this foreigner?" Then he said to him, "Rise and go; your faith has made you well."

Luke 8:38–39

The man from whom the demons had gone out begged to go with him, but Jesus sent him away, saying, "Return home and tell how much God has done for you."

Matthew 18:32–33

"I cancelled all that debt of yours because you begged me to. Shouldn't you have had mercy on your fellow servant just as I had on you?"

Colossians 2:6

So then, just as you received Christ Jesus as Lord, continue to live your lives in him, rooted and built up in him, strengthened in the faith as you were taught, and overflowing with thankfulness.

Commentary

It's not that if you read through the Gospels you will come across that many instances of Jesus giving thanks to God (as in our passage from Mark 14 above).

He gave thanks before meals, and here and there we see him give thanks in prayer. He is not recorded as specifically saying "Thank you" to people who were good to him, but he thanked them in life-changing interactions (John 4:1–42; 11:17–44; Matthew 8:14–15). His emphasis on thanksgiving concerns living out of gratitude for God's goodness and mercy rather than being careful to remember social courtesies.

In our passage from Luke 17 above, Jesus directs glory away from himself, describing the heartfelt thanks offered to him by the healed man as praise to God. In the story of the Gerasene demoniac (see the passage from Luke 8 above), Jesus gives the man the opportunity to give thanks that he longs for, in sending him home to his own people to be part of the community again and to tell of what God has done. Such a thanksgiving is surely also a continuation of the healing. In his parables (such as the passage from Matthew 18 above) Jesus challenges us to live as people who have something to be thankful for, passing the generosity on, in lives "overflowing with thankfulness", as our passage from Colossians puts it.

Questions

- The Bible says Jesus blessed food by giving thanks. What do you think is the connection between thanksgiving and blessing?
- Can you think of three things you would like to give thanks for that happened today? Then can you name three ways in which God has blessed your life? How might you show your gratitude for these three things, in the way you live from day to day?
- What is your household/individual practice about giving thanks for meals? Silently? A spoken prayer? Never thought about it? At home only? In restaurants too?

Prayer

Thank you for our homes, good Lord; may we show our gratitude for what we have in loving hospitality. Thank you for our families, Father; may we express our gratitude in the way we cherish and affirm them. Thank you, creator God, for the earth in all its wonder and beauty; may we give praise to you in using its resources responsibly and sustainably. Thank you most of all for your love shown to us in Jesus; may our lives shine forth his love every day, bringing honour and glory to his holy name, in which we make our prayer; Amen.

His proclamation of the kingdom

Bible passages

Mark 1:14

After John was put in prison, Jesus went into Galilee, proclaiming the good news of God. "The time has come," he said. "The kingdom of God has come near. Repent and believe the good news!"

Matthew 4:23

Jesus went throughout Galilee, teaching in their synagogues, proclaiming the good news of the kingdom, and healing every disease and illness among the people.

Luke 4:16–21

He went to Nazareth, where he had been brought up, and on the Sabbath day he went into the synagogue, as was his custom. He stood up to read, and the scroll of the prophet Isaiah was handed to him. Unrolling it, he found the place where it is written:

"The Spirit of the Lord is on me, because he has anointed me to proclaim good news to the poor.

He has sent me to proclaim freedom for the prisoners and recovery of sight for the blind, to set the oppressed free, to proclaim the year of the Lord's favour."

Then he rolled up the scroll, gave it back to the attendant and sat down. The eyes of everyone in the synagogue were fastened on him. He began by saying to them, "Today this scripture is fulfilled in your hearing."

Luke 4:43–44

At daybreak, Jesus went out to a solitary place. The people were looking for him and when they came to where he was, they tried to keep him from leaving them. But he said, "I must proclaim the good news of the kingdom of God to the other towns also, because that is why I was sent." And he kept on preaching in the synagogues of Judea.

Luke 17:20–21

Once, on being asked by the Pharisees when the kingdom of God would come, Jesus replied, "The coming of the kingdom of God is not something that can be observed, nor will people say, 'Here it is,' or 'There it is,' because the kingdom of God is in your midst."

Commentary

At the beginning of the Bible (and the beginning of the universe), God said, "Let there be light!" – and there was light (Genesis 1:3)! When Jesus healed people, he didn't pray to God asking him to heal them; he announced their healing: "Your faith has made you whole," or "Take up your bed and walk," or "Your sins are forgiven." This pattern of bringing things into being by announcing them is indicative of a spiritual principle; it's how life works. Because we are made in the image of God, it works that way for us, too. What we believe and declare forms up into concrete reality in our lives.

Part of the prophetic and creative ministry of Jesus was his announcement, or proclamation, of the kingdom; declaring as present reality the reign of God which exists in seed form. It's as though a farmer at sowing time came home and remarked to his wife, "The wheat's in, now!" He might say the exact same words at harvest time when the grain is safely gathered in; it's all the same – what is sown will surely grow to a harvest.

Jesus proclaimed the arrival of the kingdom: "Today this scripture is fulfilled"; "The kingdom of God is in your midst". But he also made the point (in our passage from Luke 17 above) that it cannot be delineated or defined – it is diffused among us. It's in the quality of our relationships, the peace of our family life, our generosity as neighbours, our kindness to those in need, our gentleness, our mercy, our willingness to forgive. The kingdom of God is not built with concrete and steel; it has no bank reserves or border checkpoints featuring men in gun-towers. The kingdom of God is within you, and you can access it at any time you wish. The doorway is the present moment.

Questions

- Do you feel part of the kingdom of God, or does it feel like something you are still waiting for?
- Can you think of incidents when you felt you glimpsed the kingdom?
- The kingdom of God has begun, but we have a way to go in building it. How can we work to bring it to completion, realistically, in our daily lives?

Prayer

Thy kingdom come, O Lord, thy will be done on earth as it is in heaven. May the kingdom be realized in our midst and our lives be transformed, not by might, not by power, but by the Holy Spirit – we ask this with confidence in the holy name of Jesus; Amen.

His teaching about freedom

Bible passages

John 8:31–35

To the Jews who had believed him, Jesus said, "If you hold to my teaching, you are really my disciples. Then you will know the truth, and the truth will set you free."

They answered him, "We are Abraham's descendants and have never been slaves of anyone. How can you say that we shall be set free?"

Jesus replied, "Very truly I tell you, everyone who sins is a slave to sin. Now a slave has no permanent place in the family, but a son belongs to it for ever. So if the Son sets you free, you will be free indeed."

Matthew 10:8

"Freely you have received; freely give."

Luke 4:18 (Jesus quotes Isaiah 61:1–2; 58:6)

"He has sent me to proclaim freedom for the prisoners and recovery of sight for the blind, to set the oppressed free..."

Luke 13:10–13

On a Sabbath Jesus was teaching in one of the synagogues, and a woman was there who had been crippled by a spirit for eighteen years. She was bent over and could not straighten up at all. When Jesus saw her, he called her forward and said to her, "Woman, you are set free from your infirmity." Then he put his hands on her, and immediately she straightened up and praised God.

Matthew 6:12

"And forgive us our debts, as we also have forgiven our debtors."

Romans 8:1–2

Therefore, there is now no condemnation for those who are in Christ Jesus, because through Christ Jesus the law of the Spirit who gives life has set you free from the law of sin and death.

1 Corinthians 10:23–24

"I have the right to do anything," you say – but not everything is beneficial. "I have the right to do anything"– but not everything is constructive. No one should seek their own good, but the good of others.

Commentary

While Jesus was still growing in her womb, his mother was singing about freedom: "He has brought down rulers from their thrones, but has lifted up the humble" (Luke 1:52). You might say the whole of his ministry was about setting people free – from sickness, sin, and the grip of Mammon. Jesus has the power to set us free from crippling patterns of thought, from the chains of grudges and resentment, from the paralysis of shame.

The freedom of Jesus is exercised by particular disciplines in our lives (see our passages above). 1) Faith in Jesus sets us free from the grip of sin into the new creation of grace. 2) Truth sets us free – that means honesty, integrity, authenticity, and insight or discernment; and truth is also the childlike spirit, the way of simplicity. 3) Generosity sets us free – as we give freely, so we are released from fear, from the belief that there is not enough to go round. 4) Healing sets us free; in all kinds of ways we receive Christ's healing, and taking the trouble to follow a healthy lifestyle is part of our discipleship. 5) Avoiding debt and releasing others from debt bring freedom, and this was an important practical New Testament principle. 6) Self-discipline and self-restraint bring freedom; the escape from addictions, compulsions, and impulsivity is part of our healing in Christ and brings great peace.

Questions

- Can you identify areas in your life where you have found freedom through your faith in Jesus?
- Can you think of any areas in your life where you long to experience deeper freedom?
- How is the freedom of Jesus different from permissiveness?

Prayer

God of life, when we are set free by your truth, we are free indeed! We thank you for the freedom won for us by Jesus. We thank you for the spaciousness of his love, which lets us breathe again, which breaks the chain of hopelessness and sin. There is such joy in your freedom, dear Lord, and such peace. All our lives may we be led by your Spirit into the way of perfect freedom. Give us grace and wisdom to discern the way of life; help us to be self-controlled and prudent in our choices. Give us the insight, sensitivity, and generosity to help others to step into freedom. We ask these things in Jesus' holy name; Amen.

His relationship with creation

Bible passages

Romans 8:19–21

For the creation waits in eager expectation for the children of God to be revealed. For the creation was subjected to frustration, not by its own choice, but by the will of the one who subjected it, in hope that the creation itself will be liberated from its bondage to decay and brought into the freedom and glory of the children of God.

Mark 4:36–41

Leaving the crowd behind, they took him along, just as he was, in the boat. There were also other boats with him. A furious squall came up, and the waves broke over the boat, so that it was nearly swamped. Jesus was in the stern, sleeping on a cushion. The disciples woke him and said to him, "Teacher, don't you care if we drown?"

He got up, rebuked the wind and said to the waves, "Quiet! Be still!" Then the wind died down and it was completely calm.

He said to his disciples, "Why are you so afraid? Do you still have no faith?"

They were terrified and asked each other, "Who is this? Even the wind and the waves obey him!"

Colossians 1:15–17

The Son is the image of the invisible God, the firstborn over all creation. For in him all things were created: things in heaven and on earth, visible and invisible, whether thrones or powers or rulers or authorities; all things have been created through him and for him. He is before all things, and in him all things hold together.

John 1:1–4

In the beginning was the Word, and the Word was with God, and the Word was God. He was with God in the beginning. Through him all things were made; without him nothing was made that has been made. In him was life, and that life was the light of all mankind.

Commentary

During the cultural period of the Enlightenment in the eighteenth century, our attitude to creation changed. During that time, the scientific view developed of nature as a mere resource, animals as soulless mechanisms, and only humans as being capable of relationship with God. But this is not a biblical view.

The Bible teaches that God has a covenant relationship with the whole of creation (see for example Genesis 9:16) and an intimate personal connection with all life (see Psalm 104:4, 21, 27–30).

In the New Testament we learn that the work of Jesus in his death on the cross not only won salvation for humankind but also redeemed all creation from the bondage into which it had been subjected by human folly and sin (see our passages from Romans and Colossians above). The cross of Jesus now sits at the heart of creation, holding all things together in a living, holistic unity, with all things working together for good.

In his ministry on earth, Jesus identified himself as messiah in part by his relationship with creation – his ability to calm the storm at a word, to make people's bodies well at a touch or a word, to call people back from death, to walk on the water, and to multiply food. The earth is not a dead store cupboard of resources, or a kind of machine; it is alive and full of life, and all life responds to the God who called it into being with praise and adoration. As we are the people of God it is part of our calling to respect, cherish, and lovingly steward the living earth, which God has entrusted to our care. Just as Jesus did, we are to work for its health, peace, and well-being.

Questions

- How might a person who lives in an urban apartment express their stewardship of the earth that God has entrusted to us?
- Many people feel the presence of God very strongly in nature – in the hills, by the sea, in the beauty of a flower or an animal's trusting eyes. Is this true for you? Where have you seen glimpses of the holy in creation?
- What connections can you see between Christ's command to love our neighbours and God's command to us to be stewards of the earth?

Prayer

Creator God, source of all life, how glorious is your name in all the earth! We bless you for the beauty of sea and sky, for the wonderful provision of clean water, fruit and grain to eat, the intricate web of the ecosystem in strong yet fragile interdependence. You have thought of everything! Make us strong and wise to love you, Lord, in your creatures. May the majesty of the cloud forests, the teeming life of the oceans, and the industry of ants and bees be nurtured and protected by our way of life, and so may we honour and adore you, God who created all things. Amen.

His path of simplicity

Bible passages

Luke 2:7, KJV

And she brought forth her firstborn son, and wrapped him in swaddling clothes, and laid him in a manger; because there was no room for them in the inn.

Matthew 8:18–22

When Jesus saw the crowd around him, he gave orders to cross to the other side of the lake. Then a teacher of the law came to him and said, "Teacher, I will follow you wherever you go."

Jesus replied, "Foxes have dens and birds have nests, but the Son of Man has nowhere to lay his head."

Another disciple said to him, "Lord, first let me go and bury my father."

But Jesus told him, "Follow me, and let the dead bury their own dead."

John 4:6–7

Jesus, tired as he was from the journey, sat down by the well. It was about noon. When a Samaritan woman came to draw water, Jesus said to her, "Will you give me a drink?"

John 12:12–15

The next day the great crowd that had come for the festival heard that Jesus was on his way to Jerusalem. They took palm branches and went out to meet him, shouting, "Hosanna! Blessed is he who comes in the name of the Lord! Blessed is the king of Israel!"

Jesus found a young donkey and sat upon it, as it is written: "Do not be afraid, Daughter of Zion; see, your king is coming, seated on a donkey's colt."

Luke 19:45–46

When Jesus entered the temple courts, he began to drive out those who were selling. "It is written," he said to them, "'My house will be a house of prayer'; but you have made it 'a den of robbers'."

Mark 15:20

And when they had mocked him, they took off the purple robe and put his own clothes on him. Then they led him out to crucify him.

Commentary

The life of Jesus starts with being born in a stable, continues with becoming a refugee, passes with barely a nod through his years earning his living as a carpenter, and moves on to his ministry as an itinerant preacher and healer wandering in the hills and by the lakeside before climaxing in his death outside the city gates, stripped naked and pinned on a cross, his body laid in the borrowed tomb of a friend. Somehow you can spot radical simplicity as an emergent theme!

Possibly the most challenging thing Jesus ever said is: "Those of you who do not give up everything you have cannot be my disciples" (Luke 14:33).

We quietly put our cream cake back untasted on the plate and turn the central heating down a degree or two. What are we to make of this? In Jesus we have seen hope. We have experienced his healing and his joy. We have been taught that believing in him is the way to heaven. But this? Give up *everything*? Really?

There is no way round this. Jesus did actually say it. Perhaps we have to bear in mind what the ancient Chinese sage Lao Tsu said: "A journey of a thousand miles begins with the first step."

Giving up everything surely begins with giving up *something*. We can start by decluttering our homes and schedules and by living more simply and frugally, reviewing our lives to see where we can begin introducing habits of simplicity. If we make this a pattern in our lives, maybe we can inch our way towards obedience, until we live with creative necessity.

Questions

- Jesus challenged us by his words and life to take up the way of simplicity, yet many of his followers were ordinary householders and some of them were rich. What do you think he meant in practical terms?
- Why do you think Jesus identified simplicity as important? What are its benefits?
- What are your own experiences of living simply, in your own life or the lives of people you have known?

Prayer

Beloved Jesus, some of your teachings are hard to understand, and harder still to follow. Help us to get this one right, and to remain true to you, embracing the kind of simplicity that can walk with you all the way home. Amen.

His faithfulness in prayer

Bible passages

Mark 1:35

Very early in the morning, while it was still dark, Jesus got up, left the house and went off to a solitary place, where he prayed.

Mark 9:26–29

The spirit shrieked, convulsed him violently and came out. The boy looked so much like a corpse that many said, "He's dead." But Jesus took him by the hand and lifted him to his feet, and he stood up.

After Jesus had gone indoors, his disciples asked him privately, "Why couldn't we drive it out?"

He replied, "This kind can come out only by prayer."

Matthew 14:22–23

Immediately Jesus made the disciples get into the boat and go on ahead of him to the other side, while he dismissed the crowd. After he had dismissed them, he went up on a mountainside by himself to pray. Later that night, he was there alone...

Matthew 26:36–39

Then Jesus went with his disciples to a place called Gethsemane, and he said to them, "Sit here while I go over there and pray." He took Peter and the two sons of Zebedee along with him, and he began to be sorrowful and troubled. Then he said to them, "My soul is overwhelmed with sorrow to the point of death. Stay here and keep watch with me."

Going a little farther, he fell with his face to the ground and prayed, "My Father, if it is possible, may this cup be taken from me. Yet not as I will, but as you will."

John 17:15–21

"My prayer is not that you take them out of the world but that you protect them from the evil one. They are not of the world, even as I am not of it. Sanctify them by the truth; your word is truth. As you sent me into the world, I have sent them into the world. For them I sanctify myself, that they too may be truly sanctified.

"My prayer is not for them alone. I pray also for those who will believe in me through their message, that all of them may be one, Father, just as you are in me and I am in you. May they also be in us so that the world may believe that you have sent me."

Commentary

Mahatma Gandhi described prayer as "the key of the morning and the bolt of the evening", and the first letter to the Thessalonians (5:17, KJV) encourages us to "pray without ceasing".

Of our study passages, perhaps the most sobering is the story from Mark 9, where the disciples struggled ineffectually to help the boy and were glad to have Jesus take over and sort things out. His response when they ask him the cause of their own failure later in private, "This kind can come out only by prayer," demonstrates if we needed it that prayer is not just a religious duty or a mental exercise to induce pleasant feelings of calm, but makes a material difference in both occasional crisis and regular daily life.

The life of Jesus, beset on every side by people in trouble needing his help and people who hated him plotting his downfall, shows us a man who sought prayer as a thirsty man seeks a cold drink on a hot day. Jesus depended on prayer, took refuge in prayer, drew his strength and guidance from prayer.

A striking thing Jesus said was: "Very truly I tell you, whoever believes in me will do the works I have been doing, and they will do even greater things than these, because I am going to the Father. And I will do whatever you ask in my name, so that the Father may be glorified in the Son. You may ask me for anything in my name, and I will do it" (John 14:12–14).

This offers us the challenge that, if we will immerse ourselves in prayer like Jesus and with Jesus, we too will see the wonderful works of God in our lives; we are more like Jesus than we think. The choice is ours.

Questions

- Can you think of a time when you saw prayer definitely make a difference?
- Have you read any books on prayer you could recommend?
- What are your experiences of fasting with prayer? What difference does the fasting make?

Prayer

Faithful God, you wait for us in the silence, to refresh our spirits and strengthen our souls for service. Give us the grace to turn aside and seek your presence, before the day begins, in the midst of everything, and when we lay ourselves down to rest. Thank you for being there for us; may we also be there for you. We ask it in Jesus' holy name; Amen.

His passion and death

Bible passages

Mark 8:31–37

He then began to teach them that the Son of Man must suffer many things and be rejected by the elders, the chief priests and the teachers of the law, and that he must be killed and after three days rise again. He spoke plainly about this, and Peter took him aside and began to rebuke him.

But when Jesus turned and looked at his disciples, he rebuked Peter. "Get behind me, Satan!" he said. "You do not have in mind the concerns of God, but merely human concerns."

Then he called the crowd to him along with his disciples and said: "Whoever wants to be my disciple must deny themselves and take up their cross and follow me. For whoever wants to save their life will lose it, but whoever loses their life for me and for the gospel will save it. What good is it for someone to gain the whole world, yet forfeit their soul? Or what can anyone give in exchange for their soul?"

Romans 4:25

He was delivered over to death for our sins and was raised to life for our justification.

Romans 8:1–4

Therefore, there is now no condemnation for those who are in Christ Jesus, because through Christ Jesus the law of the Spirit who gives life has set you free from the law of sin and death. For what the law was powerless to do because it was weakened by the flesh, God did by sending his own Son in the likeness of sinful flesh to be a sin offering. And so he condemned sin in the flesh, in order that the righteous requirement of the law might be fully met in us, who do not live according to the flesh but according to the Spirit.

Acts 2:23–24

This man was handed over to you by God's deliberate plan and foreknowledge; and you, with the help of wicked men, put him to death by nailing him to the cross. But God raised him from the dead, freeing him from the agony of death, because it was impossible for death to keep its hold on him.

Commentary

This word "passion" – it doesn't mean what we might at first think. It's not about strong feeling, as in "I love you passionately". It stems from the Latin word *passiō*, meaning to suffer, or to submit. Remember when Jesus says, "Suffer little children … to come unto me" (Matthew 19:14, KJV)? The word "suffer" means permit or allow. "Passion" is associated with this, and with the word "passive". The passion of Jesus is about when the time came for him to lay aside the inner strength and authority that had kept those who hated him at bay for so long, and permit them to have their way with him so that the will of God in the salvation of the world could be accomplished through his grim and agonizing death.

When we think of the death of Jesus, by which we are saved and the way to heaven is opened for us, it is important to include the passion, because passion is part of our salvation. There's a German word, *Gelassenheit* (literally "letting-go-ness"), which is about allowing things to take their course, submitting to reality and to God, not getting ourselves in the way of the flow of things or obstructing the unfolding of grace. Our salvation was won by Jesus' death, but also by his passion, his submission and humility, his self-emptying, and his laying-aside of power.

Questions

- Can you pick out, in our study passages, how the passion of Jesus is woven right in there with the story of his death?

- Many people say they fear not death itself but the helplessness and loss of independence that may precede it. Can you think of ways that focusing on the passion of Jesus may comfort us and help us with this?

- The passion and death of Jesus brought about our salvation. In what ways do you think that being a saved person therefore includes something of the flavour of sacrifice and "passion"?

Prayer

When we think of your suffering and death for our sakes, Lord Jesus, words fail us. Let us sit in silence and adore you, and pour out our love and thanksgiving in the silence of our hearts… Thank you, Lord Jesus. We adore you, Lord Jesus. For all you have done for us, for so much love, for our full and free salvation, for the abundant life you have won for us, for the healing and freedom we find in you, we bring our humble and hearty thanks. Give us grace and strength to follow you as you truly deserve, and to remain faithful to you unto our lives' end. Amen.

His work of reconciliation

Bible passages

Colossians 1:19–20

For God was pleased to have all his fullness dwell in him, and through him to reconcile to himself all things, whether things on earth or things in heaven, by making peace through his blood, shed on the cross.

2 Corinthians 5:18–19

All this is from God, who reconciled us to himself through Christ and gave us the ministry of reconciliation: that God was reconciling the world to himself in Christ, not counting people's sins against them. And he has committed to us the message of reconciliation.

Ephesians 2:14–22

For he himself is our peace, who has made the two groups one and has destroyed the barrier, the dividing wall of hostility, by setting aside in his flesh the law with its commands and regulations. His purpose was to create in himself one new humanity out of the two, thus making peace, and in one body to reconcile both of them to God through the cross, by which he put to death their hostility. He came and preached peace to you who were far away and peace to those who were near. For through him we both have access to the Father by one Spirit.

Consequently, you are no longer foreigners and strangers, but fellow citizens with God's people and also members of his household, built on the foundation of the apostles and prophets, with Christ Jesus himself as the chief cornerstone. In him the whole building is joined together and rises to become a holy temple in the Lord. And in him you too are being built together to become a dwelling in which God lives by his Spirit.

Galatians 3:26–28

So in Christ Jesus you are all children of God through faith, for all of you who were baptised into Christ have clothed yourselves with Christ. There is neither Jew nor Gentile, neither slave nor free, nor is there male and female, for you are all one in Christ Jesus.

Commentary

On a helicopter, holding the rotor blades to the main body is "the Jesus nut". The phrase is also used for other engineering components that hold everything in a machine together, with dire consequences should the part fail.

The Jesus nut is also what holds the whole of creation together (see our study on Jesus' relationship with creation on p. 210). As our passage from Colossians 1 says, "God was pleased to have all his fullness dwell in him, and through him to reconcile to himself all things, whether things on earth or things in heaven," and, as our passage from 2 Corinthians 5 says (here KJV), "God was in Christ, reconciling the world unto himself."

The cross of Jesus sits at the heart of creation, holding all things together in a living harmony. From his cross, healing flows through the whole web of all that is made. Through his cross death and life are reconciled to each other in one living entity, brought into harmony, so that death is no longer the end of life but part of life, no more than a horizon of sight. In passing from life to death and from death to life, Jesus opened a path, created a unity. He who was with the Father in the making of creation from the very beginning, with everything that was made being created through him, therefore had a right by this creative connection to redeem and reconcile the whole cosmos by surrendering himself, its Lord, to its depths. For us the cross of Jesus is our ultimate safety, the part that holds firm and keeps us aloft, the eye of any storm, the promise that will not fail, the certain hope of salvation.

Questions

- As the work of reconciliation is central to the ministry of Jesus, so it will show up in the lives of his followers. How might we take part in his work of reconciliation?
- Are there any relationships in your own life that you think could benefit from the blessing of reconciliation?
- If reconciliation is central to the ministry of Jesus, do you think all Christians have to be pacifists?

Prayer

Jesus, our rock, our strength, and our redeemer, we put our trust in you. Carry us through, Lord Jesus, any times of trouble that may be besetting us now; give us the insight we need into what you have done for us, that we may have confidence in you and trust you to the uttermost. Teach us to lean on your love, move in your power, and walk in your light. So may we become for others a rock that does not shift, a waymarker that will help them find the sure path to life and the refuge of your eternal name; Amen.

His resurrection and glorious ascension

Bible passages

John 20:26–28

Though the doors were locked, Jesus came and stood among them and said, "Peace be with you!" Then he said to Thomas, "Put your finger here; see my hands. Reach out your hand and put it into my side. Stop doubting and believe."

Thomas said to him, "My Lord and my God!"

1 Corinthians 15:3–8

For what I received I passed on to you as of first importance: that Christ died for our sins according to the Scriptures, that he was buried, that he was raised on the third day according to the Scriptures, and that he appeared to Cephas, and then to the Twelve. After that, he appeared to more than five hundred of the brothers and sisters at the same time, most of whom are still living, though some have fallen asleep. Then he appeared to James, then to all the apostles, and last of all he appeared to me also, as to one abnormally born.

1 Corinthians 15:17

If Christ has not been raised, your faith is futile; you are still in your sins.

1 Corinthians 15:42–44

The body that is sown is perishable, it is raised imperishable; it is sown in dishonour, it is raised in glory; it is sown in weakness, it is raised in power; it is sown a natural body, it is raised a spiritual body.

Ephesians 4:7–13

But to each one of us grace has been given as Christ apportioned it. This is why it says: "When he ascended on high, he took many captives and gave gifts to his people."

(What does "he ascended" mean except that he also descended to the lower, earthly regions? He who descended is the very one who ascended higher than all the heavens, in order to fill the whole universe.) So Christ himself gave the apostles, the prophets, the evangelists, the pastors and teachers, to equip his people for works of service, so that the body of Christ may be built up until we all reach unity in the faith and in the knowledge of the Son of God and become mature, attaining to the whole measure of the fullness of Christ.

Commentary

To call the resurrection of Jesus "groundbreaking" is an understatement. It changed everything. It is the basis of our faith. There is debate in the church about whether the resurrection was a physical event. The Gospel stories make it very clear that it was physical (John 20:27; 21:9, 15; Luke 24:30, 40–43), but with some very big differences – Jesus would suddenly disappear, or appear in their midst though the doors were locked. Paul addresses this in our passage from 1 Corinthians 15 above: the resurrection body is a spiritual body not a natural body – but that doesn't mean it isn't physical. Quantum physicists are discovering that physicality and spirituality belong to the same continuum, so perhaps we might see the resurrection body as a *fulfilled* body, one which has reached its full potential.

The resurrection was a wonderful event that revolutionized the whole cosmos, but it was not complete until Jesus had ascended to the Father and poured out the Spirit on us at Pentecost. In ascending to the Father and being absorbed into the Godhead, Jesus became not remote but universally accessible. In the giving of the Spirit at Pentecost he became not just accessible but fully present in our lives.

These three linked mysteries are central to the Christian faith and make it possible for us to actually, personally, experience the living Jesus literally present with us in our hearts in everyday life, in all his power and joy.

Questions

- Theologians have been arguing for centuries about the physical resurrection and the resurrection body of Jesus. What do you think about it?
- In what ways do you experience the presence of Jesus in your daily life?
- How do you see the Holy Spirit manifest in the church today?

Prayer

God of life and power, we marvel at the mystery that you have come to live with us – actually inhabit us – in the Holy Spirit, the presence of Jesus. May his indwelling of our hearts day by day work the miracle of grace within us, filling us with his joy and kindness, transforming us into the likeness of his loving face, setting us free from all that warps and diminishes us, and bringing us into the fullness of abundant life. Thank you, Father, for this mind-boggling gift of salvation; may we prove worthy of what you have entrusted to us, in Jesus' holy name; Amen.

Insights from the Law and the Prophets

(15 studies)

Putting God first
The poor and needy
Choosing life
Keeping faith with a faithful God
To do justice, to love mercy and to walk humbly with thy God

Putting God first

Bible passages

Deuteronomy 6:4–8

Hear, O Israel: the Lord our God, the Lord is one. Love the Lord your God with all your heart and with all your soul and with all your strength. These commandments that I give you today are to be on your hearts. Impress them on your children. Talk about them when you sit at home and when you walk along the road, when you lie down and when you get up. Tie them as symbols on your hands and bind them on your foreheads. Write them on the doorframes of your houses and on your gates.

Haggai 1:2–10

This is what the Lord Almighty says: "These people say, 'The time has not yet come to rebuild the Lord's house.'"

Then the word of the Lord came through the prophet Haggai: "Is it a time for you yourselves to be living in your panelled houses, while this house remains a ruin?"

Now this is what the Lord Almighty says: "Give careful thought to your ways. You have planted much, but harvested little. You eat, but never have enough. You drink, but never have your fill. You put on clothes, but are not warm. You earn wages, only to put them in a purse with holes in it."

This is what the Lord Almighty says: "Give careful thought to your ways. Go up into the mountains and bring down timber and build my house, so that I may take pleasure in it and be honoured," says the Lord. "You expected much, but see, it turned out to be little. What you brought home, I blew away. Why?" declares the Lord Almighty. "Because of my house, which remains a ruin, while each of you is busy with your own house. Therefore, because of you the heavens have withheld their dew and the earth its crops."

Matthew 6:33

"But seek first his kingdom and his righteousness, and all these things will be given to you as well."

Revelation 2:4

Yet I hold this against you: you have forsaken the love you had at first. Consider how far you have fallen! Repent and do the things you did at first.

Commentary

The foundational concept of the Law and the Prophets is that the well-being of humanity depends completely upon putting God first.

This is not because God is like an out-of-control toddler demanding attention, or an arrogant despot greedy for power; it's because all life proceeds from God: he is the source, the Alpha and the Omega. Without him nothing can start or continue; in fact, nothing can happen at all.

Unless we put God first in our personal lives, our homes, and our society, everything will rot and be blighted; everything will go wrong. But if we put God first, the material blessings that make us happy will naturally follow.

This does not mean that our lives will be all plain sailing. Adversity is our opportunity to learn and grow; it is natural to life. We are born resilient, able to meet challenges and heal from damage. God watches over us every step of the way and will supply our needs in every situation, however terrible. The shining faith and courage of Christian martyrs facing the grisliest of deaths witness to the power of trusting in God in adversity. God is with us; he will never desert us. This is not an insurance policy against mishap, but is the provision of grace we need for every circumstance of life.

It is impossible to put God first as a strategy, a trade to get the good things we want. As long as – overtly or covertly – we put ourselves first, our lives will be all out of joint. It is when we put God first in spirit and in truth that we will see the blessing promised by the Law and the Prophets.

Questions

- Would anything need to change in what you do at the moment, to put God first in your life?
- Can you think of an example of someone you know who put God first in choosing a course of action or way of life?
- When a church becomes a formal organization with buildings, charitable status, and employed staff, is it easier or harder to put God first?

Prayer

O God most holy, exalted one, king of kings, Lord of hosts, how privileged are we to sing your praises and lift high your wonderful name. Gracious God, may your Spirit so enter our hearts and take charge of our lives that we walk in your way and follow in the path of Jesus' calling, putting you first in our lives in everything. For we ask it in his holy name; Amen.

The poor and needy

Bible passages

Leviticus 19:10

Do not go over your vineyard a second time or pick up the grapes that have fallen. Leave them for the poor and the foreigner. I am the Lord your God.

Deuteronomy 15:7–11

If anyone is poor among your fellow Israelites in any of the towns of the land that the Lord your God is giving you, do not be hard-hearted or tight-fisted towards them. Rather, be open-handed and freely lend them whatever they need. Be careful not to harbour this wicked thought: "The seventh year, the year for cancelling debts, is near," so that you do not show ill will towards the needy among your fellow Israelites and give them nothing. They may then appeal to the Lord against you, and you will be found guilty of sin. Give generously to them and do so without a grudging heart; then because of this the Lord your God will bless you in all your work and in everything you put your hand to. There will always be poor people in the land. Therefore I command you to be open-handed towards your fellow Israelites who are poor and needy in your land.

Deuteronomy 24:10–15, 17

When you make a loan of any kind to your neighbour, do not go into their house to get what is offered to you as a pledge. Stay outside and let the neighbour to whom you are making the loan bring the pledge out to you. If the neighbour is poor, do not go to sleep with their pledge in your possession. Return their cloak by sunset so that your neighbour may sleep in it. Then they will thank you, and it will be regarded as a righteous act in the sight of the Lord your God.

Do not take advantage of a hired worker who is poor and needy, whether that worker is a fellow Israelite or a foreigner residing in one of your towns. Pay them their wages each day before sunset, because they are poor and are counting on it. Otherwise they may cry to the Lord against you, and you will be guilty of sin... Do not deprive the foreigner or the fatherless of justice, or take the cloak of the widow as a pledge.

Isaiah 41:17

The poor and needy search for water, but there is none; their tongues are parched with thirst. But I the Lord will answer them; I, the God of Israel, will not forsake them.

Commentary

If putting God first is the basic essential of the Law and the Prophets, caring for the poor and needy follows it as a close second.

Where the prophets speak out against the people of God, issuing dire warnings of calamity, what has triggered God's wrath is invariably turning away from true worship (that is, not putting God first) and oppressing the poor.

The expression of faith is reverence for God in all things and ensuring social justice.

Sometimes individuals or governments cut back on their care for the poor because it seems to be too big an expense, but the Law and the Prophets warn against this (see our passage from Deuteronomy 15 above), teaching that blessing flows from caring for the poor. In the Bible, blessing is in every case synonymous with increase – of flocks, crops, family, or money. So the Bible teaches us that caring for the poor will, contrary to what we might expect, not deplete but increase our resources. This will happen by every means, from the logical progression of a poor man assisted into prosperity and therefore becoming a contributor himself, to sovereign miracles of God.

Questions

- What do you think and how do you feel when you see a beggar on the street? In what way do you think we should offer help to people reduced to begging?

- We hear and see so much of overwhelming poverty afflicting some parts of our world. How might we go about choosing where and how to help?

- Are there indirect ways by which we might address poverty – for example, tackling climate change, campaigning for peace, abstaining from alcohol and cigarettes, educating about AIDS? How important are these, and what other examples can you think of?

Prayer

O God of love, you care with such passion for the poor and needy. So fill us with your Spirit that our compassion never fails despite the need all around us. Give us wisdom and discernment to know how and when and whom to help. Give us generous and trusting hearts. May we always remember our own poverty, and how much you have given us in Jesus, in whose holy name we pray; Amen.

Choosing life

Bible passage

Deuteronomy 30:11–20 (verse numbers left in as the passage is long)

Now what I am commanding you today is not too difficult for you or beyond your reach. ¹² It is not up in heaven, so that you have to ask, "Who will ascend into heaven to get it and proclaim it to us so that we may obey it?" ¹³ Nor is it beyond the sea, so that you have to ask, "Who will cross the sea to get it and proclaim it to us so that we may obey it?" ¹⁴ No, the word is very near you; it is in your mouth and in your heart so that you may obey it.

¹⁵ See, I set before you today life and prosperity, death and destruction. ¹⁶ For I command you today to love the Lord your God, to walk in obedience to him, and to keep his commands, decrees and laws; then you will live and increase, and the Lord your God will bless you in the land you are entering to possess.

¹⁷ But if your heart turns away and you are not obedient, and if you are drawn away to bow down to other gods and worship them, ¹⁸ I declare to you this day that you will certainly be destroyed. You will not live long in the land you are crossing the Jordan to enter and possess.

¹⁹ This day I call the heavens and the earth as witnesses against you that I have set before you life and death, blessings and curses. Now choose life, so that you and your children may live ²⁰ and that you may love the Lord your God, listen to his voice, and hold fast to him. For the Lord is your life, and he will give you many years in the land he swore to give to your fathers, Abraham, Isaac and Jacob.

Commentary

In the 1980s, the then British Prime Minister Margaret Thatcher was interviewed by John Humphrys on the BBC radio programme *Today*. Knowing her to be a Christian, he asked her what she considered the essence of Christianity, expecting her to reply "Love" or "Charity" and intending then to challenge the stringency of the home politics of her government. She surprised him by answering: "Choice."

Jesus taught, "By this everyone will know that you are my disciples, if you love one another" (John 13:35), and love has always been the hallmark of true Christianity. But the capacity to love assumes freedom (you cannot force or require love), exercised by making choices. Christ's emphatic teaching of love is rooted and grounded, and meant to be understood, in the context of the Old Testament teaching about choice and responsibility – personal moral accountability.

God leaves us free to choose, but makes it clear that some choices will bring life and well-being, while others will bring suffering and death. This in turn makes it clear that self-discipline, social responsibility, ethical citizenship, and reverence for the commands of God are not limitations or shackles, but the framework for freedom and peace, the root system on which the life of a society depends. The Deuteronomy passage underlines that these choices do not belong to the lofty and distant world of exalted people, but to the ordinary everyday life of us all.

Questions

- Have you made any choices you now regret? Did you foresee the consequences when you made the choice? Where do you think you went wrong?
- Can you think of examples of loving choices made to benefit others, accepting responsibility for their well-being? You may like to research Maximilian Kolbe[3] as an example of this. Are we "our brother's keeper", or can we alone bear responsibility for ourselves? Where do we draw the line?
- Can you identify moral choices you are making in your life right now? How will you discern the right way to go, that path that leads to life?

Prayer

O God of life and blessing, give us the grace, courage, and strength to choose well, to accept responsibility, to live accountably, and to love generously, so that we may show forth your gospel to the world, and live in a way that pleases you, our Master and our Lord. This we ask in Jesus' holy name; Amen.

---

3 *Maximilian Kolbe: Saint of Auschwitz* by Elaine Murray Stone, published by Paulist Press in 1997, ISBN-10: 0809166372, ISBN-13: 978-0809166374, or look him up with any online search engine.
Kolbe was a Catholic priest who, in the Auschwitz death camp, offered his life in exchange for that of a condemned man. His offer was accepted.

Keeping faith with a faithful God

Bible passages

Deuteronomy 7:7–9

The Lord did not set his affection on you and choose you because you were more numerous than other peoples, for you were the fewest of all peoples. But it was because the Lord loved you and kept the oath he swore to your ancestors that he brought you out with a mighty hand and redeemed you from the land of slavery, from the power of Pharaoh king of Egypt. Know therefore that the Lord your God is God; he is the faithful God, keeping his covenant of love to a thousand generations of those who love him and keep his commandments.

Genesis 9:8–10 (reading the whole chapter is recommended)

Then God said to Noah and to his sons with him: "I now establish my covenant with you and with your descendants after you and with every living creature that was with you – the birds, the livestock and all the wild animals, all those that came out of the ark with you – every living creature on earth."

Genesis 12:1–3 (the covenant with Abraham)

The Lord had said to Abram, "Go from your country, your people and your father's household to the land I will show you.

"I will make you into a great nation, and I will bless you; I will make your name great, and you will be a blessing. I will bless those who bless you, and whoever curses you I will curse; and all peoples on earth will be blessed through you."

Genesis 17:19 (the covenant renewed with Isaac)

"... your wife Sarah will bear you a son, and you will call him Isaac. I will establish my covenant with him as an everlasting covenant for his descendants after him."

Exodus 19:4–6; 24:7 (the covenant with Moses – in Exodus chapters 19 – 24)

"'You yourselves have seen what I did to Egypt, and how I carried you on eagles' wings and brought you to myself. Now if you obey me fully and keep my covenant, then out of all nations you will be my treasured possession. Although the whole earth is mine, you will be for me a kingdom of priests and a holy nation.' These are the words you are to speak to the Israelites."

... Then he took the Book of the Covenant and read it to the people. They responded, "We will do everything the Lord has said; we will obey."

2 Samuel 7:11–13 (the covenant with David)

"'The Lord declares to you that the Lord himself will establish a house for you: when your days are over and you rest with your ancestors, I will raise up your offspring to succeed you, your own flesh and blood, and I will establish his kingdom. He is the one who will build a house for my Name, and I will establish the throne of his kingdom for ever.'"

Commentary

The Bible tells of God entering a covenant relationship with his people, reaffirming this on a number of occasions. It is worth reading the whole chapter of Genesis 9, the story of Noah's ark and the sign of the rainbow. This is often described as God's covenant with Noah – but that misses out something important. The Genesis 9 covenant is between God and Noah and his descendants, but also between God and all the earth's animals. God's promise is not only to and for the human race; it is not only with us that he is in a living relationship, but with all other living creatures too. For this reason, we should treat them not only with compassion because of their capacity to suffer, but with respect because they like us are in a covenant relationship with God.

God also made a covenant with Abraham, and renewed this with Isaac, then with Moses, and then with David. The Law is part of this covenant relationship, and when the prophets speak of God's faithfulness, they have this in mind.

Questions

- Looking at our passages, can you see how the Old Testament covenants look forward to the coming of Jesus and his church? (See also Luke 22:20; Matthew 16:19; 26:28; 1 Peter 2:9; Hebrews 9:15.)
- Can you think of examples of God's faithfulness to us? What do you think he wants us to do, in practical everyday terms, to keep faith with him?
- In what ways do we express our faithfulness to God in our relationships with each other as part of our relationship with him?

Prayer

Ancient of Days, you have kept faith with your people in every generation, and we know we can trust you to keep faith with us too. Help us to believe in your love, walk in your way, and remain your faithful people unto our lives' end, for we ask it in Jesus' holy name; Amen.

To do justice, to love mercy and to walk humbly with thy God

Bible passages

Micah 6:6–8

> With what shall I come before the Lord
> and bow down before the exalted God?
> Shall I come before him with burnt offerings,
> with calves a year old?
> Will the Lord be pleased with thousands of rams,
> with ten thousand rivers of oil?
> Shall I offer my firstborn for my transgression,
> the fruit of my body for the sin of my soul?
> He has shown you, O mortal, what is good.
> And what does the Lord require of you?
> To act justly and to love mercy
> and to walk humbly with your God.

2 Corinthians 3:4–6

> Such confidence we have through Christ before God. Not that we are competent in ourselves to claim anything for ourselves, but our competence comes from God. He has made us competent as ministers of a new covenant – not of the letter but of the Spirit; for the letter kills, but the Spirit gives life.

Commentary

It is so easy to focus on externals. The Law was given as the framework of a just and merciful society, in which the presence and reality of the living God would always be present in the consciousness of the people (see Deuteronomy 8). Covering the details of daily life, it ensured provision for everyone. The sacrificial system was a sharing-out of bounty, as well as an offering to the Lord. The year of Jubilee gave people trapped in slavery and debt a chance to start again, and to prevent power and wealth from being stockpiled by a few, as well as being a holy feast of celebration of God's goodness. Rules about marriage, food, gleaning, and the Sabbath protected the life of the community as well as exalting the Lord.

The Law was a wonderful thing but, when applied with mechanical scrupulosity, the heart of it, the intention, its soul, were lost. It's worth reading Matthew chapter 23, Jesus' great indictment of those religious leaders who insisted on the Law being applied to the letter while letting slip its vision of creating a society both just and merciful, in which the loving purposes of God would always be remembered. In insisting on the application of its externals, they had lost sight of the vision that inspired it – the formation of a community in covenant with God.

The prophets hammer home the message that what God wants is for us to get our attitude right – to help the poor, the widow, the orphan, and the stranger; to be good neighbours, practising mercy and kindness. Again and again the prophets insist that without this core vision our practice of religion is a hollow sham.

Questions

- As we try to live our lives in the light of biblical teaching, where do you think we should draw the line between adhering to the letter and being faithful to the spirit of what we read? How do we decide which instructions are matters of basic principle and which are for all time?

- Justice is the bone, and mercy the soft tissue of society; we need both. How do we decide when to administer justice and when to temper it with mercy – for example in disciplining children, in determining the fate of asylum seekers, in considering the cases of criminal offenders?

- What might walking humbly with our God mean in real, practical terms, in daily life?

Prayer

We thank you, O God, for the framework and structure of the Law, shaping our understanding of society as an organic whole, held together by a living web of responsibility. We thank you for the prophets, for their visionary faithfulness in passing on the heart's cry of your passion for mercy and justice among your people. And we thank you for Jesus, who came to bring us the grace we needed to live justly, to know mercy, and to walk in humility, hand in hand with you. We make our prayer in Christ's holy name; Amen.

Also from Monarch Books:

The Road of Blessing
Penelope Wilcock
FINDING GOD'S DIRECTION FOR YOUR LIFE
ISBN: 978-1-85424-965-4   £7.99 UK / $12.99 US

Life is filled with tough choices. Whether it is choosing a career, or what to do with your money, or deciding whom to marry: things work much better if you walk the Road of Blessing, loving God and following the Maker's instructions.

As you learn to follow the Road and hear the Spirit, decisions get easier. "May the freedom and peace of the Road of Blessing refresh the roots of your soul," writes Pen Wilcock. "May the Spirit within you well up to a fountain of living water; may the Way open to you, and may you learn to trust it. It will never fail you."

"Penelope Wilcock speaks serenity and wisdom into our turbulent lives and troubled times. We need people like her" – **Ruth Valerio, author of** *L is for Lifestyle*

"Pen's love for God shines through every word. She writes as a fellow traveller. Her words are deeply rooted in truth, watered with compassion, and fed with hope. This is a must-have book" – **Malcolm Duncan, Senior Pastor, Gold Hill Baptist Church and author of** *Kingdom Come*

"At last, a book on being blessed that does not fall into the trap of divorcing the spiritual and the material. I found this book profound and practical, and greatly enjoyed the author's holistic vision of the Christian life"
– **Dr Mark Stibbe, author of** *I am Your Father*

In Celebration of Simplicity
Penelope Wilcock
THE JOY OF LIVING LIGHTLY
ISBN (UK): 978-1-85424-912-8   £8.99
ISBN (US): 978-1-85424-984-5 $14.99

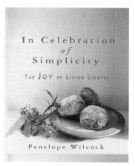

This practical yet visionary book offers a model for a truly healthy life based on gospel simplicity. Ditch the stuff that gets in the way, and your heart is free to respond to God.

"What an illuminating book! Pen goes right to the heart of the gospel with her rich understanding of what it means to walk the road of simplicity. Living lightly allows space for people, fun, prayer – all the good things of life"
– **Dr Elaine Storkey**

"I have always admired Pen's writing. She has an immense talent for putting words together in the most effective way possible. This book invites the reader to join her in a fascinating journey of thought and sentiment. Don't worry about agreeing or disagreeing – just go. A wonderful collection of quotes will accompany you"
– **Adrian Plass**

Route 66
Krish Kandiah

A CRASH COURSE IN NAVIGATING LIFE WITH THE BIBLE

ISBN: 978-0-85721-018-0   £8.99 UK / $13.99 US

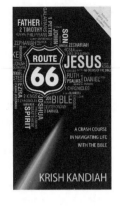

Route 66 is an inspirational eight-week challenge for you, your small group, or your whole church to get in gear with the Bible.

"Connects the reader to the Bible in fresh, motivational and life-changing ways" – **David Jackman, Founder of the Cornhill Training Course**

"I can't wait to use this book and give it to others. I sense that here is something very special indeed" – **Rob Parsons, Founder and Chairman, Care for the Family**

"A fantastic resource, packed with great teaching. If you want to understand the Bible better and to fall in love with God more deeply, then this book is a must" – **Vicky Beeching, worship leader, songwriter, and blogger**

"A great aid to understanding the Bible" – **Graeme Goldsworthy, Moore College, Sydney**

"A most extraordinary book" – **Revd Dr Michael Jensen, Moore College, Sydney**

"A really useful tool to help people get to know the Bible better" – **Revd Dr Graham Tomlin, Dean, St Mellitus College**

"Top of my list for what I'll be doing next with my church small group" – **Ruth Valerio, author and Director of A Rocha's** Living Lightly

"It is the ideal introduction for exploring every part of Scripture *and applying it to* every part of life*"* – **Jonathan Lamb, Director, Langham Preaching, and Chairman, Keswick Ministries**

Dr Krish Kandiah is a Director of the Evangelical Alliance. He is in demand as a Bible teacher and has written numerous books relating the Bible to everyday life. Krish is also a film buff, a fan of Liverpool FC, a husband, a father, and a foster carer.

Co-published with Elevation and Spring Harvest.

www.lionhudson.com/monarch

Church Actually
Gerard Kelly

REDISCOVERING THE BRILLIANCE OF GOD'S PLAN

ISBN: 978-0-85721-231-3   £8.99 UK / $14.99 US

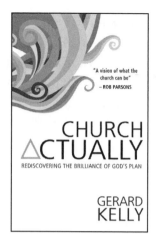

"A vision of what the church can be"
– ROB PARSONS

"Creative and inspiring – Gerard paints a vision of what the church can be – **Rob Parsons**

What happened to the fountain God switched on at Pentecost? Where did the joy go?

"In recent years," says Gerard Kelly, "I have wrestled with the loss of colour that so many people describe in their experience of the Christian faith. How has a movement that began as an explosion of life become so bland – so grey – in our experience?"

Church attendance in the West has declined in recent years, but not because of a lack of interest in spirituality. There has been a boom in spiritual exploration, just without the church. The Christian story has lost its hold on our imaginations.

Can we break out of the greyness of our church experience to discover the riot of colour God intended? Is there a route back to the brilliance of God's plan?

"A fizzing, popping read... dazzling" – **Viv Thomas**

"Rich, evocative, beautifully written, and heart-expanding" – **Mark Greene**

"Sheer genius. Gerard celebrates all that is good about the church" – **Debra Green**

"Gerard's fusion of theology, philosophy and poetry... great!" – **Dave Wiles**

"I can't think of a more timely, important, or indeed prophetic exploration of God at work among his people" – **Steve Clifford**

"Buy it. Read it. Reflect on it. Let the living colours of its message warm you" – **Danielle Strickland**

"A marvellous picture of the church as God always has planned it" – **Paul Francis**

"Gerard is a poet of the Spirit. A book I have longed to see. I love it" – **David White**

"Sparkles with humour, cut-diamond insights, and inspiration... delightful" – **Mark Roques**

"A picture of a beautiful, vibrant, colourful church... deserves to be studied by everyone trying to create something beautiful for God" – **David Lawrence**

Gerard Kelly is an author, poet, thinker, evangelist, and pastor who currently runs a centre for missional spirituality in France. He regularly speaks at large Christian gatherings and is author of a number of books, including *Breakfast with God* and *Twitturgies*. He is a leader of the Bless Network, www.blessnet.eu

Co-published with Elevation and Spring Harvest.